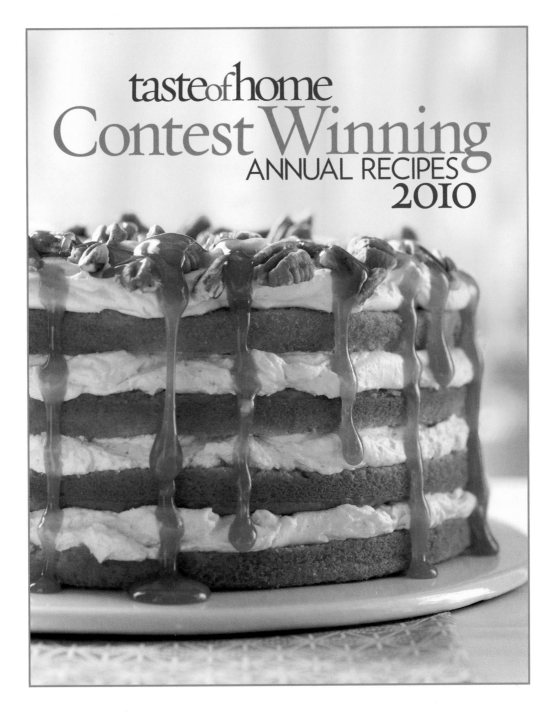

tasteofhome
Contest Winning
ANNUAL RECIPES
2010

taste of home
Contest Winning
ANNUAL RECIPES
2010

Senior Vice President, Editor in Chief: Catherine Cassidy
Vice President, Executive Editor/Books: Heidi Reuter Lloyd
Creative Director: Ardyth Cope
Food Director: Diane Werner RD
Senior Editor/Books: Mark Hagen
Editor: Michelle Bretl
Art Director: Gretchen Trautman
Content Production Supervisor: Julie Wagner
Design Layout Artist: Kathy Crawford
Proofreaders: Linne Bruskewitz, Victoria Soukup Jensen
Recipe Asset System Manager: Coleen Martin
Premedia Supervisor: Scott Berger
Recipe Testing & Editing: Taste of Home Test Kitchen
Food Photography: Taste of Home Photo Studio
Administrative Assistant: Barb Czysz

U.S. Chief Marketing Officer: Lisa Karpinski
Vice President/Book Marketing: Dan Fink
Creative Director/Creative Marketing: Jim Palmen

THE READER'S DIGEST ASSOCIATION, INC.
President and Chief Executive Officer: Mary G. Berner
President, U.S. Affinities: Suzanne M. Grimes
SVP, Global Chief Marketing Officer: Amy J. Radin

Taste of Home Books
© 2010 Reiman Media Group, Inc.
5400 S. 60th St., Greendale WI 53129
International Standard Book Number (10): 0-89821-805-5
International Standard Book Number (13): 978-0-89821-805-3
International Standard Serial Number: 1548-4157

PICTURED ON FRONT COVER:
Pumpkin Torte (p. 217). Photography by Jim Wieland.
Food styled by Kaitlyn Besasie. Set styled by Melissa Haberman.

For other Taste of Home books and products, visit **www.ShopTasteofHome.com**.

Table of Contents

Sensational Slush, p. 12

Garlic Tomato Soup, p. 57

Chicken with Mushroom Sauce, p. 96

Easy Potato Rolls, p. 152

Blond Brownies a la Mode, p. 174

Introduction 4

Snacks & Beverages 6

Special Salads 20

Soups & Sandwiches.............................38

Breakfast & Brunch...............................60

Main Dishes...82

Side Dishes & Condiments.................118

Breads & Rolls.....................................138

Cookies, Bars & Candy 156

Cakes & Pies 182

Just Desserts 206

Index...228

Over 300 National Contest Winners— All Right Here in One Big Cookbook!

COOKS who know where to find the best recipes look to *Taste of Home*, the world's #1 food source. And for the "best of the best" in one convenient cookbook series, they rely on *Contest Winning Annual Recipes*.

The all-new seventh edition, *Contest Winning Annual Recipes 2010* is packed from cover to cover with even more specialties for you to enjoy. In fact, you get hundreds of top-rated recipes—over 300 in all!

Every single dish was a prize winner in either *Taste of Home* magazine or one of its sister magazines— *Simple & Delicious, Healthy Cooking, Country* and *Country Woman*. That's the best from five different publications, all in one handy resource.

Plus, this special cookbook includes an entire year's worth of Grand Prize winners. It's a one-of-a-kind collection that's truly the "cream of the crop."

How does a recipe become a winner? First, home cooks from coast to coast read our contest announcement and enter their all-time best dishes—the must-have favorites family and friends request again and again.

Next, our Test Kitchen experts sort through the many recipes we receive and test the most promising entries. They prepare the top choices for our judging panel, which includes experienced food editors and home economists. After much sampling (yum!), the judges pick a Grand Prize winner and runners-up.

Winners from Dozens of Contests

The contests featured in this cookbook cover a wide variety of foods—snacks and beverages; salads; soups and sandwiches; breakfast dishes; main courses; sides and condiments; breads and rolls; cookies, bars and candy; cakes and pies; and desserts. No matter what type of recipe you're looking for, you're sure to find it here.

For a complete list of chapters, please see the Table of Contents on page 3. Below, we've included a quick summary of the year's worth of contests in this book and the top prize winner of each:

- **Candy Creations:** In this contest for sweet-as-can-be treats, tantalizing Cookie Dough Truffles (p. 164) snatched up the Grand Prize.
- **Choice Chicken:** When it comes to a family-pleasing main course, why wing it? Choose sure-to-satisfy Spinach Crab Chicken (p. 106).
- **Best-Ever Brownies:** Pans and pans of entries squared off in this competition, but yummy Blond Brownies a la Mode (p. 174) took highest honors.
- **Sensational Strawberries:** Breakfast will be on a roll when you make luscious Strawberry Cream Crepes (p. 74) part of your morning menu.
- **Carrot Call-Out:** Looking for a standout side dish every "bunny" will love? Dig right into the creamy, cheesy goodness of Party Carrots (p. 132).
- **Crisps and Cobblers:** Apple Crumble (p. 212) tops off meals with a comforting, home-style dessert you'll want to serve again and again.
- **Swift Skillet Side Dishes:** Rely on your stovetop to put an exceptional accompaniment—Tomatoes with Horseradish Sauce (p. 124)—on the table anytime.
- **Beat-the-Clock Breads:** Dozens of golden goodies vied for the Grand Prize, but it was Marmalade Monkey Bread (p. 142) that rose to the occasion.

Bacon Clam Chowder, p. 48

Harvest Green Salad, p. 37

- **Speedy Brunch:** Ready to wake up taste buds? Our contest judges did just that when they tried scrumptious Florentine Egg Bake (p. 70).

- **10-Minute Mainstays:** Count down to mealtime with Fiery Chicken Spinach Salad (p. 24), and you'll have a delicious entree in mere moments.

- **Swift After-School Snacks:** PB&J Spirals (p. 150) will tide the kids over until supper...but don't be surprised if these bites go over big with adults, too!

- **In-a-Dash Desserts:** Quick finales for fall and winter meals don't get much better than this contest's winner, Butter Pecan Pumpkin Pie (p. 184).

- **Country Casseroles:** Hot from the oven comes Ole Polenta Casserole (p. 90), packed with ground beef, cheese, mushrooms and more.

- **Three Cheers for Cherries:** Decadent White Chocolate Mousse Cherry Pie (p. 196) was our panel's top pick from the orchard of entries.

- **Grilled to Perfection:** Add spark to your next backyard cookout, summer picnic or other feast with a surefire winner—Southern Barbecued Chicken (p. 98).

- **Savory Sandwiches:** With apples, dried cranberries, walnuts and more, Curried Chicken Salad Sandwiches (p. 42) stacked up to the very best.

- **Tasty Taters:** At the root of this contest were special spuds...and the bountiful harvest of recipes included praiseworthy Swirled Potato Bake (p. 120).

- **Holiday Pies:** Any way you slice it, crowd-pleasing Cranberry Pear Pie (p. 202) makes a festive seasonal dessert for your Thanksgiving or Christmas table.

- **Trimmed-Down Treats:** Craving sweets but not all of the calories? You'll love this Grand Prize winner, Martha Washington Pies (p. 190).

- **Tantalizing Tenderloin:** When this popular cut of meat was the order of the day, we received mouth-watering Spicy Pork Tenderloin Salad (p. 32).

- **Sensational Salads:** Many tasty medleys were tossed into the bowl of entries, but Grilled Chicken and Pear Salad (p. 28) was the favorite.

- **30-Minute Entrees:** For dinner, think fast! Delicious Turkey Pasta Soup (p. 46) takes just half an hour to get on the table for you and your family.

- **Pare Down with Peppers:** Readers picked their best light recipe, and our judges considered Sweet Pepper Sandwiches (p. 50) to be the peppiest of the bunch.

- **Creative with Cranberries:** Cran-Apple Tea Ring (p. 64) is always a "berry" good choice for a holiday brunch or weekend breakfast.

When you create menus using the prize-worthy delights showcased in *Contest Winning Annual Recipes 2010*, you'll have unforgettable meals your family and friends will talk about—and ask for—again and again. One thing's guaranteed—every single dish you have to choose from in this cookbook is hard to beat!

Butter Pecan Pumpkin Pie, p. 184

Sensational Slush, p. 12

Roasted Carrot Dip, p. 9

Granola Trail Mix, p. 19

Snacks & Beverages

Whether you want festive finger foods for a holiday celebration, casual munchies for a sports party or something to tide over the kids after school, rely on Bacon Nachos, Sweet Gingered Chicken Wings, Banana Shakes and the other recipes here.

Crimson Cranberry Punch.....................8

Italian Snack Mix...............................8

Roasted Carrot Dip............................9

Sauerkraut Ham Balls 10

Mini Bagelizzas................................10

Chocolate Fruit Dip..........................11

Fried Shoestring Carrots...................11

Sensational Slush.............................12

Swiss Walnut Cracker Snack...............13

Dilly Veggie Pizza............................13

Bacon-Wrapped Stuffed Jalapenos........14

Banana Shakes 14

Sweet Gingered Chicken Wings.........15

Pepper Avocado Salsa 16

Bacon Nachos 17

Cranberry Spritzer 17

Cherry Berry Smoothies....................18

Sweet 'n' Crunchy Mix.....................18

Honey-Mustard Turkey Meatballs........19

Granola Trail Mix.............................19

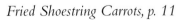

Fried Shoestring Carrots, p. 11

🎗 🎗 🎗
Crimson Cranberry Punch

Prep: 20 min. + freezing

Judie White, Florien, Louisiana

This ruby-red punch is a real crowd-pleaser and a breeze to stir together with only a few ingredients. The pretty ice ring filled with cranberries keeps it refreshing.

- 1/2 cup frozen cranberries
- 3-1/2 cups cold water
- 1 bottle (48 ounces) white grape juice, chilled
- 2 cans (12 ounces *each*) frozen cranberry juice concentrate, thawed
- 4 cans (12 ounces *each*) diet lemon-lime soda, chilled
- 3 orange slices
- 3 lemon slices

1. Place the cranberries in a 4-1/2-cup ring mold coated with cooking spray. Slowly pour a small amount of cold water into the mold to barely cover berries; freeze until solid. Add remaining water; freeze until solid.

2. Just before serving, combine the grape juice and cranberry juice concentrate in a large punch bowl; stir in soda. Unmold ice ring; place fruit side up in punch bowl. Add orange and lemon slices. **Yield:** 5 quarts.

- 8 cups Crispix
- 4 cups sourdough pretzel nuggets
- 3 tablespoons canola oil
- 1/4 cup grated Parmesan cheese
- 1 tablespoon spaghetti sauce mix
- 2 teaspoons garlic powder

In a 2-gal. resealable plastic bag, combine the cereal and pretzels. Drizzle with oil; seal bag and toss to coat. Combine the cheese, spaghetti sauce mix and garlic powder; sprinkle over cereal mixture. Seal bag and toss to coat. **Yield:** about 3 quarts.

🎗 🎗 🎗
Italian Snack Mix

Prep/Total Time: 15 min.

Nancy Zimmerman, Cape May Court House, New Jersey

With a hint of garlic and Parmesan cheese, this pretzel-and-cereal combination makes a terrific after-school treat. The no-bake medley keeps well in an airtight container.

Great Grating

If you want to grate your own Parmesan cheese for Italian Snack Mix or another recipe, grate a chunk of cheese using the finest section on your grating tool. Or, grate the cheese using your blender or food processor. Just cut the cheese into 1-inch cubes and process 1 cup of cubes at a time on high until finely grated.

✿✿✿
Roasted Carrot Dip

Prep: 15 min. **Bake:** 45 min.

Alana Rowley, Calgary, Alberta

Once you start eating this delicious dip, it's difficult to stop! The carrot flavor is great with the pita wedges in the recipe.

- 10 **medium carrots**
- 5 **garlic cloves, peeled**
- 2 **tablespoons olive oil**
- 6 to 8 **tablespoons water**
- 2 **teaspoons white wine vinegar**
- 1/2 **cup mayonnaise**
- 1/4 **cup sour cream**
- 1/8 **teaspoon sugar**
- 1/8 **teaspoon salt**
- 1/8 **teaspoon pepper**
- 4 to 6 **pita breads (6 inches)**
- 2 to 3 **tablespoons butter, melted**

1. Cut carrots in half widthwise; cut lengthwise into 1/2-in.-thick slices. In a large bowl, combine the carrots, garlic and oil; toss to coat. Transfer the mixture to a greased 15-in. x 10-in. x 1-in. baking pan.

2. Bake, uncovered, at 425° for 20 minutes. Stir; bake 15-20 minutes longer or until carrots are tender. Cool slightly.

3. In a blender, combine 6 tablespoons water, vinegar, mayonnaise, sour cream, sugar, salt, pepper and carrot mixture; cover and process until smooth. Add the additional water if needed to achieve the desired consistency. Transfer to a large bowl and refrigerate until serving.

4. Brush both sides of the pita breads with butter. Cut in half; cut each half into six wedges. Place on ungreased baking sheets.

5. Bake at 350° for 4 minutes on each side or until lightly browned. Serve pita wedges with carrot dip. **Yield:** 8-10 servings.

1 pound ground fully cooked ham
1 jar (16 ounces) sauerkraut, drained and chopped
1/4 cup finely chopped onion
2 tablespoons plus 3/4 cup dry bread crumbs, *divided*
1 package (3 ounces) cream cheese, softened
2 tablespoons minced fresh parsley
1 tablespoon prepared mustard
1/4 teaspoon garlic powder
1/8 teaspoon pepper
1/4 to 1/2 cup all-purpose flour
2 eggs
1/4 cup milk
Oil for deep-fat frying

1. In a large bowl, combine the ham, sauerkraut, onion and 2 tablespoons bread crumbs. In another bowl, combine the cream cheese, parsley, mustard, garlic powder and pepper; stir into sauerkraut mixture. Chill for 1 hour or overnight.

2. Shape into 3/4-in. balls; coat with flour. In a small bowl, beat eggs and milk. Dip ham balls into the egg mixture, then roll in the remaining bread crumbs.

3. In a deep-fat fryer or electric skillet, heat oil to 375°. Fry ham balls until golden brown; drain on paper towels. **Yield:** 5 dozen.

Editor's Note: Recipe can be made into larger balls and served as a main dish.

Sauerkraut Ham Balls

Prep: 30 min. + chilling **Cook:** 20 min.

Lillian Thomas, Toledo, Ohio

I've always enjoyed cooking…particularly when I'm doing it for people who enjoy eating! These balls are so well liked in my family that I'll buy a ham just so I can make them.

Mini Bagelizzas

Prep/Total Time: 25 min.

Stephanie Klos-Kohr, Moline, Illinois

Garlic powder gives these speedy mini pizzas extra piz-zazz. They're a snap to put together, and my husband loves them. Plus, the ingredient list is easy on my pocketbook!

8 miniature bagels, split
1 cup spaghetti sauce with miniature meatballs
32 slices pepperoni
3/4 teaspoon garlic powder
2 cups (8 ounces) shredded part-skim mozzarella cheese

1. Spread the cut sides of bagels with spaghetti sauce. Top each with two slices of pepperoni; sprinkle with garlic powder and cheese.

2. Place on ungreased baking sheets. Bake at 350° for 15-20 minutes or until cheese is melted and bubbly. **Yield:** 8 servings.

🎗🎗🎗
Chocolate Fruit Dip
Prep/Total Time: 10 min.

Sarah Maury Swan, Granite, Maryland

Neighbors of mine joke that I'm not allowed to attend neighborhood parties unless I bring this dip! It's always a hit. I usually serve it with strawberries and pineapple, but it's also good with other fruits, such as apples and melon.

> 1 package (8 ounces) cream cheese, softened
> 1/3 cup sugar
> 1/3 cup baking cocoa
> 1 teaspoon vanilla extract
> 2 cups whipped topping
> **Assorted fruit for dipping**

In a large bowl, beat cream cheese and sugar until smooth. Beat in cocoa and vanilla. Beat in whipped topping until smooth. Serve with fruit. **Yield:** 2 cups.

🎗🎗🎗
Fried Shoestring Carrots
Prep/Total Time: 25 min.

Kim Gammill, Raymondville, Texas

I came up with these fun, simple snacks as an alternative to the usual french fries. We like to serve them hot with ranch-style salad dressing as a dipping sauce.

> 2 cups self-rising flour
> 1-1/2 cups water
> 1 teaspoon salt, *divided*
> 3/4 teaspoon cayenne pepper, *divided*
> 1/2 teaspoon pepper, *divided*
> 10 cups shredded carrots
> **Oil for frying**

1. In a large bowl, whisk flour, water, 1/2 teaspoon salt, 1/4 teaspoon cayenne and 1/4 teaspoon pepper until smooth. Stir in carrots. In a small bowl, combine the remaining salt, cayenne and pepper; set aside.

2. In an electric skillet or deep-fat fryer, heat oil to 375°. Drop spoonfuls of carrot mixture, a few at a time, into oil; cook for 3-4 minutes or until golden brown, stirring frequently. Drain on paper towels; sprinkle with reserved seasoning mixture. **Yield:** 10 servings.

Editor's Note: As a substitute for each cup of self-rising flour, place 1-1/2 teaspoons baking powder and 1/2 teaspoon salt in a measuring cup. Add all-purpose flour to measure 1 cup.

🎗️🎗️🎗️
Sensational Slush

Prep: 25 min. + freezing

Connie Friesen, Altona, Manitoba

Colorful and refreshing, this sweet-tart slush has become a favorite. I freeze the mix in 2- and 4-cup containers so it can be served either in small portions for individuals or in large portions for the whole family. I also freeze crushed strawberries to make the preparation even simpler.

   1/2 cup sugar
   1 package (3 ounces) strawberry gelatin
   2 cups boiling water
   1 cup unsweetened pineapple juice
   2 cups sliced fresh strawberries
   1 can (12 ounces) frozen lemonade concentrate, thawed
   1 can (12 ounces) frozen limeade concentrate, thawed
   2 cups cold water
   2 liters lemon-lime soda, chilled

1. In a large bowl, dissolve the sugar and gelatin in boiling water. In a blender, combine pineapple juice and strawberries; cover and process until blended. Add to gelatin mixture. Stir in the concentrates and cold water. Cover and freeze for 8 hours or overnight.

2. Remove from the freezer 45 minutes before serving. For each serving, combine 1/2 cup slush mixture with 1/2 cup lemon-lime soda; stir well. **Yield:** 20 servings.

Swiss Walnut Cracker Snack

Prep: 10 min. + chilling

Geraldine Muth, Black River Falls, Wisconsin

This cheese spread is simple to prepare and makes an excellent snack for holiday and family gatherings. It features lots of "Dairy State" products and gets a nice crunch from the nuts.

  1 package (8 ounces) cream cheese, softened
1-1/2 cups (6 ounces) shredded Swiss cheese
  1/2 cup sour cream
    2 tablespoons Dijon mustard
  1/3 cup chopped walnuts
  1/3 cup minced fresh parsley
  1/4 cup chopped green onions
Crackers and/or bagel chips

1. In a large bowl, beat cream cheese until smooth. Add the Swiss cheese, sour cream and mustard. Stir in the walnuts, parsley and onions.

2. Refrigerate cheese spread for at least 1 hour before serving. Serve spread with crackers and/or bagel chips. **Yield:** 2 cups.

Dilly Veggie Pizza

Prep: 20 min. **Bake:** 10 min. + cooling

Heather Ahrens, Avon, Ohio

This appetizer pizza is one of my favorite ways to take advantage of leftover chopped veggies…or to use new ones! Feel free to alter the mixture to suit your family's taste buds.

  1 tube (8 ounces) refrigerated crescent rolls
1-1/2 cups vegetable dill dip
    2 medium carrots, chopped
    1 cup finely chopped fresh broccoli
    1 cup chopped seeded tomatoes
    4 green onions, sliced
    1 can (2-1/4 ounces) sliced ripe olives, drained

1. Unroll crescent dough into one long rectangle. Press onto bottom of a greased 13-in. x 9-in. baking pan; seal seams. Bake at 375° for 10-12 minutes or until golden brown. Cool completely on a wire rack.

2. Spread dip over crust; sprinkle with the carrots, broccoli, tomatoes, onions and olives. Cut into squares. Refrigerate leftovers. **Yield:** 15 servings.

Tomato Tip

To remove the seeds from a tomato for Dilly Veggie Pizza, cut the tomato in half horizontally and remove the stem. Holding a tomato half over a bowl or sink, either scrape out the seeds with a small spoon or squeeze the tomato to force out the seeds. Then chop the seeded tomato as directed for the recipe.

Sunday is grill-out day for my husband, and this zesty recipe is one of his specialties. We often feature the stuffed jalapenos at our annual Daytona 500 party as well, and they're snatched up from the appetizer tray in no time.

- 24 **medium jalapeno peppers**
- 1 **pound uncooked chorizo or bulk spicy pork sausage**
- 2 **cups (8 ounces) shredded cheddar cheese**
- 12 **bacon strips, cut in half**

1. Make a lengthwise cut in each jalapeno, about 1/8 in. deep; remove seeds. Combine the sausage and cheese; stuff into jalapenos. Wrap each with a piece of bacon; secure with toothpicks.

2. Prepare grill for indirect heat, using a drip pan. Place jalapenos over pan; grill, covered, over indirect medium heat for 17-20 minutes on each side or until a meat thermometer inserted into filling reads 160°. Grill, covered, over direct heat 1-2 minutes longer or until bacon is crisp. **Yield:** 2 dozen.

Editor's Note: When cutting hot peppers, disposable gloves are recommended. Avoid touching your face.

🎗🎗🎗
Bacon-Wrapped Stuffed Jalapenos

Prep: 1 hour **Grill:** 35 min.

Therese Pollard, Hurst, Texas

🎗🎗🎗
Banana Shakes

Prep/Total Time: 10 min.

Martha Miller, APO, AP

We're stationed overseas, and I've fixed these made-in-moments drinks for my children since they were tots. Pop the shakes into the freezer for a few minutes if you like them thicker.

- 1 **cup half-and-half cream**
- 4 **cups vanilla ice cream, softened**
- 1 **medium banana, sliced**
- 1/4 **teaspoon banana extract**

In a blender, combine all of the ingredients; cover and process until smooth. Pour into chilled glasses; serve immediately. **Yield:** 4 servings.

Soft Solution

To soften ice cream in the refrigerator, transfer the ice cream from the freezer to the refrigerator 20-30 minutes before using. Or let it stand at room temperature for 10-15 minutes.

🏵 🏵 🏵
Sweet Gingered Chicken Wings

Prep: 10 min. **Bake:** 1 hour

Debbie Dougal, Roseville, California

When I prepare this recipe for parties or other get-togethers, it's one of the first things to disappear. I've used these easy, lip-smacking wings not only as an appetizer, but also as a main course. The four-ingredient sauce requires just honey, orange juice concentrate, ginger and parsley.

> 1 cup all-purpose flour
> 2 teaspoons salt
> 2 teaspoons paprika
> 1/4 teaspoon pepper
> 24 chicken wings

SAUCE:
> 1/4 cup honey
> 1/4 cup thawed orange juice concentrate
> 1/2 teaspoon ground ginger

Minced fresh parsley, optional

1. In a large resealable plastic bag, combine the flour, salt, paprika and pepper. Add chicken wings, a few at a time; seal bag and toss to coat.

2. Place wings on a large greased baking sheet. Bake at 350° for 30 minutes. Remove from oven and drain.

3. Combine honey, orange juice concentrate and ginger; brush generously over chicken wings. Reduce heat to 325°.

4. Bake for 30-40 minutes or until the chicken juices run clear, basting occasionally with more sauce. Sprinkle with fresh parsley before serving if desired. **Yield:** 2 dozen.

🏅🏅🏅
Pepper Avocado Salsa
Prep: 15 min. + chilling

Theresa Mullens, Gill, Massachusetts

Peppers and avocados are popular in my family, and much of our summer menu is prepared on the grill. That led me to create this recipe. It not only makes a terrific appetizer, but also helps spice up our barbecued entrees.

- 2 medium tomatoes, diced
- 1/4 cup *each* diced green, sweet red and yellow pepper
- 1/4 cup diced red onion
- 2 tablespoons olive oil
- 2 tablespoons lime juice
- 1 tablespoon white wine vinegar
- 1 garlic clove, minced
- 1 tablespoon minced fresh basil *or* 1 teaspoon dried basil
- 1 tablespoon minced fresh dill *or* 1 teaspoon dill weed
- 1 teaspoon sugar
- 3/4 teaspoon minced fresh thyme *or* 1/4 teaspoon dried thyme
- Dash hot pepper sauce
- 1 large ripe avocado

In a large bowl, combine the first 12 ingredients. Cover and refrigerate. Just before serving, peel and chop the avocado; stir into salsa. **Yield:** 3-1/2 cups.

🎀🎀🎀
Bacon Nachos

Prep/Total Time: 20 min.

Ruth Ann Bott, Lake Wales, Florida

These crispy nachos have been a big hit in our house. Topped with kid-friendly ingredients such as ground beef and cheddar cheese, they're always popular with children. And older kids like the fact that they can microwave the snacks themselves.

> 1/2 **pound ground beef**
> 4 **cups tortilla chips**
> 1/4 **cup real bacon bits**
> 2 **cups (8 ounces) shredded cheddar cheese**
> 1/2 **cup guacamole dip**
> 1/2 **cup sour cream**

Chopped tomatoes and green onions, optional

1. In a small skillet, cook the beef over medium heat until no longer pink; drain. Place tortilla chips on a microwave-safe serving plate. Layer with the beef, bacon and cheese.

2. Microwave, uncovered, on high for 1-2 minutes or until cheese is melted. Top with guacamole and sour

cream. Sprinkle with tomatoes and onions if desired. **Yield:** 4-6 servings.

Editor's Note: This recipe was tested in a 1,100-watt microwave.

🎀🎀🎀
Cranberry Spritzer

Prep/Total Time: 10 min.

LaVonne Hegland, St. Michael, Minnesota

This tangy spritzer is my version of a cranberry drink I've had many times at a local restaurant. Lemon-lime soda puts the fizz in this thirst-quenching juice blend.

> 1 **can (12 ounces) lemon-lime soda, chilled**
> 1 **cup cranberry juice, chilled**
> 1/2 **cup unsweetened pineapple juice, chilled**
> 1/4 **cup orange juice, chilled**

Ice cubes

In a pitcher, combine the soda and juices. Serve over ice. **Yield:** 2 servings.

Festive Finish

Garnish each glass of this spritzer with fresh cranberries. Or, cut out fun shapes from orange or lemon rind using mini cookie cutters.

🎖🎖🎖
Cherry Berry Smoothies
Prep/Total Time: 5 min.

Macy Plummer, Avon, Indiana

You'll need just four ingredients to blend together these super-fast, refreshing smoothies. Try them on a hot summer's day.

1-1/2 cups unsweetened apple juice
   1 cup frozen unsweetened raspberries
   1 cup frozen pitted dark sweet cherries
1-1/2 cups raspberry sherbet

In a blender, combine the apple juice, raspberries and cherries. Add the sherbet; cover and process until well blended. Pour into chilled glasses; serve immediately. **Yield:** 4 servings.

Easy Change-Up

Feel free to vary this recipe using different fruits...or by adding more. You could also substitute a different flavor of sherbet or juice.

🎖🎖🎖
Sweet 'n' Crunchy Mix
Prep/Total Time: 30 min.

Amy Briggs, Zimmerman, Minnesota

My kids like snacks with lots of crunch. When I combined a few of their favorite ingredients to create this mix, it was a hit.

2-1/2 cups Rice Chex
2-1/2 cups Honey-Nut Cheerios
   1 package (10 ounces) honey bear-shaped crackers
   2 cups miniature pretzels
 1/2 cup butter, melted
 1/3 cup packed brown sugar
4-1/2 teaspoons ground cinnamon

1. In a large bowl, combine cereals, graham crackers and pretzels. In a small bowl, combine the butter, brown sugar and cinnamon; pour over the cereal mixture and toss to coat. Spread into two ungreased 15-in. x 10-in. x 1-in. baking pans.

2. Bake at 275° for 10 minutes. Stir; bake 10 minutes longer. Store in an airtight container. **Yield:** about 1-1/2 quarts.

🎀🎀🎀
Honey-Mustard Turkey Meatballs

Prep: 20 min. **Bake:** 30 min.

Bonnie Durkin, Nescopeck, Pennsylvania

I serve these often during the holiday season. The tangy meatballs can be prepared ahead and frozen, so even drop-in guests can be treated to a hot appetizer.

- 1 egg, lightly beaten
- 3/4 cup crushed butter-flavored crackers
- 1/2 cup shredded part-skim mozzarella cheese
- 1/4 cup chopped onion
- 1/2 teaspoon ground ginger
- 6 tablespoons Dijon mustard, *divided*
- 1 pound ground turkey
- 1 tablespoon cornstarch
- 1/4 teaspoon onion powder
- 1-1/4 cups unsweetened pineapple juice
- 1/4 cup chopped green pepper
- 2 tablespoons honey

1. In a large bowl, combine the egg, cracker crumbs, cheese, onion, ginger and 3 tablespoons mustard. Crumble turkey over mixture and mix well. Shape into 30 (1-in.) balls.

2. Place meatballs on a greased rack in a shallow baking pan. Bake, uncovered, at 350° for 20-25 minutes or until juices run clear; drain.

3. In a small saucepan, combine the cornstarch and onion powder. Stir in the pineapple juice until smooth.

Add pepper and honey. Bring to a boil; cook and stir 2 minutes or until thickened. Reduce heat; stir in remaining mustard until smooth.

4. Brush meatballs with about 1/4 cup sauce and bake 10 minutes longer. Serve remaining sauce as a dip for meatballs. **Yield:** 2-1/2 dozen.

🎀🎀🎀
Granola Trail Mix

Prep/Total Time: 5 min.

Shelley Riddlespurger, Amarillo, Texas

My family has always enjoyed this crunchy, four-ingredient snack. When we go camping, each person includes one additional ingredient, such as mini marshmallows, corn chips or cookie pieces. The taste is never the same, and we're often surprised by the yummy combinations we come up with.

- 1 package (16 ounces) banana-nut granola
- 1 package (15 ounces) raisins
- 1 package (14 ounces) milk chocolate M&M's
- 1 can (12 ounces) honey-roasted peanuts

In a large bowl, combine all ingredients. Store in an airtight container. **Yield:** 11 cups.

Blue Cheese 'n' Fruit Tossed Salad, p. 27

Pecan Spinach Salad, p. 30

Calico Cranberry Couscous Salad, p. 36

Special Salads

Toss together these memorable medleys for neighborhood potlucks, Sunday picnics, weekday dinners and everything in between. No matter what the occasion, you'll find just the right main dish or side to round out your menu.

Green Bean Tossed Salad....................22

Asparagus Berry Salad.......................22

Polynesian Shrimp Salad...................23

Tangerine Tossed Salad 23

Summer Chicken Salad.....................24

Fiery Chicken Spinach Salad...............24

Chicken Salad with Crispy Wontons....26

Sunny Carrot Salad...........................26

Blue Cheese 'n' Fruit Tossed Salad 27

Cajun Potato Salad...........................27

Beef Fajita Salad..............................28

Grilled Chicken and Pear Salad.........28

Greek Veggie Salad 30

Pecan Spinach Salad..........................30

Cucumber Couscous Salad.................31

Colorful Coleslaw.............................31

Vegetarian Taco Salad........................32

Spicy Pork Tenderloin Salad...............32

Frozen Date Salad............................34

Crispy Chicken Strip Salad.................34

Misty Melon Salad...........................35

Blue Cheese Pear Salad......................35

Calico Cranberry Couscous Salad........36

Tangy Potato Salad...........................36

Harvest Green Salad..........................37

Flavorful Cranberry Gelatin Mold........37

Harvest Green Salad, p. 37

6 to 8 tablespoons olive oil
1/4 cup cider vinegar
3 to 4 teaspoons sugar
1/2 to 1 teaspoon salt
1/4 teaspoon pepper
4 cups torn mixed salad greens
1 ripe avocado, peeled and sliced
1/2 cup chopped pecans

1. Place the beans in a large saucepan and cover with water; bring to a boil. Cook, uncovered, for 8-10 minutes or until crisp-tender. Drain and rinse in cold water.

2. In a large bowl, combine the beans, oranges and onion. In a small bowl, whisk the oil, vinegar, sugar, salt and pepper. Pour over bean mixture and toss to coat. Cover and refrigerate for at least 2 hours. Just before serving, add the salad greens, avocado and pecans; toss gently. **Yield:** 8-9 servings.

When to Measure

If the word "chopped" comes before the ingredient when listed in a recipe, then chop the ingredient before measuring it. If the word "chopped" comes after the ingredient, then chop after measuring.

🎗 🎗 🎗
Green Bean Tossed Salad

Prep: 20 min. + chilling

Shirley Kosto, Chugiak, Alaska

To spruce up a salad recipe featuring mandarin oranges, red onion and lettuce, I decided to add some fresh green beans. This unusual medley was the tasty result.

1-1/2 pounds fresh green beans, trimmed
1 can (11 ounces) mandarin oranges, drained
1 medium red onion, thinly sliced

🎗 🎗 🎗
Asparagus Berry Salad

Prep/Total Time: 30 min.

Trisha Kruse, Eagle, Idaho

This sensational salad is such a treat when asparagus and strawberries are at their peak. I like to serve it for brunch or dinner…and I sometimes add grilled chicken or salmon to create a refreshing but filling main dish.

1 pound fresh asparagus, trimmed and cut into 1-inch pieces
3 tablespoons olive oil, *divided*
1/4 teaspoon salt
1/4 teaspoon coarsely ground pepper
8 cups spring mix salad greens
3 cups sliced fresh strawberries
1/2 small red onion, thinly sliced
1/2 cup chopped walnuts, toasted
2 tablespoons balsamic vinegar
2 teaspoons sugar

1. In a large bowl, toss the asparagus with 1 tablespoon oil. Spread in a greased 15-in. x 10-in. x 1-in. baking

pan. Sprinkle with salt and pepper. Bake at 400° for 15-20 minutes or until tender.

2. In a large salad bowl, toss the greens, strawberries, onion, walnuts and asparagus. In a small bowl, whisk the vinegar, sugar and remaining oil. Pour over salad; toss to coat. **Yield:** 6-8 servings.

Polynesian Shrimp Salad

Prep: 20 min. + chilling

Elaine Carncross, Hilo, Hawaii

Pineapple is one of our state's best-known products, and I make the most of that tangy fruit in recipes such as this one. With plenty of shrimp and pasta, this salad is a real crowd-pleaser and a fantastic choice for summertime luncheons.

> 1 can (20 ounces) pineapple chunks
> 2 teaspoons cornstarch
> 1/2 to 1 teaspoon curry powder
> 1/8 teaspoon salt
> 1/8 teaspoon pepper
> 1/3 cup mayonnaise
> 1/3 cup sour cream
> 1 pound cooked medium shrimp, peeled and deveined
> 2 cups cooked medium pasta shells
> 1 can (8 ounces) sliced water chestnuts, drained
> 1/4 cup chopped sweet red pepper

1. Drain the pineapple, reserving 3/4 cup juice; set pineapple aside. In a small saucepan, combine the cornstarch, curry powder, salt, pepper and reserved pineapple juice until smooth. Bring to a boil; cook and stir for 1 minute or until thickened. Remove from the heat; cool to room temperature. Stir in mayonnaise and sour cream.

2. In a large bowl, combine the shrimp, pasta, water chestnuts, red pepper and reserved pineapple. Add dressing and toss to coat. Cover and refrigerate for at least 2 hours before serving. **Yield:** 6-8 servings.

Tangerine Tossed Salad

Prep: 40 min.

Helen Musenbrock, O'Fallon, Missouri

I learned to cook from my mother when I was a young girl. One of my favorite recipes is this green salad, which features a combination of sweet tangerines and crunchy caramelized almonds.

> 1/2 cup sliced almonds
> 3 tablespoons sugar, *divided*
> 2 medium tangerines *or* navel oranges
> 6 cups torn lettuce
> 3 green onions, chopped
> 2 tablespoons cider vinegar
> 2 tablespoons olive oil
> 1/4 teaspoon salt
> 1/4 teaspoon pepper

1. In a small skillet, cook and stir the almonds and 2 tablespoons sugar over medium-low heat for 25-30 minutes or until the sugar is melted and the almonds are toasted. Remove from the heat. Peel and section the tangerines, reserving 1 tablespoon juice.

2. In a large bowl, combine lettuce, onions, tangerines and almonds. In a small bowl, whisk the vinegar, oil, salt, pepper, reserved juice and remaining sugar. Pour over salad; toss to coat. **Yield:** 6 servings.

4 boneless skinless chicken breast halves
  (4 ounces *each*)
1 can (14-1/2 ounces) chicken broth
6 cups torn mixed salad greens
2 cups halved fresh strawberries
CITRUS DRESSING:
1/2 cup fresh strawberries, hulled
1/3 cup orange juice
2 tablespoons canola oil
1 tablespoon lemon juice
2 teaspoons grated lemon peel
1 teaspoon sugar
1/2 teaspoon chili powder
1/4 teaspoon salt
1/4 teaspoon pepper
1/4 cup chopped walnuts, toasted

1. Place chicken in a large skillet; add broth. Bring to a boil. Reduce heat; cover and simmer for 20-25 minutes or until a meat thermometer reads 170°. Drain; cover and refrigerate. In a large bowl, combine greens and sliced strawberries; refrigerate.

2. In a blender, combine the hulled strawberries, orange juice, oil, lemon juice and lemon peel, sugar, chili powder, salt and pepper. Cover and process until smooth. Pour into a small saucepan. Bring to a boil. Reduce heat; simmer for 5-6 minutes until slightly thickened. Cool slightly.

3. Drizzle half of the dressing over greens and berries; toss to coat. Divide among four plates. Cut chicken into 1/8-in. slices; arrange over salads. Drizzle the remaining dressing over chicken; sprinkle with walnuts. **Yield:** 4 servings.

🎗🎗🎗

Summer Chicken Salad

Prep: 10 min. **Cook:** 25 min. + chilling

Nancy Whitford, Edwards, New York

I found this recipe many years ago in a church cookbook. With a tangy citrus dressing, the summery salad is special enough for a fancy dinner but easy enough to fix for a light lunch. Even my picky son enjoys it.

Fiery Chicken Spinach Salad

Prep/Total Time: 10 min.

6 frozen breaded spicy chicken breast strips, thawed
1 package (6 ounces) fresh baby spinach
1 medium tomato, cut into 12 wedges
1/2 cup chopped green pepper
1/2 cup fresh baby carrots
1 can (15 ounces) black beans, rinsed and drained
1 can (11 ounces) Mexicorn, drained
3 tablespoons salsa
3 tablespoons barbecue sauce

3 tablespoons prepared ranch salad dressing
2 tablespoons shredded Mexican cheese blend

1. Heat chicken strips in a microwave according to package directions. Meanwhile, arrange the spinach on individual plates; top with the tomato, green pepper, carrots, beans and corn.

2. In a small bowl, combine salsa, barbecue sauce and ranch dressing. Place chicken over salads. Drizzle with dressing; sprinkle with cheese. **Yield:** 6 servings.

Editor's Note: This recipe was tested in a 1,100-watt microwave.

KATI SPENCER TAYLORSVILLE, UTAH

With packaged chicken breast strips as well as canned black beans and Mexicorn, this hearty salad is easy to throw together when I get home from work. I sometimes add a can of ripe olives and fresh cherry tomatoes from our garden.

❧❧❧ Chicken Salad with Crispy Wontons

Prep/Total Time: 30 min.

Kylea Rorabaugh, Kansas City, Missouri

My mother often made this when I was growing up. When I starting fixing it myself, I added veggies and lightened up the dressing. I also bake the wontons instead of frying them.

☑ This recipe includes Nutrition Facts and Diabetic Exchanges.

- 10 wonton wrappers, cut into 1/4-inch strips
- 1/4 cup cider vinegar
- 3 tablespoons canola oil
- 3/4 teaspoon sesame oil
- 2 tablespoons sugar
- 3/4 teaspoon salt
- 1/4 teaspoon pepper
- 5 cups torn romaine
- 3 cups cubed cooked chicken breast
- 1 medium sweet red pepper, cut into 1/4-inch strips
- 1 medium sweet yellow pepper, cut into 1/4-inch strips
- 1/2 cup halved grape tomatoes

1. Lightly spritz both sides of the wonton strips with cooking spray; place on a baking sheet. Broil 4-6 in. from the heat for 2-3 minutes or until golden brown.

Turn the strips over; broil 2-3 minutes longer or until golden brown. Remove to wire racks to cool.

2. For dressing, in a small bowl, whisk the vinegar, canola oil, sesame oil, sugar, salt and pepper; set aside. In a large bowl, combine the romaine, chicken, peppers and tomatoes. Just before serving, drizzle with dressing and toss to coat. Top with wonton strips. **Yield:** 10 servings.

Nutrition Facts: 1 cup equals 149 calories, 6 g fat (1 g saturated fat), 33 mg cholesterol, 253 mg sodium, 10 g carbohydrate, 1 g fiber, 14 g protein. **Diabetic Exchanges:** 2 very lean meat, 1 fat, 1/2 starch.

❧❧❧ Sunny Carrot Salad

Prep/Total Time: 10 min.

Barb Hunter, Ponder, Texas

Almonds and sunflower kernels give a pleasing crunch to this speedy twist on carrot-raisin salad. If you prefer a nuttier flavor, use 1/2 cup of sunflower kernels instead of 1/3 cup.

- 3 cups shredded carrots
- 2 cups unsweetened crushed pineapple, drained
- 1/2 cup golden raisins
- 1/3 cup mayonnaise
- 1/2 cup sliced almonds
- 1/3 cup unsalted sunflower kernels

In a large serving bowl, combine the carrots, pineapple and golden raisins. Stir in the mayonnaise. Cover salad and refrigerate until serving. Just before serving, add the almonds and sunflower kernels; toss to coat. **Yield:** 5 servings.

❦❦❦
Blue Cheese 'n' Fruit Tossed Salad

Prep/Total Time: 20 min.

Michel Larson, Chandler, Arizona

I discovered a version of this refreshing salad recipe in the newspaper and changed it a bit to suit my family. I serve the homemade oil-and-vinegar dressing on the side so each person can add as much or as little as desired.

- 1/4 cup canola oil
- 2 tablespoons water
- 2 tablespoons plus 1-1/2 teaspoons cider vinegar
- Sugar substitute equivalent to 1 tablespoon sugar
- 1-1/4 teaspoons poppy seeds
- 3/4 teaspoon grated onion
- 1/2 teaspoon ground mustard
- 1/4 teaspoon salt
- 4 cups torn romaine
- 2 medium unpeeled Granny Smith apples, chopped
- 1 can (11 ounces) mandarin oranges, drained
- 1/3 cup pecan halves, toasted
- 1/2 cup crumbled blue cheese

1. In blender, combine the first eight ingredients; cover and process until blended. In a large bowl, combine the romaine, apples, mandarin oranges and pecans. Add the dressing and toss to coat; sprinkle with blue cheese. **Yield:** 8 servings.

Editor's Note: This recipe was tested with Splenda no-calorie sweetener.

❦❦❦
Cajun Potato Salad

Prep: 35 min. **Cook:** 25 min.

Rita Futral, Starkville, Mississippi

I experimented to come up with this recipe, and I think it's one of the most unique potato salads I've ever tasted. The addition of shrimp makes it hearty enough to be a main dish.

- 5 medium red potatoes
- 6 cups water
- 3 tablespoons seafood seasoning
- 1 tablespoon salt
- 1 pound medium uncooked shrimp
- 1/4 cup chopped green onions
- 1 jar (2 ounces) diced pimientos, drained
- 1/2 cup mayonnaise
- 1 teaspoon cider vinegar
- 1/2 teaspoon sugar
- Additional salt to taste

1. Place the potatoes in a large saucepan; add water, seafood seasoning and salt. Bring to a boil. Reduce heat; cover and simmer for 25 minutes.

2. Add the shrimp; cover and cook for 5 minutes or until shrimp turn pink and potatoes are tender. Drain. Peel and dice potatoes. Peel and devein the shrimp; cut into pieces.

3. In a large bowl, combine the potatoes, shrimp, onions and pimientos. In a small bowl, combine the mayonnaise, vinegar and sugar. Add to potato mixture; gently toss to coat. Season with the additional salt. Cover and refrigerate for at least 1 hour before serving. **Yield:** 8-10 servings.

1/4 cup lime juice
2 tablespoons minced fresh cilantro
1 garlic clove, minced
1 teaspoon chili powder
3/4 pound beef top sirloin steak, cut into thin strips
1 medium green pepper, julienned
1 medium sweet red pepper, julienned
1 medium onion, sliced and halved
1 teaspoon olive oil
1 can (16 ounces) kidney beans, rinsed and drained
4 cups torn mixed salad greens
1 medium tomato, chopped
4 tablespoons fat-free sour cream
2 tablespoons salsa

🎗 🎗 🎗
Beef Fajita Salad

Prep/Total Time: 30 min.

Ardeena Harris, Roanoke, Alabama

This easy Southwestern salad is delicious and on the lighter side, too. It features colorful peppers, beans, tomato and tender strips of beef, which marinate for just 10 minutes but get great flavor from the lime juice, cilantro and chili powder.

✓ This recipe includes Nutrition Facts and Diabetic Exchanges.

1. In a large resealable plastic bag, combine the lime juice, cilantro, garlic and chili powder; add the beef. Seal bag and turn to coat; refrigerate for 10 minutes, turning once.

2. Meanwhile, in a nonstick skillet, cook peppers and onion in oil over medium-high heat for 5 minutes or until tender. Remove and keep warm. Add beef with marinade to the skillet; cook and stir for 4-5 minutes or until meat is tender and mixture comes to a boil. Add beans and pepper mixture; heat through.

3. Divide salad greens and tomato among four bowls; top each with 1-1/4 cups beef mixture, 1 tablespoon sour cream and 1-1/2 teaspoons salsa. **Yield:** 4 servings.

Nutrition Facts: 1 serving equals 291 calories, 6 g fat (2 g saturated fat), 50 mg cholesterol, 291 mg sodium, 34 g carbohydrate, 9 g fiber, 27 g protein. **Diabetic Exchanges:** 2 lean meat, 2 vegetable, 1-1/2 starch.

Grilled Chicken and Pear Salad

Prep/Total Time: 25 min.

5 boneless skinless chicken breast halves (4 ounces *each*)
7 cups torn mixed salad greens
2 ounces Brie cheese, cubed
2 medium pears, chopped
1/4 cup chopped pecans, toasted
1/4 cup thawed apple juice concentrate
2 tablespoons canola oil
4-1/2 teaspoons cider vinegar
2 teaspoons Dijon mustard
1/4 teaspoon salt
1/8 teaspoon pepper

1. Coat the grill rack with cooking spray before starting the grill. Grill chicken, covered, over medium heat for 6-8 minutes on each side or until a meat thermometer reads 170°.

2. Arrange the salad greens, cheese, pears and pecans on individual plates. Slice chicken; arrange over salad. Whisk the apple juice concentrate, oil, vinegar, mustard, salt and pepper. Drizzle over salad. **Yield:** 5 servings.

JANET DURAN DES MOINES, WASHINGTON

When I served this fresh-tasting salad at a shower, I received many compliments and requests for the recipe. The toasted pecans provide a fun crunch, and the vinaigrette wonderfully accents the grilled chicken and Brie cheese.

Grand
Prize
Winner

3 medium tomatoes, cut into wedges
3 medium green peppers, julienned
2 medium cucumbers, peeled and sliced
2 medium onions, coarsely chopped
1/4 cup olive oil
2 tablespoons plus 2 teaspoons red wine vinegar
1 tablespoon minced fresh dill
1 garlic clove, minced
1/2 teaspoon minced fresh oregano
1/8 teaspoon salt
Dash pepper
1 cup (4 ounces) crumbled feta cheese
12 pitted Greek olives
6 anchovy fillets, halved

In a large bowl, combine the tomatoes, green peppers, cucumbers and onions. Whisk together the oil, vinegar, dill, garlic, oregano, salt and pepper. Pour over the tomato mixture; toss to coat. Cover and refrigerate for at least 2 hours. Top with the cheese, olives and anchovies. **Yield:** 12 servings.

Nutrition Facts: 1 cup equals 105 calories, 7 g fat (2 g saturated fat), 7 mg cholesterol, 254 mg sodium, 7 g carbohydrate, 2 g fiber, 4 g protein. **Diabetic Exchanges:** 1-1/2 fat, 1 vegetable.

Greek Veggie Salad

Prep: 25 min. + chilling

Sue Dannahower, Fort Pierce, Florida

Cucumbers, feta cheese and anchovies make this colorful salad a winner. The vinegar-and-oil dressing offers a touch of garlic and herbs, which helps pull all of the flavors together.

Pecan Spinach Salad

Prep/Total Time: 10 min.

Karen Robinson, Calgary, Alberta

Coated with a pleasant homemade vinaigrette and topped with toasted pecans and blue cheese, this salad both looks and tastes impressive. It can be prepared in 10 minutes or less, but your guests will never believe it!

3 cups fresh baby spinach
1/2 cup chopped pecans, toasted
1/3 cup real bacon bits
1/4 cup crumbled blue cheese
DRESSING:
1/3 cup olive oil
2 tablespoons cider vinegar
2 teaspoons brown sugar
1/2 teaspoon dried thyme
1/2 teaspoon minced garlic
1/4 teaspoon salt

In a large salad bowl, combine the spinach, pecans, bacon and blue cheese. In a small bowl, whisk the dressing ingredients. Pour over salad; toss to coat. **Yield:** 4 servings.

1-1/4 cups water
  1 cup uncooked couscous
  2 medium cucumbers, peeled, quartered
    lengthwise and sliced
  1 cup chopped sweet red pepper
1/4 cup thinly sliced green onions
1/2 cup buttermilk
1/4 cup reduced-fat plain yogurt
  2 tablespoons minced fresh dill
  2 tablespoons white vinegar
  1 tablespoon olive oil
1/2 teaspoon salt
1/4 teaspoon pepper

1. In a small saucepan, bring water to a boil. Stir in couscous. Remove from heat; cover and let stand for 5 minutes. Fluff with a fork. Cool to room temperature.

2. In a large bowl, combine the couscous, cucumbers, red pepper and onions. Whisk together the buttermilk, yogurt, dill, vinegar, oil, salt and pepper. Pour over couscous mixture. Cover and refrigerate for at least 1 hour. **Yield:** 8 servings.

Nutrition Facts: 2/3 cup equals 126 calories, 2 g fat (trace saturated fat), 1 mg cholesterol, 172 mg sodium, 22 g carbohydrate, 2 g fiber, 5 g protein. **Diabetic Exchanges:** 1 starch, 1 vegetable, 1/2 fat.

🏅🏅🏅
Cucumber Couscous Salad

Prep: 25 min. + chilling

Evelyn Lewis, Independence, Missouri

Try chicken or grilled salmon as a main course alongside this refreshing medley. Its combination of cucumber and dill tastes great, and couscous makes it a hearty side dish.

✓ This recipe includes Nutrition Facts and Diabetic Exchanges.

- -

🏅🏅🏅
Colorful Coleslaw

Prep: 25 min. + chilling

Jeanette Jones, Muncie, Indiana

It seems every time I prepare this versatile coleslaw recipe, I adjust the ingredients a bit. I think this version tastes the best, and it also has the fewest calories.

  5 cups shredded cabbage
  1 *each* medium green, sweet red and yellow
    pepper, julienned
  2 cups julienned carrots
  6 green onions, thinly sliced
DRESSING:
2/3 cup rice vinegar
1/4 cup olive oil
Sugar substitute equivalent to 1/3 cup sugar
1/4 cup reduced-fat creamy peanut butter
  1 teaspoon salt
  1 teaspoon minced fresh gingerroot
1/2 teaspoon pepper

In a large bowl, combine the cabbage, peppers, carrots and onions. In a blender, combine the dressing ingredients; cover and process until smooth. Drizzle over the

vegetables and toss to coat. Cover and refrigerate for at least 1 hour. Toss; serve with a slotted spoon. **Yield:** 8 servings.

Editor's Note: This recipe was tested with Splenda no-calorie sweetener.

🎗 🎗 🎗
Vegetarian Taco Salad

Prep/Total Time: 25 min.

Susan LeBrun, Sulphur, Louisiana

The cute tortilla bowls that hold this Southwestern salad are a snap to bake in the oven. We use canned beans that include hot spices to punch up the flavor.

✓ This recipe includes Nutrition Facts and Diabetic Exchanges.

4 whole wheat tortillas (8 inches)
6 cups shredded romaine
1/2 cup canned pinto beans, rinsed and drained
1 small tomato, chopped
1/4 cup shredded reduced-fat cheddar cheese
1/4 cup chopped green onions
2 tablespoons sliced ripe olives, drained
Sliced jalapeno peppers, optional
DRESSING:
1/2 cup fat-free sour cream
2 tablespoons fat-free ranch salad dressing
1 teaspoon taco seasoning
1/4 teaspoon hot pepper sauce, optional

1. Place four 10-oz. custard cups upside down in a shallow baking pan; set aside. Place the tortillas in a single layer on ungreased baking sheets.

2. Bake at 425° for 1 minute. Place a tortilla over each custard cup, pinching sides to form a bowl shape. Bake for 7-8 minutes or until crisp. Remove tortillas from cups to cool on wire racks.

3. In a large bowl, combine the romaine, beans, tomato, cheese, onions, olives and jalapenos if desired. In a small bowl, whisk the dressing ingredients. Pour over the salad; toss to coat. Serve salad in the tortilla bowls. **Yield:** 4 servings.

Editor's Note: When cutting hot peppers, disposable gloves are recommended. Avoid touching your face.

Nutrition Facts: 1 tortilla bowl with 1-1/4 cups dressed salad equals 257 calories, 5 g fat (1 g saturated fat), 10 mg cholesterol, 485 mg sodium, 40 g carbohydrate, 6 g fiber, 11 g protein. **Diabetic Exchanges:** 2 starch, 1 lean meat, 1 vegetable.

Spicy Pork Tenderloin Salad

Prep: 20 min. **Cook:** 35 min.

4-1/2 teaspoons lime juice
1-1/2 teaspoons orange juice
1-1/2 teaspoons Dijon mustard
1/2 teaspoon curry powder
1/4 teaspoon salt
1/8 teaspoon pepper
2 tablespoons olive oil
SPICE RUB:
1/2 teaspoon salt
1/2 teaspoon ground cumin
1/2 teaspoon ground cinnamon
1/2 teaspoon chili powder
1/4 teaspoon pepper
1 pork tenderloin (1 pound)
2 teaspoons olive oil
1/3 cup packed brown sugar
6 garlic cloves, minced
1-1/2 teaspoons hot pepper sauce
1 package (6 ounces) fresh baby spinach

1. In a small bowl, whisk the first six ingredients; gradually whisk in oil. Cover and refrigerate vinaigrette. Combine the salt, cumin, cinnamon, chili powder and pepper; rub over meat.

2. In a ovenproof skillet, brown the meat on all sides in oil, about 8 minutes. Combine the brown sugar, garlic and hot pepper sauce; spread the mixture over the meat.

3. Bake at 350° for 25-35 minutes or until a meat thermometer reads 160°. Let stand for 5 minutes before slicing.

4. Toss spinach with vinaigrette. Arrange spinach on four salad plates; top with sliced pork. Drizzle with pan juices. **Yield:** 4 servings.

PAT SELLON MONTICELLO, WISCONSIN

A friend served this curry-flavored dish at a luncheon, and I tweaked the recipe a bit to fit my family's tastes. The salad is not only great for entertaining, but also for weeknight dinners. Hot sauce adds a bit of a kick.

Grand Prize Winner

🎀🎀🎀
Frozen Date Salad

Prep: 10 min. + freezing

Margaret Dowdy, North Vassalboro, Maine

Vermont is known for its delicious maple syrup, and that's where I discovered this recipe. With cream cheese, dates and walnuts, this salad complements many meals.

- 1 package (8 ounces) cream cheese, softened
- 1 cup maple syrup
- 1 can (20 ounces) unsweetened crushed pineapple, drained
- 1 cup chopped dates
- 1 cup chopped walnuts
- 1 carton (8 ounces) frozen whipped topping, thawed

1. Line a 9-in. x 5-in. loaf pan with plastic wrap. In a small bowl, beat cream cheese and syrup until smooth.

Fold in pineapple, dates, walnuts and whipped topping. Spoon into prepared pan; cover with foil. Freeze for at least 8 hours or overnight. May be frozen for up to 3 months.

2. Remove the salad from the freezer 20 minutes before serving. Invert onto a serving plate; cut into slices. **Yield:** 8 servings.

🎀🎀🎀
Crispy Chicken Strip Salad

Prep: 40 min. **Cook:** 10 min.

Lillian Julow, Gainesville, Florida

Serve this attractive salad for a luncheon, and you're sure to win raves. Well-seasoned chicken strips, raspberries and candied pecans top a bed of greens dressed with a fruity vinaigrette.

- 1 tablespoon butter
- 1/2 cup pecan halves
- 2 tablespoons sugar
- 3/4 cup all-purpose flour
- 2 tablespoons minced fresh tarragon *or* 2 teaspoons dried tarragon
- 1 tablespoon grated lemon peel
- 2 eggs
- 1 pound boneless skinless chicken breast, cut into 1-inch strips
- 2 tablespoons canola oil
- 4 cups spring mix salad greens
- 1 cup torn Bibb *or* Boston lettuce
- 1/2 cup raspberry vinaigrette
- 2 cups fresh *or* frozen unsweetened raspberries

1. In a small skillet, melt butter. Add pecans and cook over medium heat until the nuts are toasted, about 4 minutes. Sprinkle with sugar. Cook and stir for 2-4 minutes or until sugar is melted. Transfer to a greased foil-lined baking sheet; cool completely.

2. In a large resealable bag, combine the flour, tarragon and lemon peel. In a shallow bowl, beat the eggs. Add the chicken strips to flour mixture in batches; seal and shake to coat. Dip in eggs, then return to bag and coat again.

3. In a large skillet over medium heat, cook chicken in oil for 6-8 minutes or until no longer pink.

4. Break the pecans apart. Toss the greens and lettuce with vinaigrette; arrange on individual plates. Top with the raspberries, chicken strips and pecans. **Yield:** 4 servings.

🎀🎀🎀
Misty Melon Salad

Prep: 20 min. + chilling

Rita Reifenstein, Evans City, Pennsylvania

The poppy seed dressing in this recipe perfectly complements the mix of cantaloupe, honeydew, strawberries and pineapple. It's a salad that always adds refreshing flavor to your table.

- 1 medium cantaloupe, cut into cubes
- 1 medium honeydew, cut into cubes
- 2 cups fresh strawberries, halved
- 1 can (20 ounces) pineapple chunks
- 1/2 cup sugar
- 1 tablespoon chopped onion
- 1 teaspoon salt
- 1 teaspoon ground mustard
- 1/2 cup canola oil
- 2 to 3 teaspoons poppy seeds

1. In a large bowl, combine the cantaloupe, honeydew and strawberries. Drain pineapple, reserving 1/3 cup juice; set juice aside. Add pineapple to fruit mixture; cover and refrigerate until chilled.

2. For dressing, in a blender, combine the sugar, onion, salt, mustard and reserved pineapple juice; cover and process until blended. While processing, gradually add oil in a steady stream. Stir in poppy seeds. Cover and refrigerate until chilled. Serve with fruit salad. **Yield:** 10-12 servings.

🎀🎀🎀
Blue Cheese Pear Salad

Prep/Total Time: 20 min.

Tina Green, Albany, Oregon

I toss together this fresh-tasting medley either as a main course on hot days or as a side with grilled meat. The salad takes only a few minutes to prepare while the grill is warming.

- 3 tablespoons sugar
- 2 tablespoons chopped walnuts
- 1-1/2 cups torn Bibb *or* Boston lettuce
- 1/2 cup cubed cheddar cheese
- 1 medium pear, thinly sliced
- 1 slice sweet onion, separated into rings
- 2 tablespoons crumbled blue cheese
- 3 tablespoons poppy seed salad dressing

1. In a small heavy skillet, melt sugar over low heat. Add walnuts and stir to coat. Remove from the heat.

2. Divide lettuce between two serving plates; top with the cheddar cheese, pear and onion. Sprinkle with blue cheese and sugared walnuts. Drizzle with dressing. **Yield:** 2 servings.

1 cup water
3/4 cup uncooked couscous
1/2 cup dried cranberries
1/2 cup chopped celery
1/2 cup shredded carrot
1/4 cup chopped green onions
1/4 cup slivered almonds, toasted

DRESSING:
3 tablespoons red wine vinegar
1 tablespoon olive oil
1 tablespoon Dijon mustard
1/4 teaspoon salt
1/4 teaspoon pepper

🏅🏅🏅
Calico Cranberry Couscous Salad

Prep/Total Time: 20 min.

Rosemarie Matheus, Germantown, Wisconsin

A simple, homemade Dijon dressing jazzes up couscous, dried cranberries and green onions in this tasty salad. It can be served either chilled or at room temperature—we like it both ways.

1. In a small saucepan, bring water to a boil. Stir in couscous; cover and remove from the heat. Let stand for 5 minutes. Fluff with a fork; cool.

2. In a serving bowl, combine couscous, cranberries, celery, carrot, onions and almonds.

3. In a small bowl, whisk the dressing ingredients. Pour over the salad and toss to coat. Serve at room temperature or chilled. **Yield:** 6 servings.

Nutrition Facts: 1/2 cup equals 171 calories, 5 g fat (1 g saturated fat), 0 cholesterol, 176 mg sodium, 29 g carbohydrate, 3 g fiber, 5 g protein. **Diabetic Exchanges:** 1-1/2 starch, 1 fat, 1/2 fruit.

🏅🏅🏅
Tangy Potato Salad

Prep: 30 min. **Cook:** 15 min.

Ruth Towle, Belmont, New Hampshire

I downsized one of my recipes to come up with a creamy classic that serves just two. When my sister visits, I often put this potato salad on the menu alongside green beans and chicken.

2 medium potatoes, peeled
1/2 teaspoon cider vinegar
2 tablespoons diced sweet red pepper
2 tablespoons frozen peas, thawed
2 tablespoons chopped cucumber
1 tablespoon finely chopped onion
1/3 cup mayonnaise
1/3 cup sour cream
1/2 teaspoon prepared horseradish
1/8 teaspoon salt
1/8 teaspoon pepper

1. Place potatoes in a small saucepan and cover with water. Bring to a boil. Reduce heat; cover and cook for 15-20 minutes or until tender. Drain. Sprinkle with the vinegar.

2. When potatoes are cool enough to handle, cube and place in a small bowl. Add the red pepper, peas, cucumber and onion; toss gently to combine.

3. In a small bowl, combine the mayonnaise, sour cream, horseradish, salt and pepper. Pour over potato mixture; toss to coat. Cover and refrigerate until serving. **Yield:** 2 servings.

3 whole medium fresh beets
1 large sweet potato, peeled and cubed
2 tablespoons water
1/2 cup reduced-fat balsamic vinaigrette
2 tablespoons jellied cranberry sauce
1 package (5 ounces) spring mix salad greens
1/2 cup dried cranberries
4 ounces crumbled Gorgonzola cheese

1. Wash beets; trim stem and leave root intact. Wrap beets in aluminum foil. Place on a baking sheet. Bake at 400° for 1 hour or until tender. Remove foil and cool.

2. In a microwave-safe bowl, combine the sweet potato and water. Cover and microwave on high for 4-5 minutes or until tender. Cool.

3. In a blender, combine vinaigrette and cranberry sauce; cover and process until smooth. Peel beets and cut into slices. On six salad plates, arrange the greens, beets and sweet potatoes. Sprinkle with cranberries and cheese. Drizzle with dressing. **Yield:** 6 servings.

Editor's Note: Use plastic gloves when peeling beets to avoid stains. This recipe was tested in a 1,100-watt microwave.

🎖️ 🎖️ 🎖️

Harvest Green Salad

Prep: 25 min. **Bake:** 1 hour + cooling

Beth Royals, Richmond, Virginia

Whenever I serve this green salad chock-full of cranberries, beets, sweet potato and cheese, it gets rave reviews. Guests say it fills them up without weighing them down.

🎖️ 🎖️ 🎖️

Flavorful Cranberry Gelatin Mold

Prep: 10 min. + chilling

Jenice Gibson, Oregon City, Oregon

I make this traditional gelatin featuring cranberry sauce, pineapple and walnuts for our holiday dinners. A little port or Merlot wine provides a delicious twist.

☑ This recipe includes Nutrition Facts and Diabetic Exchanges.

2 packages (.3 ounce *each*) sugar-free raspberry gelatin
1-1/2 cups boiling water
1 can (20 ounces) unsweetened crushed pineapple, drained
1 can (14 ounces) whole-berry cranberry sauce
1/2 cup chopped walnuts
1/3 cup port wine *or* red grape juice
Mint leaves for garnish, optional

1. In a large bowl, dissolve gelatin in boiling water. Stir in pineapple, cranberry sauce, walnuts and wine.

2. Pour into a 5-cup mold coated with cooking spray. Run a knife through the gelatin mixture to evenly distribute the fruit. Refrigerate mixture for 2-1/2 hours or until firm.

3. Unmold onto a serving plate. Garnish with mint if desired. **Yield:** 8 servings.

Nutrition Facts: 1/2 cup equals 193 calories, 4 g fat (trace saturated fat), 0 cholesterol, 66 mg sodium, 33 g carbohydrate, 2 g fiber, 3 g protein. **Diabetic Exchanges:** 1 starch, 1 fruit, 1 fat.

Italian Chicken Wraps, p. 45

Curried Chicken Salad Sandwiches, p. 42

Mexican Shrimp Bisque, p. 54

Soups & Sandwiches

That classic combo of soup and sandwich only gets better thanks to the winning creations here. Choose from Rocky Ford Chili, Pineapple-Stuffed Burgers, Bacon Clam Chowder, Beef Gyros and more…you just can't go wrong!

Fresh Mozzarella Sandwiches.............40

Rocky Ford Chili...........................40

Genoa Sandwich Loaf.....................41

Tuna Puff Sandwiches 41

Two-Potato Soup..........................42

Curried Chicken Salad Sandwiches......42

Black Bean Soup with Fruit Salsa 44

Beefy Mushroom Soup.....................44

Mushroom Potato Soup....................45

Italian Chicken Wraps.....................45

Grilled Beef Tenderloin Sandwiches......46

Turkey Pasta Soup.........................46

Hearty Country Burgers....................48

Bacon Clam Chowder.......................48

Zesty Garlic-Avocado Sandwiches........49

Chipotle Turkey Chili 49

Florentine Chicken Soup...................50

Sweet Pepper Sandwiches.................50

Buffalo Chicken Wraps.....................52

Roast Beef Barbecue.......................52

Open-Faced Crab Salad Sandwiches....53

Bacon 'n' Egg Salad Sandwiches.............53

Hearty Muffuletta..........................54

Mexican Shrimp Bisque....................54

Southwestern Chicken Soup...............56

Beef Gyros..................................56

Buffalo Chicken Sandwiches..............57

Garlic Tomato Soup........................57

Chicken Tortilla Soup......................58

Pineapple-Stuffed Burgers.................58

Garlic Tomato Soup, p. 57

Fresh Mozzarella Sandwiches

Prep: 25 min. **Cook:** 35 min.

Kristine Chayes, Smithtown, New York

As children, my sisters and I always helped our mother fix these hearty melted cheese sandwiches. Served with a robust tomato sauce for dipping, they made a quick, nutritious lunch or dinner. Now, I prepare them for my own family.

- 1/4 **cup chopped onion**
- 2 **tablespoons olive oil**
- 1 **garlic clove, minced**
- 1 **can (28 ounces) crushed tomatoes in puree**
- 1 **teaspoon grape jelly**
- 1/2 **teaspoon dried oregano**
- 1/2 **teaspoon dried basil**
- 1/2 **teaspoon salt**
- 1/8 **teaspoon pepper**

SANDWICHES:
- 1 **pound fresh mozzarella cheese, cut into 1/2-inch slices**
- 8 **slices sourdough bread (3/4 inch thick)**
- 2 **eggs, lightly beaten**
- 3/4 **cup milk**
- 1/2 **teaspoon salt**
- 1/4 **teaspoon pepper**
- 2 **tablespoons butter**

1. In a large saucepan, saute onion in oil until tender. Add garlic; cook 1 minute longer. Stir in the tomatoes, jelly, oregano, basil, salt and pepper. Bring to a boil. Reduce the heat; simmer, uncovered, for 20 minutes, stirring several times.

2. Meanwhile, for sandwiches, arrange cheese on four slices of bread to within 1/2 in. of edges. Top with remaining bread. In a shallow bowl, combine the eggs, milk, salt and pepper. Dip sandwiches in egg mixture.

3. Melt 1 tablespoon butter in a large skillet over medium heat. Add two sandwiches; toast over medium heat for 4-5 minutes on each side or until golden brown and the cheese is melted. Repeat with the remaining sandwiches and butter. Serve with tomato sauce for dipping. **Yield:** 4 servings.

Rocky Ford Chili

Prep/Total Time: 10 min.

Karen Golden, Phoenix, Arizona

When my brother and sister were in grade school in Colorado, this comforting chili was served in the school cafeteria. My siblings described it to my mom so she could make it at home.

- 2 **cans (14.3 ounces *each*) chili with beans**
- 1 **package (10 ounces) frozen corn**
- 4 **cups corn chips**
- 1 **cup shredded lettuce**
- 1 **cup (4 ounces) shredded Mexican cheese blend**
- 1 **can (2-1/4 ounces) sliced ripe olives, drained**
- 1/4 **cup sour cream**
- 1/4 **cup salsa**

1. In a large microwave-safe bowl, microwave chili and corn on high for 2-4 minutes or until heated through. Place corn chips in four large soup bowls;

top with the chili mixture, lettuce, cheese, olives, sour cream and salsa. **Yield:** 4 servings.

Editor's Note: This recipe was tested in a 1,100-watt microwave.

✿✿✿
Genoa Sandwich Loaf

Prep: 20 min. **Bake:** 15 min. + standing

Melita Doyle, Milton Freewater, Oregon

I'm an Italian American and love this open-faced sandwich because it tastes like the "old country." I fix it for family gatherings, and my Irish husband enjoys it just as much as my relatives do. The homemade pesto adds a special touch.

1/3	cup olive oil
1-1/4	cups packed minced fresh parsley
1	cup minced fresh basil
1/2	cup shredded Parmesan cheese, *divided*
4	garlic cloves, peeled
1/4	teaspoon ground nutmeg
1	package (8 ounces) cream cheese, softened
1	loaf (1 pound) French bread, halved lengthwise
1	pound thinly sliced hard salami
2	large tomatoes, thinly sliced

1. For pesto, in a blender, combine the oil, parsley, basil, 1/4 cup Parmesan cheese, garlic and nutmeg. Cover and process on high until blended.

2. Spread the cream cheese over cut sides of bread; spread with pesto. Layer the salami and tomatoes over pesto; sprinkle with the remaining Parmesan cheese. Place on an ungreased baking sheet. Bake at 350° for 15-20 minutes or until cheese is melted. Let stand for 10 minutes before cutting. **Yield:** 8-10 servings.

✿✿✿
Tuna Puff Sandwiches

Prep/Total Time: 30 min.

Stella Dobmeier, Kamloops, British Columbia

My husband and I can't get enough of this great supper sandwich. The cheese-covered tomato slices deliciously top off the mild tuna salad. Sometimes I replace the tuna with canned salmon, ham, chicken or turkey.

3/4	cup mayonnaise, *divided*
2	tablespoons chopped green pepper
1-1/2	teaspoons grated onion
1-1/2	teaspoons prepared mustard
1/4	teaspoon Worcestershire sauce
1	pouch (7.1 ounces) tuna
3	hamburger buns, split
6	slices tomato
3/4	cup shredded cheddar cheese

1. In a small bowl, combine 1/4 cup mayonnaise, green pepper, onion, mustard and Worcestershire sauce; stir in tuna. Spread over each bun half; top each with a tomato slice. Arrange sandwiches on a baking sheet.

2. In another bowl, combine the cheese and remaining mayonnaise; spoon cheese mixture over tomato. Bake at 400° for 11-13 minutes or until topping is puffy and golden brown. **Yield:** 6 servings.

1/2 **pound small unpeeled red potatoes, cut into chunks**
1/2 **pound medium russet potatoes, peeled and cut into chunks**
1 **can (14-1/2 ounces) reduced-sodium chicken broth**
1 **cup water**
1/4 **cup chopped onion**
2 **teaspoons canola oil**
1 **tablespoon all-purpose flour**
1/4 **cup 2% milk**
2 **tablespoons evaporated milk**
3 **tablespoons cream cheese, cubed**
1 **tablespoon minced fresh parsley**
1/4 **teaspoon salt**
1/8 **teaspoon white pepper**
1/3 **cup shredded Swiss cheese**

1. Place the potatoes in a large saucepan; add broth and water. Bring to a boil. Reduce heat; cover and cook for 10-15 minutes or until almost tender. Meanwhile, in a small skillet, saute onion in oil until tender; add to potatoes.

2. In a small bowl, combine flour, milk and evaporated milk until smooth; add to the potato mixture. Bring to a boil; cook and stir for 2 minutes or until thickened. Reduce heat; stir in the cream cheese, parsley, salt and pepper. Cover and simmer for 5-10 minutes or until the cream cheese is melted and the potatoes are tender, stirring occasionally. Garnish with Swiss cheese. **Yield:** about 3 cups.

Nutrition Facts: 1 cup (prepared with reduced-fat cream cheese, fat-free evaporated milk and reduced-fat Swiss cheese) equals 245 calories, 8 g fat (3 g saturated fat), 17 mg cholesterol, 689 mg sodium, 33 g carbohydrate, 3 g fiber, 12 g protein.

🎀 🎀 🎀
Two-Potato Soup
Prep/Total Time: 30 min.

Pamela Reiling-Kemp, Roselle, Illinois

Potato chunks, Swiss cheese and onions fill this creamy soup recipe that came from my mother. It's especially good on crisp autumn and cold winter afternoons. For variety, I sometimes add chopped celery and a dash of green hot sauce.

Curried Chicken Salad Sandwiches
Prep/Total Time: 20 min.

2 **cups cubed cooked chicken breast**
3/4 **cup chopped apple**
3/4 **cup dried cranberries**
3/4 **cup mayonnaise**
1/2 **cup chopped walnuts**
1/2 **cup chopped celery**
2 **teaspoons lemon juice**
1 **tablespoon chopped green onion**

1 **teaspoon curry powder**
6 **lettuce leaves**
6 **croissants, split**

In a large bowl, combine the chicken, apple, dried cranberries, mayonnaise, walnuts, celery, lemon juice, onion and curry powder. Place the lettuce on croissants. Top with the chicken salad mixture. **Yield:** 6 servings.

CAROLE MARTIN COFFEEVILLE, MISSISSIPPI

This is the perfect sandwich to serve when you're having company and want to "show off" a little. It has an interesting blend of chicken, walnuts, dried cranberries, curry and more. I mix it up the night before so the flavors have time to blend.

Grand Prize Winner

🎀🎀🎀
Black Bean Soup With Fruit Salsa

Prep: 20 min. **Cook:** 20 min.

Michaela Rosenthal, Woodland Hills, California

Peppers and cumin bring Southwestern flair to this flavorful, filling soup, and a bowlful is a complete meal-in-one. The fruit salsa makes an unusual but refreshing topping.

- 1/4 cup diced seeded peeled cucumber
- 1/4 cup diced peeled mango
- 1/4 cup diced fresh pineapple
- 2 tablespoons chopped sweet onion
- 4-1/2 teaspoons lime juice
- 1-1/2 teaspoons grated lime peel
- 1-1/2 teaspoons minced fresh cilantro
- 1/4 teaspoon chopped seeded jalapeno pepper

SOUP:

- 3 bacon strips, diced
- 3/4 cup chopped red onion
- 1 Anaheim pepper, seeded and chopped
- 2 garlic cloves, minced
- 2 cups reduced-sodium chicken broth
- 1 can (15 ounces) black beans, rinsed and drained
- 4 teaspoons lime juice
- 1 teaspoon ground cumin
- 1/2 teaspoon lemon-pepper seasoning
- 1/2 teaspoon ground coriander

1. For salsa, combine the first eight ingredients in a small bowl; set aside. In a saucepan, saute bacon and onion until bacon is crisp and onion is tender. Add Anaheim pepper and garlic; cook 1 minute longer. Stir in the remaining ingredients. Bring to a boil. Reduce heat; simmer, uncovered, for 10 minutes. Cool slightly.

2. Puree half of the soup in a blender; return to pan. Bring to a boil. Reduce heat; simmer for 5 minutes. Serve with fruit salsa. **Yield:** 3 cups.

Editor's Note: When cutting hot peppers, disposable gloves are recommended. Avoid touching your face.

🎀🎀🎀
Beefy Mushroom Soup

Prep/Total Time: 30 min.

Ginger Ellsworth, Caldwell, Idaho

Here's a great way to use up leftover roast or steak and get a quick supper on the table at the same time. The rich taste of this satisfying mushroom soup is sure to please.

- 1 medium onion, chopped
- 1/2 cup sliced fresh mushrooms
- 2 tablespoons butter
- 2 tablespoons all-purpose flour
- 2 cups reduced-sodium beef broth
- 2/3 cup cubed cooked roast beef
- 1/2 teaspoon garlic powder
- 1/4 teaspoon paprika
- 1/4 teaspoon pepper
- 1/8 teaspoon salt

Dash hot pepper sauce

- 1/4 cup shredded part-skim mozzarella cheese, optional

1. In a large saucepan, saute the onion and mushrooms in butter until the onion is tender; remove with a slotted spoon and set aside. In a small bowl, whisk the flour and broth until smooth; gradually add to the pan. Bring to a boil; cook and stir for 1-2 minutes or until thickened.

2. Add the roast beef, garlic powder, paprika, pepper, salt, pepper sauce and onion mixture; cook and stir until heated through. Garnish with cheese if desired. **Yield:** 3 cups.

Mushroom Potato Soup

Prep: 15 min. **Cook:** 25 min.

Clare Wallace, Lynchburg, Virginia

Plenty of veggies make this cream soup hearty and warming. It really hits the spot, especially on a cold fall or winter day. For potatoes that hold together well in boiling water, try waxy red ones or all-purpose Yukon Golds.

- 2 medium leeks, sliced
- 2 large carrots, sliced
- 6 tablespoons butter, *divided*
- 6 cups chicken broth
- 5 cups diced peeled potatoes
- 1 tablespoon minced fresh dill
- 1 teaspoon salt
- 1/8 teaspoon pepper
- 1 bay leaf
- 1 pound sliced fresh mushrooms
- 1/4 cup all-purpose flour
- 1 cup heavy whipping cream

1. In a Dutch oven or soup kettle, saute leeks and carrots in 3 tablespoons butter for 5 minutes or until tender. Stir in the broth, potatoes, dill, salt, pepper and bay leaf. Bring to a boil. Reduce heat; cover and simmer for 15-20 minutes or until potatoes are tender.

2. Meanwhile, in a large skillet, saute mushrooms in remaining butter for 4-6 minutes or until tender. Discard bay leaf from soup. Stir in mushroom mixture.

3. In a small bowl, combine the flour and cream until smooth; gradually stir into the soup. Bring to a boil; cook and stir for 2 minutes or until thickened. **Yield:** 12 servings (3 quarts).

Italian Chicken Wraps

Prep/Total Time: 25 min.

Cathy Hofflander, Adrian, Michigan

After enjoying a chicken wrap at a restaurant, I experimented at home to create something similar. This five-ingredient version with veggies and Parmesan cheese is fast and delicious.

- 1 package (16 ounces) frozen stir-fry vegetable blend
- 2 packages (6 ounces *each*) ready-to-use grilled chicken breast strips
- 1/2 cup fat-free Italian salad dressing
- 3 tablespoons shredded Parmesan cheese
- 6 flour tortillas (8 inches), room temperature

1. In a large saucepan, cook vegetables according to package directions; drain. Stir in the chicken, salad dressing and cheese. Simmer, uncovered, for 3-4 minutes or until heated through.

2. Spoon about 3/4 cup down center of each tortilla; roll up tightly. **Yield:** 6 servings.

🏅🏅🏅
Grilled Beef Tenderloin Sandwiches

Prep: 15 min. + marinating **Cook:** 70 min.

Ruth Lee, Troy, Ontario

Sweet-sour onions and fresh mushrooms are perfect over the tender beef and lip-smacking garlic mayonnaise in these sandwiches. Give them a try when you want a change of pace from the usual beef burgers on the grill.

> 1 tablespoon brown sugar
> 2 garlic cloves, minced
> 1/2 teaspoon coarsely ground pepper
> 1/4 teaspoon salt
> 1 beef tenderloin roast (1 pound)
> 1 whole garlic bulb
> 1/2 teaspoon canola oil
> 1/4 cup *each* fat-free mayonnaise and plain yogurt
> ONION TOPPING:
> 1 tablespoon olive oil
> 1 large sweet onion, thinly sliced
> 1/2 pound sliced fresh mushrooms
> 2 tablespoons balsamic vinegar
> 1-1/2 teaspoons sugar
> 1/8 teaspoon salt
> 1/8 teaspoon pepper
> 4 slices French bread (3/4 inch thick)
> 1 cup fresh arugula

1. Combine the first four ingredients; rub over meat. Refrigerate for 2 hours. Remove papery outer skin from garlic (do not peel or separate cloves). Cut top off of garlic. Brush with canola oil.

2. Wrap bulb in heavy-duty foil. Bake at 425° for 30-35 minutes or until softened. Cool for 10-15 minutes. Squeeze garlic into food processor; add mayonnaise and yogurt. Process until smooth; chill.

3. In a large nonstick skillet, heat olive oil and saute onion for 5 minutes. Reduce heat; cook and stir for 10-12 minutes or until onion is golden. Add mushrooms; cook and stir until tender. Add next four ingredients; cook until reduced slightly.

4. Coat grill rack with cooking spray before starting the grill. Grill beef, covered, over medium heat for 5-6 minutes on each side or until meat reaches desired doneness (for medium-rare, a meat thermometer should read 145°; medium, 160°; well-done, 170°). Let stand for 10 minutes before cutting into 4 slices.

5. Serve warm on bread with garlic mayonnaise, arugula and onion mixture. **Yield:** 4 servings.

Turkey Pasta Soup
Prep/Total Time: 30 min.

> 1 cup uncooked small pasta shells
> 1 pound lean ground turkey
> 2 medium onions, chopped
> 2 garlic cloves, minced
> 3 cans (14-1/2 ounces *each*) reduced-sodium chicken broth
> 2 cans (15 ounces *each*) white kidney or cannellini beans, rinsed and drained
> 2 cans (14-1/2 ounces *each*) Italian stewed tomatoes
> 2 teaspoons dried oregano
> 2 teaspoons dried basil
> 1 teaspoon fennel seed, crushed
> 1 teaspoon pepper
> 1/2 teaspoon salt
> 1/4 teaspoon crushed red pepper flakes

1. Cook the pasta according to package directions. Meanwhile, in a large stockpot, cook the turkey, onions and garlic over medium heat until meat is no longer pink; drain. Stir in the broth, beans, tomatoes and seasonings. Bring to a boil. Reduce heat; simmer, uncovered, for 10 minutes.

2. Drain pasta and add to the soup. Cook 5 minutes longer or until heated through. **Yield:** 10 servings.

MARIE EWERT RICHMOND, MICHIGAN

This quick but filling soup has such terrific flavor that everyone I've shared it with has asked for the recipe. I've found that it simmers up nicely in a slow cooker as well as on the stove. Serve it with your favorite sandwiches or rolls.

2 garlic cloves, minced
1 tablespoon olive oil
1/3 cup plus 1 teaspoon lime juice, *divided*
2 tablespoons cola, *divided*
1 tablespoon orange juice
1 tablespoon soy sauce
1 pound ground beef
1/2 teaspoon garlic powder
4 slices provolone cheese
4 bacon strips, halved and cooked
4 hamburger buns, split and toasted
4 lettuce leaves
4 slices tomato
1 slice onion, separated into rings

1. In a small skillet, saute the garlic in oil for 1 minute or until golden. Stir in 1/3 cup lime juice, 1 tablespoon cola, orange juice and soy sauce. Bring to a boil; cook and stir for 5-6 minutes or until slightly thickened. Set aside for basting.

2. Crumble beef into a large bowl. Sprinkle with the garlic powder and remaining lime juice and cola; mix well. Shape into four 3/4-in.-thick patties.

3. Grill, covered, over medium heat for 8-9 minutes on each side or until a meat thermometer reads 160°, basting occasionally with sauce. During the last 2 minutes, top burgers with cheese and bacon. Serve on buns with lettuce, tomato and onion. **Yield:** 4 servings.

🎀 🎀 🎀
Hearty Country Burgers

Prep: 15 min. **Grill:** 20 min.

Gladys Gibbs, Brush Creek, Tennessee

When I'm planning a menu for a casual country cookout, these dressed-up burgers are at the top of my list. Bacon, lettuce, tomato, cheese and a touch of sauce really boost the flavor. Plus, the mildly seasoned meat always turns out nice and juicy.

🎀 🎀 🎀
Bacon Clam Chowder

Prep: 15 min. **Cook:** 25 min.

Betty Lineaweaver, Paradise, California

Chopping the clams into tiny pieces adds big flavor to this full-bodied chowder. Everyone says it's the best they've ever tasted. I like to serve it with garlic bread or a side salad.

1 can (6-1/2 ounces) minced clams
1 cup reduced-sodium chicken broth
1 medium potato, peeled and cubed
1/2 cup chopped celery
1/4 cup chopped onion
1/2 teaspoon chicken bouillon granules
1/4 teaspoon dried thyme
1 tablespoon cornstarch
1/2 cup half-and-half cream
1-1/2 teaspoons butter
Dash cayenne pepper
2 bacon strips, cooked and crumbled

1. Drain the clams, reserving juice; set aside. Place the clams in a food processor; cover and process until finely chopped. Set aside.

2. In a large saucepan, combine broth, potato, celery, onion, bouillon and thyme. Bring to a boil. Reduce heat; simmer, uncovered, for 10-12 minutes or until vegetables are tender. Stir in the reserved clam juice.

3. Combine the cornstarch and cream until smooth; gradually stir into soup. Bring to a boil; cook and stir for 2 minutes or until thickened. Stir in the butter, cayenne and clams. Cook and stir over medium heat for 3-4 minutes or until heated through. Garnish with bacon. **Yield:** 3 cups.

This is a satisfying meatless sandwich I developed using several of our family's favorite ingredients—garlic, avocado, cream cheese and bagels. Any leftover spread makes an excellent dip for vegetables. For a twist, add some chopped fresh chives or minced sun-dried tomato to the cream cheese.

🎗️ 🎗️ 🎗️

Zesty Garlic-Avocado Sandwiches

Prep/Total Time: 30 min.

Tricia Farnum, Branson West, Missouri

1 package (8 ounces) cream cheese, softened
2 medium ripe avocados, peeled
1 garlic clove, minced
1/8 teaspoon salt
6 whole grain bagels, split and toasted
6 slices tomato
1/2 cup sliced cucumber
6 slices red onion
6 sweet red pepper rings
6 lettuce leaves

In a small bowl, beat the cream cheese, avocados, garlic and salt until smooth. Spread on the bagels; top with the tomato, cucumber, red onion, red pepper rings and lettuce. **Yield:** 6 servings.

🎗️ 🎗️ 🎗️

Chipotle Turkey Chili

Prep: 25 min. **Cook:** 1-1/2 hours

Christie Ladd, Mechanicsburg, Pennsylvania

I combined a few of my chili recipes and came up with this spicy variety that uses ground turkey instead of beef. It's a terrific meal served with crusty rolls or baked tortilla chips.

1 can (7 ounces) chipotle peppers in adobo sauce
1-1/4 pounds lean ground turkey
3 medium carrots, chopped
1 medium green pepper, chopped
1/2 cup chopped onion
4 garlic cloves, minced
1 can (28 ounces) crushed tomatoes
1 can (14-1/2 ounces) reduced-sodium chicken broth
1 can (8 ounces) tomato sauce
1-1/2 teaspoons dried oregano
1-1/2 teaspoons dried basil
1 teaspoon chili powder
1/2 teaspoon ground cumin
1 can (16 ounces) kidney beans, rinsed and drained
1 can (15 ounces) garbanzo beans or chickpeas, rinsed and drained

1. Drain chipotle peppers; set aside 2 tablespoons adobo sauce. Seed and chop three peppers; set aside. (Save remaining peppers and sauce for another use.)

2. In a large Dutch oven or soup kettle coated with cooking spray, cook the turkey, carrots, green pepper,

onion, garlic and reserved peppers over medium heat until meat is no longer pink; drain if necessary. Stir in the tomatoes, broth, tomato sauce, oregano, basil, chili powder, cumin and reserved adobo sauce. Bring to a boil. Reduce heat; cover and simmer for 1 hour.

3. Stir in beans. Cover and simmer for 15-20 minutes or until heated through. **Yield:** 8 servings.

Editor's Note: When cutting hot peppers, disposable gloves are recommended. Avoid touching your face.

1 jar (7 ounces) roasted sweet red peppers, drained and sliced
3 fresh rosemary sprigs, chopped
1/2 teaspoon garlic powder
1/4 teaspoon pepper
1 tablespoon butter
1-1/2 cups reduced-sodium chicken broth
3/4 cup Alfredo sauce
3 tablespoons prepared pesto
2 tablespoons pine nuts, toasted
1 tablespoon shredded Parmesan cheese

1. Cook pasta according to package directions. Meanwhile, in a large saucepan, saute chicken, spinach, red peppers, rosemary, garlic powder and pepper in butter until spinach is wilted. Stir in broth, sauce and pesto; cook for 4-5 minutes or until heated through.

2. Drain pasta and add to the soup. Sprinkle with pine nuts and cheese. **Yield:** 5 cups.

Florentine Chicken Soup

Prep/Total Time: 30 min.

Cindie Henf, Sebastian, Florida

My husband likes Alfredo sauce, so I'm always looking for new variations. This easy-to-fix soup is wonderful with crusty Italian bread and a tomato-mozzarella-basil salad. Best of all, the recipe makes the perfect amount for the two of us.

1 cup uncooked penne pasta
1 package (6 ounces) ready-to-use chicken breast cuts
4 cups chopped fresh spinach

Noodle Know-How

When pasta is cooked in soup, it absorbs quite a bit of liquid and gives off starch. This makes the noodles very mushy and the soup broth very thick. To avoid this, try cooking the pasta separately, then adding it to the soup at the end of the cooking time.

Sweet Pepper Sandwiches

Prep/Total Time: 25 min.

✓ This recipe includes Nutrition Facts and Diabetic Exchanges.

1 *each* small green, sweet red and yellow pepper, thinly sliced
1 small onion, thinly sliced
1 tablespoon olive oil
1 garlic clove, minced
1 tablespoon balsamic vinegar
2 ounces fresh mozzarella cheese
1/4 cup fat-free mayonnaise
1/2 teaspoon prepared horseradish
4 hard rolls, split and toasted
8 fresh basil leaves
1 plum tomato, thinly sliced

1. In a large nonstick skillet, saute peppers and onion in oil until crisp-tender. Add the garlic; cook 1 minute longer. Drizzle with vinegar; toss to coat.

2. Cut mozzarella cheese into four slices. Combine the mayonnaise and horseradish; spread over cut sides of rolls. Spoon the vegetable mixture onto the bottom halves; top with cheese.

3. Broil 4-6 in. from the heat for 2-4 minutes or until the cheese is melted. Top with the basil leaves and tomato. Replace roll tops. **Yield:** 4 servings.

Nutrition Facts: 1 sandwich equals 278 calories, 10 g fat (3 g saturated fat), 13 mg cholesterol, 456 mg sodium, 39 g carbohydrate, 3 g fiber, 9 g protein.
Diabetic Exchanges: 2 starch, 1-1/2 fat, 1 vegetable.

CARA NETH FORT COLLINS, COLORADO

We love this recipe because it's easy to get on the table...and a great choice as a meatless meal. Family members assemble their own sandwiches to their liking, then I pop everyone's creations in the oven for a few minutes.

Grand
Prize
Winner

🎗🎗🎗
Buffalo Chicken Wraps
Prep/Total Time: 25 min.

Athena Russell, Florence, South Carolina

Blue cheese dressing and hot pepper sauce bring a kick to these tongue-tingling tortilla wraps. Filled with chicken, cheese, lettuce and tomatoes, they're fun to eat…and portable, too!

- 1 cup all-purpose flour
- 1 teaspoon salt
- 1/4 teaspoon pepper
- 1/2 cup buttermilk
- 4 boneless skinless chicken breast halves (4 ounces *each*)
- 1 cup canola oil
- 1/2 cup hot pepper sauce
- 1/4 cup butter, melted
- 4 spinach tortillas (10 inches)
- 1 cup shredded lettuce
- 1 cup (4 ounces) shredded cheddar cheese
- 2/3 cup chopped tomatoes
- 1/2 cup blue cheese salad dressing

1. In a shallow bowl, combine the flour, salt and pepper. Place buttermilk in another shallow bowl. Dip chicken in buttermilk, then roll in flour mixture.

2. In a large skillet, cook chicken in oil for 4-5 minutes on each side or until a meat thermometer reads 170°. Drain on paper towels; cut into strips.

3. In a small bowl, combine the hot pepper sauce and butter. Dip chicken strips into mixture, coating both sides. Place chicken in the center of each tortilla. Layer with the lettuce, cheese and tomatoes; drizzle with salad dressing. Bring up sides of tortillas; secure with toothpicks if desired. **Yield:** 4 servings.

🎗🎗🎗
Roast Beef Barbecue
Prep/Total Time: 10 min.

Agnes Ward, Stratford, Ontario

When I'm in a hurry and want something satisfying, this sandwich really fills the bill. It tastes great with a salad and baked beans on the side. For extra zip, I sometimes skip the ketchup and use barbecue sauce with a little Tabasco.

- 2/3 pound thinly sliced deli roast beef
- 1/2 cup water
- 1/4 cup ketchup
- 1 tablespoon brown sugar
- 1/2 teaspoon prepared mustard
- 1/4 teaspoon hot pepper sauce
- 1/8 teaspoon salt
- 1/8 teaspoon pepper
- 1/8 teaspoon chili powder
- 4 hamburger buns, split

In a small saucepan, combine first nine ingredients. Cook over medium-high heat for 4-6 minutes or until heated through. Serve on hamburger buns, using a slotted spoon. **Yield:** 4 servings.

🎗🎗🎗
Open-Faced Crab Salad Sandwiches

Prep/Total Time: 25 min.

Lanie Kappe, Santa Ana, California

Everyone loved the crab salad my mother-in-law contributed to a family gathering. When I got the recipe, I reduced the fat a bit to come up with this version. Serve it in hot or cold sandwiches… or as a spread for your favorite crackers.

- 1/2 cup reduced-fat mayonnaise
- 1/8 teaspoon salt
- 1/8 teaspoon pepper
- 2 packages (8 ounces *each*) imitation crabmeat, chopped
- 1 cup (4 ounces) shredded part-skim mozzarella cheese
- 1/4 cup chopped sweet red pepper
- 1/4 cup chopped green onions
- 1/4 cup chopped celery
- 1 loaf (8 ounces) unsliced French bread, halved lengthwise

1. In a large bowl, combine the mayonnaise, salt and pepper. Stir in the crab, cheese, red pepper, onions and celery. Spoon over bread halves.

2. Place on a baking sheet. Broil 5 in. from the heat for 7-8 minutes or until lightly browned. Cut into 3-in. pieces. **Yield:** 8 servings.

🎗🎗🎗
Bacon 'n' Egg Salad Sandwiches

Prep: 25 min. + chilling

Jane Ozment, Purcell, Oklahoma

When I don't have much time to cook, this yummy egg salad dressed up with cheddar cheese and crumbled bacon is the perfect option. The recipe calls for croissants, but it's also good with toasted bread or English muffins.

- 4 bacon strips, cooked and crumbled
- 1/2 cup shredded cheddar cheese
- 1/2 cup sour cream
- 1/3 cup mayonnaise
- 2 tablespoons minced chives
- 1/4 teaspoon salt
- 1/4 teaspoon pepper
- 10 hard-cooked eggs, chopped
- 8 lettuce leaves
- 8 croissants, split

In a large bowl, combine the first seven ingredients. Add the eggs and mix well. Cover and refrigerate for at least 2 hours. Serve on lettuce-lined croissants. **Yield:** 8 servings.

1/4 cup minced fresh parsley
3 tablespoons lemon juice
1 teaspoon dried oregano
1 garlic clove, minced
1/8 teaspoon pepper
1 round loaf (24 ounces) unsliced Italian bread
1/4 pound thinly sliced hard salami
1/4 pound provolone cheese
1/4 pound thinly sliced deli ham

1. In a large bowl, combine the first 12 ingredients. Cover; refrigerate for at least 8 hours. Drain, reserving 2 tablespoons liquid.

2. Cut the loaf of bread in half; hollow out top and bottom, leaving a 1-in. shell (discard removed bread or save for another use). Brush cut sides of bread with reserved liquid. Layer the bottom of the bread shell with salami, half of the olive mixture, cheese, remaining olive mixture and ham. Replace bread top. Cut into wedges. **Yield:** 8-10 servings.

Editor's Note: Giardiniera is a vegetable mixture available in mild and hot varieties. Look for it in the Italian or pickle section of your local grocery store.

🎗 🎗 🎗
Hearty Muffuletta
Prep: 55 min. + chilling

Ruth Hayward, Lake Charles, Louisiana

Famous here in Louisiana, muffulettas feature cold cuts, cheese and olive salad layered in an Italian bread shell. I was thrilled when a friend gave me this recipe so I could make them myself. More than a meal, it's a dining experience!

1/2 cup finely chopped celery
1/2 cup sliced pimiento-stuffed olives, drained
1/2 cup sliced ripe olives, drained
1/2 cup giardiniera
1/3 cup finely chopped onion
1/3 cup olive oil
1/4 cup finely chopped green onions

Made Meatless

Prefer a Hearty Muffuletta without meat? Experiment with replacing the salami and ham with grilled portobello mushroom caps, fresh tomato slices and spinach leaves.

Mexican Shrimp Bisque
Prep/Total Time: 30 min.

1/2 cup chopped onion
1 tablespoon olive oil
2 garlic cloves, minced
1 tablespoon all-purpose flour
1 cup water
1/2 cup heavy whipping cream
1 tablespoon chili powder
2 teaspoons chicken bouillon granules
1/2 teaspoon ground cumin
1/2 teaspoon ground coriander
1/2 pound uncooked medium shrimp, peeled and deveined
1/2 cup sour cream
Fresh cilantro and cubed avocado, optional

1. In a large saucepan, saute the onion in oil until tender. Add garlic; cook 1 minute longer. Stir in flour until blended. Stir in the water, heavy whipping cream, chili powder, bouillon, cumin and coriander; bring to a boil. Reduce heat; cover and simmer for 5 minutes.

2. Cut the shrimp into bite-size pieces; add to the soup. Simmer 5 minutes longer or until the shrimp turn pink.

3. Gradually stir 1/2 cup hot soup into sour cream; return all to the pan, stirring constantly. Heat through (do not boil). Garnish with cilantro and avocado if desired. **Yield:** 3 cups.

KAREN HARRIS CASTLE ROCK, COLORADO

I'm a fan of both Cajun and Mexican cuisine, and this rich, elegant soup combines the best of both worlds. I often serve big bowlfuls with a crispy green salad and glasses of our favorite white wine for a simple but special meal.

Grand
Prize
Winner

1/2 pound boneless skinless chicken breast, cut into 1/2-inch cubes
1/4 cup finely chopped onion
2 tablespoons olive oil
2 garlic cloves, minced
1 can (15-1/4 ounces) whole kernel corn, drained
1 can (15 ounces) black beans, rinsed and drained
1 can (14-1/2 ounces) chicken broth
1 can (10 ounces) diced tomatoes and green chilies, undrained
1 teaspoon ground cumin
1/2 teaspoon salt
1/2 teaspoon chili powder
1/8 teaspoon cayenne pepper
Plain yogurt and minced fresh cilantro

🎀🎀🎀
Southwestern Chicken Soup

Prep: 10 min. **Cook:** 25 min.

Terri Stevens, Ardmore, Oklahoma

This simple-to-fix soup is seasoned Southwestern-style and chock-full of chicken, corn, black beans and diced tomatoes. To round out your meal, try Mexican corn bread.

1. In a large skillet over medium heat, cook chicken and onion in oil until chicken is no longer pink. Add garlic; cook 1 minute longer.

2. Stir in the corn, beans, broth, tomatoes, cumin, salt, chili powder and cayenne. Bring to a boil. Reduce heat; cover and simmer for 10-15 minutes. Garnish with yogurt and cilantro. **Yield:** 4 servings.

🎀🎀🎀
Beef Gyros

Prep/Total Time: 30 min.

Sheri Scheerhorn, Hills, Minnesota

Going out to restaurants for gyros got to be expensive for our family, so I came up with this homemade version. I usually set out the fixings so everyone can assemble their own. My husband and our two busy teens request them often.

1 cup ranch salad dressing
1/2 cup chopped seeded peeled cucumber
1 pound beef top sirloin steak, cut into thin strips
2 tablespoons olive oil
5 whole gyro-style pitas (6 inches)
1 medium tomato, chopped
1 can (2-1/4 ounces) sliced ripe olives, drained
1/2 small onion, thinly sliced
1 carton (4 ounces) crumbled feta cheese
2-1/2 cups shredded lettuce

1. In a small bowl, combine the salad dressing and cucumber; set aside. In a large skillet, brown beef in oil over medium heat until no longer pink.

2. Layer half of each pita with the steak, tomato, olives, onion, feta cheese, lettuce and dressing mixture. Bring edges of each pita over filling and secure with a toothpick. **Yield:** 5 servings.

Here's a simple but sensational way to dress up breaded chicken patties. We like these sandwiches with additional blue cheese dressing for dipping. Or try them with Monterey Jack cheese and ranch dressing instead.

> 2 refrigerated breaded chicken patties
> 1/4 cup Louisiana-style hot sauce
> 2 teaspoons canola oil
> 2 tablespoons butter, softened
> 2 sandwich buns, split
> 2 slices provolone cheese
> 2 tablespoons blue cheese salad dressing

Lettuce, tomato and red onion slices
Additional hot sauce

1. Place chicken patties in a large resealable plastic bag; add hot sauce. Seal bag and turn to coat. In a large skillet, brown patties in oil over medium heat for 1-2 minutes on each side or until heated through. Remove and keep warm.

2. Spread butter over cut sides of buns. In the same skillet, toast buns, buttered side down, over medium heat for 1-2 minutes or until lightly browned. Top with a chicken patty, provolone cheese, salad dressing, lettuce, tomato and onion. Serve with additional hot sauce. **Yield:** 2 servings.

🏵🏵🏵
Buffalo Chicken Sandwiches
Prep/Total Time: 10 min.
Dawn Onuffer, Crestview, Florida

🏵🏵🏵
Garlic Tomato Soup
Prep: 30 min. Cook: 30 min.
Marilyn Coomer, Louisville, Kentucky

Roasted garlic adds a mellow background flavor to this rich, creamy creation. Using convenient canned tomatoes and tomato puree, the soup is a year-round favorite for both lunch and dinner. Store-bought varieties just can't measure up!

> 12 garlic cloves, peeled and sliced
> 1-1/2 teaspoons olive oil
> 1 can (14-1/2 ounces) diced tomatoes, undrained
> 1 cup tomato puree
> 1 pint heavy whipping cream
> 1/4 teaspoon dried oregano
> 1/4 teaspoon minced fresh basil
> 1/4 teaspoon salt
> 1/8 teaspoon pepper

1. In a 3-cup baking dish, combine the garlic and oil. Cover and bake at 300° for 25-30 minutes or until lightly browned.

2. In a large saucepan, bring the garlic, tomatoes and tomato puree to a boil. Reduce heat; cover and simmer for 30 minutes.

3. Add the cream, oregano, basil, salt and pepper. Cool slightly. Place half of the soup at a time in a blender; cover and process until pureed. Return to the pan; heat through. **Yield:** about 4 cups.

🎀🎀🎀 Chicken Tortilla Soup

Prep: 30 min. **Cook:** 25 min.

Kathy Averbeck, Dousman, Wisconsin

This Southwestern soup is ideal for using up your fresh garden bounty. To add richness, I first grill the chicken and veggies.

- 2 medium tomatoes
- 1 small onion, cut into wedges
- 1 garlic clove, peeled
- 4 teaspoons canola oil, *divided*
- 1 boneless skinless chicken breast half (6 ounces)
- 1/4 teaspoon lemon-pepper seasoning
- 1/8 teaspoon salt
- 2 corn tortillas (6 inches)
- 1/2 cup diced zucchini
- 2 tablespoons chopped carrot
- 1 tablespoon minced fresh cilantro
- 3/4 teaspoon ground cumin
- 1/2 teaspoon chili powder
- 1 cup reduced-sodium chicken broth
- 1/2 cup spicy hot V8 juice
- 1/3 cup frozen corn
- 2 tablespoons tomato puree
- 1-1/2 teaspoons chopped seeded jalapeno pepper
- 1 bay leaf
- 1/4 cup cubed *or* sliced avocado
- 1/4 cup shredded Mexican cheese blend

1. Brush the tomatoes, onion and garlic with 1 teaspoon oil. Broil 4 in. from the heat for 3-4 minutes on each side or until tender. Peel and discard charred skin from tomatoes; place in a blender. Add onion and garlic; cover and process for 1-2 minutes or until smooth.

2. Sprinkle the chicken with lemon-pepper and salt; broil for 5-6 minutes on each side or until a meat thermometer reads 170°. Cut one tortilla into 1/4-in. strips; coarsely chop remaining tortilla.

3. In a large saucepan, heat the remaining oil. Fry the tortilla strips until crisp and browned; remove with a slotted spoon. Set aside.

4. In the same pan, cook the zucchini, carrot, cilantro, cumin, chili powder and chopped tortilla over medium heat for 4 minutes. Stir in the tomato mixture, broth, V8 juice, corn, tomato puree, jalapeno and bay leaf. Bring to a boil. Reduce heat; simmer, uncovered, for 20 minutes.

5. Cut the chicken into strips and add to soup; simmer 5 minutes longer or until chicken is no longer pink. Discard bay leaf. Garnish with the avocado, cheese and tortilla strips. **Yield:** 3-1/2 cups.

Editor's Note: When cutting hot peppers, disposable gloves are recommended. Avoid touching your face.

Pineapple-Stuffed Burgers

Prep/Total Time: 30 min.

- 1/4 cup packed brown sugar
- 1/4 cup ketchup
- 1 tablespoon prepared mustard
- 1/2 pound lean ground beef (90% lean)
- 2 slices unsweetened pineapple
- 1/8 teaspoon salt
- 1/8 teaspoon pepper
- 2 hamburger buns, split
- 2 lettuce leaves

1. In a small saucepan, combine brown sugar, ketchup and mustard. Cook over medium heat for 2-3 minutes, stirring occasionally.

2. Meanwhile, shape beef into four patties. Place pineapple slices on two patties; top with remaining patties. Seal edges; sprinkle with salt and pepper.

3. Coat the grill rack with cooking spray before starting the grill. Grill the burgers, covered, over medium-hot heat for 7-9 minutes on each side or until a meat thermometer reads 160° and juices run clear. Serve on the buns with sauce and lettuce. **Yield:** 2 servings.

ANN COUCH HALIFAX, NORTH CAROLINA

These special beef burgers have a "surprise" inside—tangy pineapple slices. With brown sugar, mustard and ketchup, the homemade sauce makes these tropical grilled sandwiches even better. They're sure to please at backyard barbecues.

Grand
Prize
Winner

Cran-Apple Tea Ring, p. 64

Cherry Cream Cheese Coffee Cake, p. 72

Mashed Potato Kolachkes, p. 77

Breakfast & Brunch

Wake up your taste buds with the exceptional daybreak delights here. Thanks to treats such as Cherry Cream Cheese Coffee Cake, Pecan-Stuffed Waffles and Florentine Egg Bake, morning just might become your favorite part of the day!

Puffy Apple Omelet............................62

Apple Puff Pancake............................62

Sunshine Sweet Rolls.......................63

Almond Chip Scones 64

Cran-Apple Tea Ring.......................64

Great-Grandma's Prune Roll..............66

French Toast Supreme.......................66

Turkey Potato Pancakes......................67

Chocolate Croissants 67

Wild Rice Brunch Casserole..............68

Pecan-Stuffed Waffles 68

Speedy Sausage Squares.......................69

Peach Coffee Cake..............................69

French Banana Pancakes......................70

Florentine Egg Bake..........................70

Special Stuffed French Toast..............72

Cherry Cream Cheese Coffee Cake 72

Reuben Brunch Bake.......................73

Tacoed Eggs....................................73

Salmon Quiche.................................74

Strawberry Cream Crepes 74

Caramel Sweet Rolls.......................76

Cinnamon-Nut Coffee Cake...............76

Mashed Potato Kolachkes 77

Brunch Lasagna 78

Coconut-Chip Coffee Cake...............78

Chocolate-Cherry Cream Crepes........79

Pumpkin Pancakes............................79

Pumpkin Coffee Cake........................80

Almond Streusel Rolls.......................80

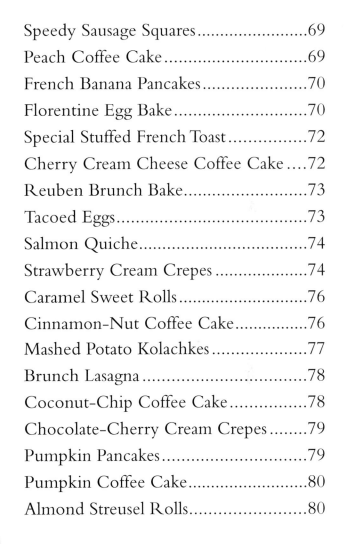

Sunshine Sweet Rolls, p. 63

3 tablespoons all-purpose flour
1/4 teaspoon baking powder
1/8 teaspoon salt, optional
2 eggs, *separated*
3 tablespoons milk
1 tablespoon lemon juice
3 tablespoons sugar
TOPPING:
1 large baking apple, peeled and thinly sliced
1 teaspoon sugar
1/4 teaspoon ground cinnamon

1. In a small bowl, combine the flour, baking powder and salt if desired. In a small bowl, whisk the egg yolks, milk and lemon juice. Stir into dry ingredients and mix well; set aside.

2. In another small bowl, beat egg whites on medium speed until soft peaks form. Gradually beat in the sugar, 1 tablespoon as a time, on high until stiff peaks form. Fold into yolk mixture.

3. Pour into a shallow 1-1/2-qt. baking dish coated with cooking spray. Arrange apple slices on top. Combine sugar and cinnamon; sprinkle over apples.

4. Bake, uncovered, at 375° for 18-20 minutes or until a knife inserted near the center comes out clean. Serve immediately. **Yield:** 2 servings.

Puffy Apple Omelet

Prep/Total Time: 30 min.

Melissa Davenport, Campbell, Minnesota

With all of the eggs our chickens produce, I could make this omelet every day! I often choose it for special occasions, but you could fix it anytime—whether for breakfast or supper.

Apple Puff Pancake

Prep/Total Time: 25 min.

Linda Hubbuch, Versailles, Kentucky

This thick, puffy pancake sprinkled with nuts looks and tastes so good, it gets high praise from family and company alike. For an extra-special touch, top each serving with warm maple syrup and a dollop of whipped cream.

1/3 cup butter
1 cup all-purpose flour
4 eggs
1 cup milk
Dash salt
1 can (21 ounces) apple *or* peach pie filling
Toasted walnuts, optional

1. Place butter in a 10-in. ovenproof skillet. Place in a 425° oven just until melted. In a large bowl, beat the flour, eggs, milk and salt until smooth. Leaving 1 tablespoon melted butter in the skillet, stir the remaining butter into the batter.

2. Pour the batter into the hot skillet. Bake for 15-20 minutes or until edges are golden brown.

3. Meanwhile, in a small saucepan, warm pie filling over low heat until heated through. Pour into center of puff pancake. Sprinkle with walnuts if desired. Serve immediately. **Yield:** 4 servings.

🎗🎗🎗
Sunshine Sweet Rolls

Prep: 30 min. + rising **Bake:** 25 min.

Alice Vivian Shepherd, Maryville, Tennessee

Here's a bread-machine recipe I love. The cream cheese filling and drizzled citrus icing make these golden brown rolls a real treat for breakfast or snacking.

1-1/2 cups warm water (110° to 115°)
1/4 cup canola oil
1/4 cup shredded carrot
4-1/2 cups all-purpose flour
1/4 cup sugar
1-1/2 teaspoons salt
2 teaspoons active dry yeast
FILLING:
1 package (8 ounces) cream cheese, softened
1/4 cup sugar
1 teaspoon vanilla extract
1 package (3 ounces) cook-and-serve vanilla pudding mix
1 jar (6 ounces) carrot baby food
1 teaspoon ground cinnamon
GLAZE:
1/2 cup confectioners' sugar
2 to 3 teaspoons orange juice
1/2 teaspoon grated orange peel
1/4 teaspoon vanilla extract

1. In bread machine pan, place first seven ingredients in order suggested by manufacturer. Select the dough setting (check dough after 5 minutes of mixing; add 1 to 2 tablespoons of water or flour if needed).

2. Meanwhile, in a small bowl, beat the cream cheese, sugar and vanilla extract until smooth; set aside. In a microwave-safe bowl, combine pudding mix, baby food and cinnamon until smooth. Cover and microwave on high for 2 minutes; stir.

3. When cycle is completed, turn dough onto a lightly floured surface. Divide in half; shape each portion into a ball. Roll each into a 9-in. x 8-in. rectangle. Spread cream cheese mixture to within 1/2 in. of edges; top with the carrot mixture. Roll up jelly-roll style, starting with a long side; pinch seam to seal.

4. Cut each into six rolls. Place cut side up in two greased 9-in. square baking pans. Cover and let rise in a warm place until doubled, about 30 minutes.

5. Bake at 350° for 25-30 minutes or until golden brown. Cool on wire racks for 5 minutes. Combine glaze ingredients; drizzle over warm rolls. **Yield:** 1 dozen.

Editor's Note: This recipe was tested in a 1,100-watt microwave.

3-1/2 cups all-purpose flour
2 tablespoons sugar
5 teaspoons baking powder
1 teaspoon salt
1/2 cup cold butter
4 eggs
1 cup heavy whipping cream
1-1/2 to 2 teaspoons almond extract
1 cup (6 ounces) semisweet chocolate chips
1/2 cup slivered almonds, toasted

Almond Chip Scones

Prep/Total Time: 30 min.

Heidi Rowley, Baton Rouge, Louisiana

For bridal showers or other special occasions, I often triple the recipe for these moist scones. Feel free to use blueberries instead of chocolate chips and almonds.

1. In a large bowl, combine the flour, sugar, baking powder and salt. Cut in butter until mixture resembles coarse crumbs.

2. In a small bowl, whisk 3 eggs, cream and extract; add to crumb mixture just until moistened. Gently stir in chips and almonds. Turn onto a floured surface; knead 6-8 times.

3. On a greased baking sheet, pat the dough into a 10-1/2-in. circle, about 3/4 in. thick. Cut into eight wedges. Beat the remaining egg; brush over dough. Slightly separate wedges.

4. Bake at 425° for 10-15 minutes or until golden brown. Serve warm. **Yield:** 8 servings.

Cran-Apple Tea Ring

Prep: 45 min. + rising **Bake:** 20 min. + cooling

1 package (1/4 ounce) active dry yeast
1/4 cup warm water (110° to 115°)
1/2 cup warm fat-free milk (110° to 115°)
1 egg
2 tablespoons butter, softened
1 tablespoon grated orange peel
1 teaspoon salt
3 tablespoons plus 1/2 cup sugar, *divided*
2-3/4 to 3-1/4 cups all-purpose flour
1 cup thinly sliced peeled apple
1 cup dried cranberries
1/2 cup chopped walnuts, toasted
1-1/2 teaspoons ground cinnamon
1 egg white
1 tablespoon water
1/2 cup confectioners' sugar
1 tablespoon orange juice

1. In a large bowl, dissolve yeast in warm water. Add the milk, egg, butter, orange peel, salt, 3 tablespoons sugar and 1 cup flour; beat until smooth. Stir in enough remaining flour to form a soft dough.

2. Turn onto a floured surface; knead until smooth and elastic, about 6-8 minutes. Place in a bowl coated with cooking spray; turn once to coat top. Cover and let rise in a warm place for 1 hour.

3. In a bowl, toss the apple, cranberries, walnuts, cinnamon and remaining sugar; set aside. Punch dough down; turn onto a lightly floured surface. Roll into a 20-in. x 10-in. rectangle. Combine egg white and water; chill 3 tablespoons. Brush remaining mixture over dough. Spoon the fruit mixture to within 1 in. of edges. Roll up tightly jelly-roll style, starting with a long side; seal ends.

4. Place seam side down in a 15-in. x 10-in. x 1-in. baking pan coated with cooking spray; pinch ends to form a ring. With scissors, cut from outside edge two-thirds of the way toward center of ring at 1-in. intervals. Separate strips slightly; twist so filling shows. Cover and let rise until doubled, about 40 minutes.

5. Brush with reserved egg white mixture. Bake at 375° for 20-25 minutes or until golden brown (cover with foil during the last 10 minutes). Remove to a wire rack to cool. Combine confectioners' sugar and orange juice; drizzle over ring. **Yield:** 16 servings.

NELLIE GRIMES JACKSONVILLE, TEXAS

Dried cranberries, apple slices and toasted walnuts make this citrus-glazed tea ring a wonderful addition to Sunday brunch, especially during the fall and winter seasons. Invite friends and family over to enjoy a few slices with coffee.

Grand Prize Winner

🏵🏵🏵 Great-Grandma's Prune Roll

Prep: 30 min. + rising **Bake:** 25 min.

Marci Kulla, Brush Prairie, Washington

Here's an old-fashioned favorite that brings back memories of home cooking with wholesome ingredients. A vanilla glaze drizzled over the loaves adds the perfect hint of sweetness.

> 1 package (1/4 ounce) active dry yeast
> 1 cup warm milk (110° to 115°)
> 1/2 cup butter, softened
> 1/2 cup shortening
> 3 egg yolks
> 3 tablespoons sugar
> 1 teaspoon salt
> 4 cups all-purpose flour

FILLING:

> 2 cups pitted dried plums
> 1/2 cup water
> 1/2 cup sugar
> 2 tablespoons lemon juice
> 1/4 cup butter
> 1/2 teaspoon ground cinnamon

GLAZE:

> 1 cup confectioners' sugar
> 1/4 teaspoon vanilla extract
> 2 to 3 tablespoons water

1. In a large bowl, dissolve the yeast in warm milk. Add the butter, shortening, egg yolks, sugar, salt and 3 cups flour. Beat until smooth. Stir in enough remaining flour to form a soft dough. Cover and refrigerate overnight.

2. In a large saucepan, cook the plums in water 12-15 minutes or until liquid is absorbed. Mash; add sugar and lemon juice. Cook for 8-10 minutes over low heat until thickened. Cool and refrigerate.

3. Turn dough onto a lightly floured surface; divide in half. Roll each portion into a 3-in. x 9-in. rectangle. Dot with butter; sprinkle with cinnamon. Spread about 1/3 cup plum filling down the center of each.

4. Fold a third of the dough lengthwise over filling. Fold remaining dough over top; pinch seams to seal and tuck ends under. Place seam side down in two greased 15-in. x 10-in. x 1-in. baking pans. Cover and let rise in a warm place for 2 hours or until doubled.

5. Bake at 350° for 25-30 minutes or until golden brown. Remove from the pans to wire racks to cool. Combine the glaze ingredients; drizzle over loaves. **Yield:** 2 loaves (12 slices each).

🏵🏵🏵 French Toast Supreme

Prep/Total Time: 15 min.

Elaine Bonica, Bethel, Maine

I like to use thick slices of French bread or homemade white bread when fixing these sandwiches. I served them with a fresh fruit salad at brunch, and everyone asked me for the recipe. It's easy to double or triple for a hungry crowd.

> 8 slices Texas toast
> 4 slices Canadian bacon
> 4 slices Monterey Jack cheese
> 1 egg
> 1/2 cup refrigerated French vanilla nondairy creamer

Confectioners' sugar, optional
> 1/4 cup seedless raspberry jam

1. On four slices of toast, place one slice of bacon and one slice of cheese; top with remaining toast. In a shallow bowl, whisk the egg and creamer. Dip the sandwiches into egg mixture.

2. On a hot griddle or large skillet coated with cooking spray, cook French toast for 2-3 minutes on each side or until golden brown. Sprinkle with confectioners' sugar if desired. Serve with jam. **Yield:** 4 servings.

🎗🎗🎗
Turkey Potato Pancakes

Prep: 10 min. **Cook:** 30 min.

Kathy Duerr, Fulda, Minnesota

My husband and our children like pancakes, and I appreciate quick suppers…so I gave this recipe a try. The addition of turkey turns golden potato pancakes into a heartier side dish.

        3 cups shredded peeled potatoes
    1-1/2 cups finely chopped cooked turkey
      1/4 cup sliced green onions with tops
        2 tablespoons all-purpose flour
    1-1/2 teaspoons salt
        3 eggs, lightly beaten
    Canola oil
    Cranberry sauce, optional

1. In a sieve or colander, drain the potato, squeezing to remove excess liquid. Pat dry; set aside. In a large bowl, combine turkey, onions, flour and salt. Stir in eggs until blended. Add reserved potatoes; toss to coat.

2. Heat about 2 tablespoons of oil in a large nonstick skillet over medium heat. Drop the pancake batter by 1/3 cupfuls into oil. Fry in batches until golden brown on both sides, using remaining oil as needed. Drain on paper towels.

3. Serve with the cranberry sauce if desired. **Yield:** 12 pancakes.

       12 unsliced croissants
        2 cups milk chocolate chips
      1/3 cup sugar
        1 teaspoon cornstarch
        1 teaspoon ground cinnamon
        1 cup milk
        4 eggs, lightly beaten
      1/2 cup half-and-half cream
        3 teaspoons vanilla extract

1. Cut a slit into the side of each croissant; fill with about 2 tablespoons chips. In a shallow bowl, combine the sugar, cornstarch and cinnamon; whisk in milk until smooth. Whisk in the eggs, cream and vanilla.

2. Dip croissants into egg mixture. Place in two greased 15-in. x 10-in. x 1-in. baking pans. Bake at 400° for 7-9 minutes or until golden brown. Serve warm. **Yield:** 1 dozen.

🎗🎗🎗
Chocolate Croissants

Prep/Total Time: 25 min.

Phyllis Johnston, Fayetteville, Tennessee

From time to time, we have stuffed French toast made from rich, buttery brioche. One Father's Day when I wanted to make it for my husband, the store was out of brioche, so I tried croissants instead. They turned out to be even simpler to use.

Cream Clue

Out of half-and-half? For dishes that are cooked or baked, you may substitute 4-1/2 teaspoons melted butter plus enough whole milk to equal 1 cup. One cup of evaporated milk may also be substituted for each cup of half-and-half.

CHEESE SAUCE:
- 2 tablespoons canola oil
- 3 tablespoons all-purpose flour
- 1 cup milk
- 2 cups (8 ounces) shredded Colby or Gouda cheese
- 1/2 teaspoon ground ginger
- Dash white pepper

1. Cook rice according to package directions. Spread in greased 13-in. x 9-in. baking dish; set aside.

2. Place asparagus and 1/2 in. of water in a large saucepan; bring to a boil. Reduce heat; cover and simmer for 3-5 minutes or until crisp-tender. Drain and set aside.

3. In a large skillet, saute the ham in 2 tablespoons butter until lightly browned. Spoon over wild rice.

4. In a large bowl, whisk eggs, milk, salt and pepper. In the same skillet, heat remaining butter until hot. Add egg mixture; cook and stir over medium heat until eggs are completely set. Spoon over ham; top with asparagus.

5. For sauce, heat oil in a saucepan. Stir in flour until smooth. Gradually stir in milk. Bring to a boil; cook and stir for 2 minutes or until thickened. Reduce the heat; add the cheese, ginger and pepper. Cook and stir 2 minutes longer or until cheese is melted.

6. Pour over casserole. Cover and bake at 325° for 30 minutes. Uncover; bake 10-15 minutes longer or until a thermometer reads 160°. **Yield:** 10 servings.

🎖🎖🎖
Wild Rice Brunch Casserole
Prep: 20 min. **Bake:** 40 min.

Meredith Berg, Hudson, Wisconsin

Wild rice is one of our state's prized foods, and here's a great way to enjoy it for breakfast. With asparagus, ham and a rich cheese sauce, this recipe is hard to beat.

- 1 package (4 ounces) wild rice
- 1-1/2 pounds fresh asparagus, trimmed and cut into 1-inch pieces
- 2 cups cubed fully cooked ham
- 5 tablespoons butter, *divided*
- 12 eggs
- 1/2 cup milk
- 1 teaspoon salt
- 1/4 teaspoon pepper

🎖🎖🎖
Pecan-Stuffed Waffles
Prep/Total Time: 15 min.

Jenny Flake, Gilbert, Arizona

This is a great recipe for entertaining because it's easy yet impressive. No one will guess the sugar-dusted waffles drizzled with syrup take just 15 minutes to prepare. And the sweet, creamy pecan filling between them is delectable!

- 8 frozen waffles
- 2 packages (3 ounces *each*) cream cheese, softened
- 1/2 cup packed brown sugar
- 1-1/2 teaspoons ground cinnamon
- 1 teaspoon vanilla extract
- 1/2 cup chopped pecans
- 1 cup maple syrup
- Confectioners' sugar
- 4 fresh strawberries, cut in half

1. Toast the waffles according to package directions. In a small bowl, beat the cream cheese, brown sugar, cinnamon and vanilla until smooth. Stir in pecans.

2. Spread over four waffles; top with the remaining waffles. Drizzle with syrup. Sprinkle with confectioners' sugar; garnish with a strawberry. **Yield:** 4 servings.

1 tube (8 ounces) refrigerated crescent rolls
1 pound bulk pork sausage
1/4 cup chopped onion
6 eggs, lightly beaten
3/4 cup milk
2 tablespoons chopped green pepper
1/2 teaspoon dried oregano
1/2 teaspoon pepper
1/4 teaspoon garlic salt
1 cup (4 ounces) part-skim shredded mozzarella cheese

1. Unroll crescent dough into a greased 13-in. x 9-in. baking dish; seal seams and perforations. Bake at 375° for 6 minutes or until golden brown.

2. Meanwhile, in a large skillet, cook sausage and onion over medium heat until meat is no longer pink; drain. In a small bowl, combine the eggs, milk, green pepper, oregano, pepper and garlic salt; pour over crust. Sprinkle with sausage mixture.

3. Bake for 15-20 minutes. Sprinkle with cheese; bake 5 minutes longer or until the cheese is melted. **Yield:** 12 servings.

Speedy Sausage Squares

Prep: 15 min. **Bake:** 30 min.

Miriam Yoder, Houstonia, Missouri

Whenever I want to serve something special for a family brunch, this is usually what I choose. I'll get the ingredients together the night before so it's a snap to bake the next morning.

Peach Coffee Cake

Prep: 20 min. **Bake:** 20 min. + cooling

Diana Krol, Nickerson, Kansas

This from-scratch coffee cake is quick to put together and easily serves a crowd. While it's delicious with peach or apricot pie filling, I like to give it red color during the Christmas holiday season using cherry or strawberry.

1 cup butter, softened
1-3/4 cups sugar
4 eggs
3 cups all-purpose flour
1-1/2 teaspoons salt
1-1/2 teaspoons baking powder
1 can (21 ounces) peach pie filling
ICING:
1-1/4 cups confectioners' sugar
1/2 teaspoon almond extract
3 to 4 tablespoons milk

1. In a large bowl, cream butter and sugar until light and fluffy. Add eggs, one at a time, beating well after each addition. Combine flour, salt and baking powder; add to creamed mixture and beat just until combined.

2. Spread 3-3/4 cups batter into a greased 15-in. x 10-in. x 1-in. baking pan. Carefully spoon pie filling to

within 1 in. of the edges. Spoon the remaining batter over filling.

3. Bake at 350° for 20-25 minutes or until a toothpick inserted near center comes out clean (cover loosely with foil if edges brown too quickly). Cool on a wire rack.

4. In a small bowl, combine confectioners' sugar, extract and enough milk to achieve desired consistency. Drizzle over coffee cake. **Yield:** 16-20 servings.

🎗🎗🎗
French Banana Pancakes

Prep: 10 min. **Cook:** 30 min.

Cheryl Sowers, Bakersfield, California

These dressed-up pancakes dolloped with whipped cream are a breakfast favorite in our family. Our daughters made them when they had friends over to spend the night. Afterward, their friends' mothers were asking for the recipe.

PANCAKES:
- 1 cup all-purpose flour
- 1/4 cup confectioners' sugar
- 1 cup milk
- 2 eggs
- 3 tablespoons butter, melted
- 1 teaspoon vanilla extract
- 1/4 teaspoon salt

FILLING:
- 1/4 cup butter
- 1/4 cup packed brown sugar
- 1/4 teaspoon ground cinnamon
- 1/4 teaspoon ground nutmeg
- 1/4 cup half-and-half cream
- 5 to 6 firm bananas, halved lengthwise

Whipped cream and additional cinnamon, optional

1. Sift the flour and confectioners' sugar into a bowl. Add the milk, eggs, butter, vanilla and salt; beat until smooth.

2. Heat a lightly greased 6-in. skillet and add about 3 tablespoons batter, spreading to almost cover bottom of skillet. Cook until lightly browned; turn and brown the other side. Remove to a wire rack. Repeat with the remaining batter (make 10-12 pancakes), greasing skillet as needed.

3. For filling, melt butter in large skillet. Stir in brown sugar, cinnamon and nutmeg. Stir in cream and cook until slightly thickened. Add half of the bananas at a time to skillet; heat for 2-3 minutes, spooning sauce over them. Remove from the heat.

4. Roll a pancake around each banana half and place on a serving platter. Spoon sauce over pancakes. Top with whipped cream and dash of cinnamon if desired. **Yield:** 5-6 servings.

Florentine Egg Bake

Prep: 30 min. **Bake:** 50 min. + standing

- 1 package (20 ounces) refrigerated shredded hash brown potatoes
- 1 tablespoon olive oil
- 1 package (10 ounces) frozen chopped spinach, thawed and squeezed dry
- 4 ounces Swiss cheese, cubed
- 4 ounces thinly sliced deli ham, coarsely chopped
- 8 eggs
- 1/2 cup buttermilk
- 1 tablespoon prepared pesto
- 1 cup biscuit/baking mix
- 1/4 teaspoon salt
- 1/8 teaspoon pepper
- 1-1/2 cups shredded Asiago cheese
- 2 tablespoons minced fresh basil

1. In a large bowl, combine the hash browns and oil. Press into a 13-in. x 9-in. baking dish coated with cooking spray. Bake at 350° for 25-30 minutes or until edges are golden brown.

2. Combine the spinach and Swiss cheese; sprinkle over crust. Top with ham. In a large bowl, whisk the eggs, buttermilk and pesto. Combine the biscuit mix, salt and pepper; add to egg mixture. Stir in the Asiago cheese. Pour over ham.

3. Bake, uncovered, for 25-30 minutes or until a thermometer reads 160°. Let stand for 10-15 minutes before cutting. Sprinkle with basil. **Yield:** 8 servings.

PATRICIA HARMON BADEN, PENNSYLVANIA

This flavorful breakfast bake comes together quickly using convenience foods, including refrigerated hash browns, frozen spinach, biscuit mix and store-bought pesto. For a seafood variation, replace the chopped deli ham with crabmeat.

Grand Prize Winner

✿✿✿
Special Stuffed French Toast

Prep: 20 min. **Cook:** 15 min.

Robin Perry, Seneca, Pennsylvania

For a breakfast or brunch sensation, whip up this dish show-casing cherries. The golden-brown Texas toast is delectable with cream cheese tucked between thick slices.

- 1 cup plus 2 tablespoons sugar, *divided*
- 2 tablespoons cornstarch
- 3/4 cup water
- 4 cups pitted frozen tart cherries, thawed
- 1 package (8 ounces) cream cheese, softened
- 1 cup confectioners' sugar
- 12 slices Texas toast
- 1 egg
- 1 cup milk

1. For sauce, combine 1 cup sugar and cornstarch in a small saucepan. Stir in water until smooth. Add cherries. Bring to a boil; cook and stir for 1-2 minutes or until thickened. Remove from heat and set aside.

2. In a small bowl, beat the cream cheese and the confectioners' sugar until smooth. Spread over six slices of bread; top with the remaining bread. In a shallow bowl, whisk the egg, milk and remaining sugar. Dip both sides of bread into egg mixture.

3. In a large nonstick skillet coated with cooking spray, toast bread on both sides until golden brown. Serve with cherry sauce. **Yield:** 6 servings.

✿✿✿
Cherry Cream Cheese Coffee Cake

Prep: 25 min. **Bake:** 50 min. + cooling

Linda Guiles, Belvidere, New Jersey

Everyone is sure to love this tender coffee cake sprinkled with a streusel topping. The sour cream pairs well with the cherries, and slivered almonds are a pleasantly crunchy accent.

- 2-1/4 cups all-purpose flour
- 3/4 cup sugar
- 3/4 cup cold butter, cubed
- 1/2 teaspoon baking powder
- 1/2 teaspoon baking soda
- 1/2 teaspoon salt
- 1 egg, lightly beaten
- 3/4 cup sour cream
- 1 teaspoon almond extract

FILLING:
- 1 package (8 ounces) cream cheese, softened
- 1/4 cup sugar
- 1 egg, lightly beaten
- 1 can (21 ounces) cherry pie filling
- 1/2 cup slivered almonds

1. In a large bowl, combine flour and sugar. Cut in butter until crumbly. Reserve 3/4 cup crumb mixture. Add the baking powder, baking soda and salt to remaining crumb mixture. Stir in the egg, sour cream and almond extract until blended. Press onto the bottom and 1 in. up the sides of an ungreased 9-in. springform pan with removable bottom.

2. For filling, in a large bowl, beat cream cheese and sugar for 1 minute. Add egg; beat just until combined. Spread over crust. Carefully top with pie filling. Sprinkle with almonds and reserved crumb mixture.

3. Bake at 350° for 50-60 minutes or until center is set. Cool on a wire rack. Carefully run a knife around edge of pan to loosen; remove sides of pan. Store in the refrigerator. **Yield:** 8-10 servings.

🎗🎗🎗
Reuben Brunch Bake

Prep: 15 min. + chilling **Bake:** 40 min. + standing

Janelle Reed, Merriam, Kansas

I created this when I wanted something different for a graduation brunch for two of our sons. When I realized I had most of the ingredients on hand for the Reuben dip I usually serve, I decided to use them in a make-ahead breakfast casserole instead. Everyone asked for the recipe.

- 8 eggs, lightly beaten
- 1 can (14-1/2 ounces) sauerkraut, rinsed and well drained
- 2 cups (8 ounces) shredded Swiss cheese
- 1 package (2-1/2 ounces) deli corned beef, cut into 1-inch pieces
- 1/2 cup chopped green onions
- 1/2 cup milk
- 1 tablespoon Dijon mustard
- 1/4 teaspoon salt
- 1/4 teaspoon pepper
- 3 slices rye bread, toasted and coarsely chopped
- 1/4 cup butter, melted

1. In a large bowl, combine the first nine ingredients. Pour into a greased 11-in. x 7-in. baking dish. Cover and refrigerate overnight.

2. Remove from the refrigerator 30 minutes before baking. Toss the bread pieces and butter; sprinkle over the casserole.

3. Bake, uncovered, at 350° for 40-45 minutes or until a knife inserted near the center comes out clean. Let stand for 10 minutes before serving. **Yield:** 8-12 servings.

🎗🎗🎗
Tacoed Eggs

Prep/Total Time: 20 min.

Mary Smith, Huntington, Indiana

One morning, I was searching the kitchen for a way to jazz up scrambled eggs. When I couldn't find any bacon bits, I used leftover taco filling from the night before.

- 8 eggs, beaten
- 1/2 cup shredded cheddar cheese
- 2 tablespoons finely chopped onion
- 2 tablespoons finely chopped green pepper
- 1 to 4 drops hot pepper sauce
- 1/2 cup leftover cooked taco-seasoned ground beef

Flour tortillas, warmed, optional
Salsa, optional

1. In a large bowl, combine the eggs, cheese, onion, green pepper and hot pepper sauce. Cook and stir in a nonstick skillet until eggs begin to set. Add taco meat; cook until eggs are completely set.

2. If desired, spoon onto a warmed tortilla and roll up; top with salsa. **Yield:** 4 servings.

Sweet Solution

Have extra flour tortillas? Here's another idea for breakfast, a snack or dessert. Simply spread cream cheese and fruit preserves on a flour tortilla and add sliced bananas. Then sprinkle it with cinnamon-sugar and roll it up.

1 unbaked pastry shell (10 inches)
1 medium onion, chopped
1 tablespoon butter
2 cups (8 ounces) shredded Swiss cheese
1 can (14-3/4 ounces) salmon, drained, flaked and cartilage removed
5 eggs
2 cups half-and-half cream
1/4 teaspoon salt
Minced fresh parsley, optional

🎗 🎗 🎗
Salmon Quiche
Prep: 15 min. **Bake:** 55 min.

Deanna Baldwin, Bermuda Dunes, California

This recipe came to me from my mother—it's the kind you request after just one bite! Unlike some quiches, it's hearty enough that it appeals equally to women and men.

1. Line unpricked pastry shell with a double thickness of heavy-duty foil. Bake at 450° for 8 minutes. Remove foil; bake 5 minutes longer. Cool on a wire rack.

2. In a small skillet, saute the onion in butter until tender. Sprinkle Swiss cheese in the crust; top with the salmon and onion.

3. In a small bowl, whisk the eggs, cream and salt; pour over salmon mixture. Bake at 350° for 45-50 minutes or until a knife inserted near the center comes out clean. Sprinkle with parsley if desired. Let stand 5 minutes before cutting. **Yield:** 6-8 servings.

Strawberry Cream Crepes
Prep: 25 min. + chilling **Cook:** 1 hour

1-1/2 cups milk
3 eggs
2 tablespoons butter, melted
1/2 teaspoon lemon extract
1-1/4 cups all-purpose flour
2 tablespoons sugar
Dash salt
TOPPING:
1/2 cup sugar
2 tablespoons cornstarch
3/4 cup water
1 tablespoon lemon juice
1 teaspoon strawberry extract
1/4 teaspoon red food coloring, optional
4 cups sliced fresh strawberries
FILLING:
1 cup heavy whipping cream
1 package (8 ounces) cream cheese, softened
2 cups confectioners' sugar
1 teaspoon vanilla extract

1. In a large bowl, combine the milk, eggs, butter and extract. Combine the flour, sugar and salt; add to milk mixture and mix well. Cover and refrigerate for 1 hour.

2. Heat a lightly greased 8-in. nonstick skillet over medium heat; pour 2 tablespoons batter into the center of skillet. Lift and tilt pan to coat bottom evenly. Cook until top appears dry; turn and cook 15-20 seconds longer. Remove to a wire rack. Repeat with remaining batter, greasing skillet as needed. When cool, stack crepes with waxed paper or paper towels in between.

3. In a small saucepan, combine the sugar and cornstarch; stir in water and lemon juice until smooth. Bring to a boil over medium heat; cook and stir for 1 minute or until thickened. Stir in extract and food coloring if desired. Cool. Add berries.

4. In a small bowl, beat the cream until stiff peaks form; set aside. In a large bowl, beat cream cheese, confectioners' sugar and vanilla until smooth; fold in whipped cream. Spoon 2 rounded tablespoons of filling down the center of each crepe; roll up. Top with berry topping. **Yield:** 22 crepes.

DEBRA LATTA PORT MATILDA, PENNSYLVANIA

I always feel like a French chef when I serve these pretty treats topped with strawberries. Although they take some time to prepare, they're well worth the effort. My guests say the crepes are luscious enough to be a dessert.

Grand
Prize
Winner

🎖🎖🎖
Caramel Sweet Rolls

Prep: 10 min. **Bake:** 25 min.

Krista Smith, Mentone, California

My family loves sweet rolls, and this is a great recipe because it goes together easily using a tube of ready-made breadstick dough and just five other ingredients. The fresh-baked treats taste like you spent hours making them.

> 1/2 cup packed brown sugar
> 1/3 cup heavy whipping cream
> 1/4 cup chopped walnuts
> 1 tube (11 ounces) refrigerated breadsticks
> 2 tablespoons sugar
> 1 teaspoon ground cinnamon

1. In a small bowl, combine brown sugar and cream until sugar is dissolved. Spread into a greased 8-in. square baking dish. Sprinkle with walnuts.

2. On a lightly floured surface, unroll breadstick dough (do not separate). Combine the sugar and cinnamon; sprinkle over dough. Reroll, starting with a short end. Cut into six slices. Place cut side down in prepared pan.

3. Bake at 350° for 25-30 minutes or until golden brown. Cool for 1 minute before inverting onto a serving plate. Serve warm. **Yield:** 6 servings.

Editor's Note: This recipe was tested with Pillsbury refrigerated breadsticks.

🎖🎖🎖
Cinnamon-Nut Coffee Cake

Prep: 15 min. **Bake:** 35 min.

Maxine Winternheimer, Scottsdale, Arizona

With a simple glaze and tasty layer of raisins and nuts, this buttery coffee cake reminds people of a popular variety sold in stores. I discovered the recipe in a church cookbook.

> 1 cup chopped pecans, *divided*
> 1/4 cup sugar
> 1/4 cup raisins
> 2 teaspoons ground cinnamon
> 1 package (18-1/4 ounces) yellow cake mix
> 1 package (3.4 ounces) instant vanilla pudding mix
> 3/4 cup water
> 3/4 cup canola oil
> 4 eggs
> 3 teaspoons butter flavoring
> 3 teaspoons vanilla extract
> **GLAZE:**
> 1 cup confectioners' sugar
> 1/2 teaspoon butter flavoring
> 4 to 5 teaspoons milk

1. In a small bowl, combine 1/2 cup pecans, sugar, raisins and cinnamon; set aside. In a large bowl, combine cake mix, pudding mix, water, oil, eggs, butter fla-

voring, vanilla and remaining pecans; beat on low speed for 30 seconds. Beat on medium for 2 minutes.

2. Pour half into a greased 13-in. x 9-in. baking dish. Sprinkle with reserved pecan mixture. Carefully spread remaining batter over top.

3. Bake at 350° for 40-45 minutes or until a toothpick comes out clean. Cool on a wire rack.

4. In a small bowl, combine the confectioners' sugar, butter flavoring and enough milk to achieve desired consistency. Drizzle over coffee cake. **Yield:** 12 servings.

⚜ ⚜ ⚜
Mashed Potato Kolachkes

Prep: 45 min. + rising **Bake:** 10 min.

Jan Wagner-Cuda, Deer Park, Washington

My husband's Bohemian mother brought a kolachke recipe with her when she came to America, so these rolls are a part of our family's heritage. Besides apricot and raspberry, traditional fillings are prune, poppy seed and cottage cheese.

☑ This recipe includes Nutrition Facts.

    1 medium potato, peeled and cubed
1-1/4 teaspoons active dry yeast
    2 tablespoons warm water (110° to 115°)
  3/4 cup sugar
  1/2 cup warm 2% milk (110° to 115°)
  1/4 cup shortening
    6 tablespoons butter, softened, *divided*
    1 egg, lightly beaten
  3/4 teaspoon salt
    3 to 4 cups all-purpose flour
  1/3 cup apricot cake and pastry filling
  1/3 cup raspberry cake and pastry filling
  2/3 cup confectioners' sugar
    4 teaspoons 2% milk

1. Place potato in a small saucepan and cover with water. Bring to a boil. Reduce heat; cover and cook for 10-15 minutes or until tender. Drain, reserving 1/2 cup cooking liquid. Mash potato; set aside 1/2 cup (discard or save remaining potato for another use).

2. In a large bowl, dissolve the yeast in warm water. Add the sugar, milk, shortening, 4 tablespoons butter, egg, salt, reserved cooking liquid and mashed potato. Beat in 2 cups flour until smooth. Stir in enough of the remaining flour to form a soft dough.

3. Turn onto a floured surface; knead until smooth and elastic, about 6-8 minutes. Place in a greased bowl, turning once to grease top. Cover and let rise in a warm place until doubled, about 45 minutes.

4. Turn onto a well-floured surface. Shape into 1-1/2-in. balls; place 2 in. apart on greased baking sheets. Flatten to 1/2-in. thickness. Cover; let rise for 15 minutes or until almost doubled. Melt remaining butter.

5. Using the end of a wooden spoon handle, make an indentation in the center of each ball; brush with butter and fill with a rounded teaspoon of filling.

6. Bake at 400° for 10-15 minutes or until lightly browned. Remove from pans to wire racks. Combine confectioners' sugar and milk; drizzle over rolls. **Yield:** about 2 dozen.

Editor's Note: This recipe was tested with Solo brand cake and pastry filling. Look for it in the baking aisle.

Nutrition Facts: 1 kolachke equals 161 calories, 5 g fat (2 g saturated fat), 17 mg cholesterol, 110 mg sodium, 26 g carbohydrate, 1 g fiber, 2 g protein.

🎖🎖🎖
Brunch Lasagna

Prep: 25 min. **Bake:** 45 min. + standing

Judy Munger, Warren, Minnesota

I really appreciate make-ahead dishes like this one. Pop it in the oven before guests arrive, add fresh fruit and muffins to the table, and you have an instant brunch. Drizzled with a little salsa, the lasagna makes a hearty supper, too.

   8 uncooked lasagna noodles
   8 eggs
1/2 cup milk
Butter-flavored cooking spray
   2 jars (16 ounces *each*) Alfredo sauce
   3 cups diced fully cooked ham
1/2 cup chopped green pepper
1/4 cup chopped green onions
   1 cup (4 ounces) shredded cheddar cheese
1/4 cup grated Parmesan cheese

1. Cook noodles according to package directions. Meanwhile, in a large bowl, beat eggs and milk. In a large nonstick skillet coated with butter-flavored cooking spray, cook eggs over medium-low heat until set but moist. Remove from the heat. Drain noodles.

2. Spread 1/2 cup Alfredo sauce in a greased 10-in. square or 13-in. x 9-in. baking dish. Layer with four lasagna noodles (trim noodles if necessary to fit dish), ham, green pepper and onions.

3. Top with half of the remaining Alfredo sauce and the remaining noodles. Layer with scrambled eggs, cheddar cheese and remaining Alfredo sauce. Sprinkle with Parmesan cheese.

4. Bake, uncovered, at 375° for 45-50 minutes or until heated through and bubbly. Let stand for 10 minutes before cutting. **Yield:** 10-12 servings.

The combination of chocolate, coconut and walnuts in this breakfast cake is wonderful. I serve pieces warm alongside cups of coffee, tea or hot cocoa. Using a convenient biscuit mix really saves time when stirring up the batter.

   2 cups biscuit/baking mix
1/2 cup sugar, *divided*
   1 egg
3/4 cup milk
   3 tablespoons butter, melted, *divided*
1/3 cup semisweet chocolate chips, melted
1/3 cup flaked coconut
1/4 cup chopped walnuts

1. In a large bowl, combine biscuit mix and 1/4 cup sugar. Whisk the egg, milk and 2 tablespoons butter; stir into dry ingredients just until moistened. Pour into a greased 8-in. square baking dish. Pour chocolate over the batter; cut through batter with a knife to swirl the chocolate.

2. Combine the coconut, walnuts and the remaining sugar and butter; sprinkle over the top. Bake at 400° for 25-30 minutes or until a toothpick inserted near the center comes out clean. Cool on a wire rack. **Yield:** 9 servings.

🎖🎖🎖
Coconut-Chip Coffee Cake

Prep: 15 min. **Bake:** 25 min. + cooling

Pauletta Bushnell, Lebanon, Oregon

⚜ ⚜ ⚜
Chocolate-Cherry Cream Crepes
Prep: 30 min. + chilling **Cook:** 15 min.

Kimberly Witt, Minot, North Dakota

My son calls me a gourmet cook whenever I make these treats. Sometimes I substitute apple pie filling for the cherries and drizzle the golden crepes with warm caramel sauce instead of fudge topping. Either way, they're yummy!

1-1/4 cups milk
   3 eggs
   2 tablespoons butter, melted
  3/4 cup all-purpose flour
   1 tablespoon sugar
  1/4 teaspoon salt
   1 package (8 ounces) cream cheese, softened
  1/2 cup confectioners' sugar
   1 teaspoon vanilla extract
   1 can (21 ounces) cherry pie filling
Chocolate fudge ice cream topping and whipped topping

1. In a large bowl, combine the milk, eggs and butter. Combine the flour, sugar and salt; add to egg mixture and mix well. Cover and refrigerate for 1 hour. For filling, in a small bowl, beat cream cheese until fluffy. Beat in confectioners' sugar and vanilla until smooth; set aside.

2. Heat a lightly greased 8-in. nonstick skillet; pour 2 tablespoons batter into the center of skillet. Lift and tilt pan to evenly coat bottom. Cook until top appears dry; turn and cook 15-20 seconds longer.

3. Remove to a wire rack. Repeat with remaining batter, greasing skillet as needed. Stack crepes with waxed paper between. Cover and freeze 10 crepes for another use. Crepes may be frozen for up to 3 months.

4. Pipe cream cheese filling onto the center of each remaining crepe. Top with 2 tablespoons pie filling. Fold side edges of crepe to the center. Drizzle with fudge topping and garnish with whipped topping. Serve immediately. **Yield:** 8 servings.

⚜ ⚜ ⚜
Pumpkin Pancakes
Prep/Total Time: 20 min.

Megan Schwartz, Wooster, Ohio

With four children, I'm always looking for simple, quick and tasty recipes they'll enjoy. They love pancakes, and these are great with breakfast sausage. I usually double or triple the recipe, depending on how hungry they are.

   1 cup complete buttermilk pancake mix
  1/2 teaspoon ground cinnamon
  1/8 teaspoon ground ginger
  2/3 cup cold water
  1/3 cup canned pumpkin
   1 cup maple syrup, warmed
  1/4 cup chopped pecans, toasted

1. In a large bowl, combine the pancake mix, cinnamon and ginger. In a small bowl, whisk water and pumpkin until blended; stir into dry ingredients just until moistened.

2. Pour batter by 1/4 cupfuls onto a hot griddle coated with cooking spray. Flatten with back of spoon. When underside is browned, turn pancakes and cook until second side is browned. Top with syrup and pecans. **Yield:** 6 pancakes.

1 package (16 ounces) pound cake mix
3/4 cup canned pumpkin
6 tablespoons water
2 eggs
2 teaspoons pumpkin pie spice
1 teaspoon baking soda

TOPPING:
1/2 cup chopped walnuts
1/2 cup packed brown sugar
1/4 cup all-purpose flour
3 teaspoons butter, melted

Pumpkin Coffee Cake

Prep: 15 min. **Bake:** 35 min. + cooling

Sarah Steele, Moulton, Alabama

When you taste the comforting fall flavor of this cake, it's tough to resist a second piece. The recipe is a breeze to throw together because it calls for pound cake mix and canned pumpkin.

1. In a large bowl, combine the first six ingredients; beat on low speed for 30 seconds. Beat on medium for 2 minutes. Pour half of the pumpkin mixture into a greased 9-in. square baking pan.

2. In a small bowl, combine the topping ingredients; sprinkle half over the batter. Carefully spread with remaining batter. Sprinkle with remaining topping (pan will be full).

3. Bake at 350° for 35-40 minutes or until a toothpick inserted near the center comes out clean. Cool on a wire rack. **Yield:** 9 servings.

Almond Streusel Rolls

Prep: 40 min. + rising **Bake:** 35 min. + cooling

2 packages (1/4 ounce *each*) active
  dry yeast
3/4 cup warm water (110° to 115°)
3/4 cup warm milk (110° to 115°)
1/4 cup butter, softened
1/2 cup sugar
2 eggs
1 teaspoon salt
5-1/4 to 5-1/2 cups all-purpose flour

FILLING:
1/2 cup almond paste
1/4 cup butter, softened
1/2 cup packed brown sugar
1/4 teaspoon almond extract

TOPPING:
3 tablespoons sugar
1 tablespoon all-purpose flour
1 tablespoon butter

ICING:
1-1/2 cups confectioners' sugar
1/4 teaspoon almond extract
1 to 2 tablespoons milk

1. In a large bowl, dissolve yeast in warm water. Add the milk, butter, sugar, eggs, salt and 2 cups flour. Beat until smooth. Stir in enough remaining flour to form a soft dough.

2. Turn onto a floured surface; knead until smooth and elastic, about 6-8 minutes. Place in a greased bowl, turning once to grease top. Cover and let rise in a warm place until doubled, about 1 hour.

3. Punch dough down; roll out to a 15-in. x 10-in. rectangle. In a large bowl, beat the filling ingredients until smooth. Spread over dough.

4. Roll up jelly-roll style, starting with a short side; seal seams. Cut into 12 slices. Place in a greased 13-in. x 9-in. baking pan. Cover and let rise in a warm place until doubled, about 30 minutes.

5. Combine topping ingredients; sprinkle over rolls. Bake at 350° for 35-40 minutes or until golden brown. Cool on a wire rack.

6. In a small bowl, combine confectioners' sugar, extract and enough milk to achieve drizzling consistency; drizzle over rolls. **Yield:** 1 dozen.

PERLENE HOEKEMA LYNDEN, WASHINGTON

This recipe was a collaboration between our grown daughter, Janis, and me. She developed the rolls, and I came up with the idea for the almond filling and streusel topping. They're a yummy treat on holidays or anytime.

Grand Prize Winner

Beef 'n' Chili Beans, p. 97

Louisiana Barbecue Brisket, p. 95

Herbed Cranberry Chicken, p. 93

Main Dishes

Creamy Baked Macaroni for a busy school night…Honey-Citrus Chicken Kabobs for your backyard barbecue…Brazilian-Style Turkey with Ham for a holiday dinner with family and friends…every kind of entree you need is in this chapter!

Old-Fashioned Chicken Pot Pie..........84

Caribbean Roast Pork Loin................84

Bacon-Cheese Topped Chicken.........85

Apple-Stuffed Pork Tenderloin...........86

Creamy Baked Macaroni...................87

Swordfish Shrimp Kabobs.................87

Grilled Veggie Pork Bundles...............88

Cherry-Glazed Roast Pork.................88

Brined Roasting Chicken...................89

Molasses-Glazed Baby Back Ribs.......90

Ole Polenta Casserole......................90

Chicken and Shrimp Satay.................92

Herbed Cranberry Chicken................93

Mongolian Beef..............................93

Chicken Pie in a Pan........................94

Pecan-Crusted Chicken....................94

Louisiana Barbecue Brisket................95

Chicken with Mushroom Sauce..........96

Chicken Pepper Stir-Fry...................97

Beef 'n' Chili Beans.........................97

Beef Fillets with Portobello Sauce........98

Southern Barbecued Chicken.............98

Mexican Pork Tenderloins................100

Asian Chicken Thighs......................101

Barbecued Chicken Legs.................101

Mustard-Herb Grilled Tenderloin......102

Marinated Chuck Roast...................102

Brazilian-Style Turkey with Ham........103

Beef and Potato Moussaka...............104

Easy Crab Cakes...........................105

Shrimp-Stuffed Chicken Breasts........105

Eggplant Sausage Casserole...............106

Spinach Crab Chicken.....................106

Grilled Veggie Sausage Pizza.............108

Chicken Rice Bowl.........................109

Roasted Pepper Ravioli Bake............109

Pork Tenderloin with
    Glazed Red Onions.....................110

Kitchen-Sink Soft Tacos...................110

Honey-Citrus Chicken Kabobs..........111

Chicken-Stuffed Cubanelle Peppers....112

Peking Shrimp...............................113

Bean and Pork Chop Bake...............113

Primavera Chicken.........................114

Pizza Quesadillas...........................114

Sweet 'n' Sour Cashew Pork.............115

Grilled Raspberry Chicken..............116

Creamy Prosciutto Pasta..................116

Spinach-Stuffed Beef Tenderloin........117

Tilapia with Corn Salsa...................117

1/3 cup all-purpose flour
1-1/2 cups chicken broth
1-1/2 cups milk
4 cups cubed cooked chicken breast
1 cup frozen peas
1 jar (2 ounces) diced pimientos, drained
1 teaspoon salt
BISCUIT TOPPING:
2 cups all-purpose flour
4 teaspoons baking powder
2 teaspoons sugar
1/2 teaspoon salt
1/2 teaspoon cream of tartar
1/2 cup cold butter
2/3 cup milk

🎖🎖🎖
Old-Fashioned Chicken Pot Pie

Prep: 1 hour **Bake:** 15 min.

Liliane Jahnke, Cypress, Texas

I often have leftover chicken broth on hand and use it for many dishes, including this family favorite. You can bake your own biscuits, like I do, or buy the refrigerated kind at the store.

1-1/2 cups sliced fresh mushrooms
1 cup sliced fresh carrots
1/2 cup chopped onion
1/3 cup butter

1. In a large saucepan, saute the mushrooms, carrots and onion in butter until tender; sprinkle with flour. Gradually stir in chicken broth and milk until blended. Bring to a boil; cook and stir for 2 minutes or until thickened. Add the chicken, peas, pimientos and salt; heat through. Pour into a greased shallow 2-1/2-qt. baking dish; set aside.

2. In a large bowl, combine the flour, baking powder, sugar, salt and cream of tartar. Cut in butter until mixture resembles coarse crumbs; stir in the milk just until moistened. Turn onto a lightly floured surface; knead 8-10 times. Pat or roll out to 1/2-in. thickness. Cut with a floured 2-1/2-in. biscuit cutter.

3. Place the biscuits over the chicken mixture. Bake, uncovered, at 400° for 15-20 minutes or until biscuits are golden brown. **Yield:** 6-8 servings.

🎖🎖🎖
Caribbean Roast Pork Loin

Prep: 5 min. **Bake:** 1-1/2 hours + standing

Denise Albers, Freeburg, Illinois

Here's an easy and different treatment for a boneless pork loin roast. Simply combine the oil and seasonings, rub it over the meat and bake. It always comes out tender and feeds a big group.

2 teaspoons olive oil
1 teaspoon pepper
3/4 teaspoon ground cinnamon
3/4 teaspoon ground nutmeg
1 boneless rolled pork loin roast (3-1/2 pounds)

Combine the oil, pepper, cinnamon and nutmeg; rub over roast. Place on a rack in a shallow roasting pan. Bake at 350° for 1-1/2 to 2 hours or until a meat thermometer reads 160°. Let stand for 10 minutes before slicing. **Yield:** 10-12 servings.

🎀🎀🎀
Bacon-Cheese Topped Chicken

Prep: 40 min. + marinating **Bake:** 20 min.

Melanie Kennedy, Battle Ground, Washington

Fresh mushrooms, bacon strips and Monterey Jack cheese top these tender marinated chicken breasts, which get rave reviews whenever I serve them. It's flavorful dining with minimal fuss.

    1/2 cup Dijon mustard
    1/2 cup honey
4-1/2 teaspoons canola oil, *divided*
    1/2 teaspoon lemon juice
      4 boneless skinless chicken breast halves
    1/4 teaspoon salt
    1/8 teaspoon pepper
Dash paprika
      2 cups sliced fresh mushrooms
      2 tablespoons butter
      1 cup (4 ounces) shredded Monterey Jack cheese
      1 cup (4 ounces) shredded cheddar cheese
      8 bacon strips, partially cooked
      2 teaspoons minced fresh parsley

1. In a small bowl, combine the mustard, honey, 1-1/2 teaspoons oil and lemon juice. Pour 1/2 cup into a large resealable plastic bag; add the chicken. Seal the bag and turn to coat; refrigerate for 2 hours. Cover and refrigerate the remaining marinade.

2. Drain and discard the marinade from the chicken. In a large skillet over medium heat, brown the chicken in the remaining oil on all sides. Sprinkle with the salt, pepper and paprika. Transfer to a greased 11-in. x 7-in. baking dish.

3. In the same skillet, saute the mushrooms in butter until tender. Spoon reserved marinade over chicken. Top with cheeses and mushrooms. Place bacon strips in a crisscross pattern over chicken.

4. Bake, uncovered, at 375° for 20-25 minutes or until a meat thermometer reads 170°. Sprinkle with parsley. **Yield:** 4 servings.

🎀🎀🎀
Apple-Stuffed Pork Tenderloin

Prep: 30 min. **Bake:** 25 min.

Sandra Harrison, Viera, Florida

My mother used to make stuffed pork tenderloin, but I added apples and nuts to the stuffing to make it more nutritious. I also reduced the amount of croutons and used the fat-free variety.

✓ This recipe includes Nutrition Facts and Diabetic Exchanges.

  6 tablespoons reduced-sodium chicken broth, divided
  2 tablespoons raisins
1/2 cup chopped apple
  1 celery rib, chopped
  2 tablespoons chopped onion
  1 garlic clove, minced
1-1/2 cups fat-free Caesar croutons
  2 tablespoons sliced almonds, toasted
1/8 teaspoon pepper
  1 pork tenderloin (1 pound)

1. In a small saucepan, bring 4 tablespoons broth to a boil. Remove from the heat; add raisins. Let stand for 5 minutes.

2. In a nonstick skillet coated with cooking spray; saute the apple, celery and onion for 3-4 minutes or until tender. Add the garlic; cook 1 minute longer. Remove from heat; stir in the broth mixture, croutons, nuts, pepper and the remaining broth.

3. Make a lengthwise slit down the center of the roast to within 1/2 in. of bottom. Open roast so it lies flat and cover with plastic wrap. Flatten to 1/2-in. thickness. Remove plastic wrap; fill with stuffing mixture. Close roast; tie at 2-in. intervals with kitchen string and secure ends with toothpicks.

4. Place on a rack in a shallow baking pan coated with cooking spray. Bake at 425° for 25-30 minutes or until a meat thermometer reads 160°. Let stand for 5 minutes before slicing. **Yield:** 3 servings.

Nutrition Facts: 6 ounces stuffed cooked pork tenderloin equals 336 calories, 7 g fat (2 g saturated fat), 84 mg cholesterol, 417 mg sodium, 27 g carbohydrate, 2 g fiber, 35 g protein. **Diabetic Exchanges:** 4 lean meat, 1-1/2 starch.

✿✿✿ Creamy Baked Macaroni

Prep: 20 min. Bake: 25 min.

Heather Eplett, Mossley, Ontario

Here's comfort food at its yummiest! Old-fashioned macaroni casserole gets a tasty new twist thanks to the Gouda cheese in this recipe. The crumb-topped dish bakes up nice and creamy with just a hint of zip from the hot sauce.

1-2/3 cups uncooked elbow macaroni
  1 can (10-3/4 ounces) condensed cream of
      chicken soup, undiluted
  1 cup milk
  1 tablespoon minced chives
1/2 teaspoon ground mustard
1/4 teaspoon hot pepper sauce
1-1/2 cups (6 ounces) Gouda *or* cheddar cheese
      (1/2-inch cubes)
  2 tablespoons dry bread crumbs
  1 tablespoon butter, melted

1. Cook macaroni according to package directions; drain. In a large bowl, combine the soup, milk, chives, mustard and hot pepper sauce. Stir in the macaroni and cheese.

2. Spoon into a greased shallow 2-qt. baking dish. Combine bread crumbs and butter; sprinkle over top. Bake, uncovered, at 400° for 25-30 minutes or until heated through and bubbly. **Yield:** 4-6 servings.

✿✿✿ Swordfish Shrimp Kabobs

Prep: 20 min. + marinating Grill: 10 min.

Weda Mosellie, Phillipsburg, New Jersey

I love kabobs made with beef and lamb, but I've been trying to fit more fish into my diet. Since I also love grilling, these grilled seafood skewers are a terrific choice.

1/4 cup olive oil
  2 tablespoons balsamic vinegar
1/2 teaspoon crushed red pepper flakes
1/2 teaspoon dried oregano
1/4 teaspoon salt
1/8 teaspoon pepper
1/2 pound swordfish steak, skin removed and cut
      into 1-inch chunks
  8 uncooked large shrimp, peeled and deveined
  8 cherry tomatoes
1/2 medium red onion, cut into 4 wedges
1/2 medium sweet yellow pepper, cut into
      8 chunks

1. In a small bowl, combine the oil, vinegar and seasonings. Place 3 tablespoons in a large resealable plastic bag; add the swordfish and shrimp. Seal the bag and turn to coat; refrigerate for up to 1 hour. Set remaining marinade aside for basting.

2. On four metal or soaked wooden skewers, thread swordfish, tomatoes, shrimp, onion and yellow pepper.

3. Coat grill rack with cooking spray before starting grill. Grill kabobs, uncovered, over medium heat for 3 minutes, turning once. Baste with some of reserved marinade. Grill 3-4 minutes longer or until the fish just turns opaque and the shrimp turn pink, turning and basting frequently. **Yield:** 2 servings.

We enjoy these colorful, bacon-wrapped bundles with a side of rice and iced tea. For variety, try them with provolone cheese or red sweet peppers...or substitute chicken breast for the pork chops.

- 4 bacon strips
- 2 boneless pork loin chops (4 ounces *each*)
- 1/8 teaspoon salt
- 1/8 teaspoon pepper
- 2 slices onion (1/4 inch thick)
- 2 slices tomato (1/2 inch thick)
- 1/2 medium green pepper, cut in half
- 2 slices Swiss cheese

1. Cross two bacon strips to form an X; repeat. Sprinkle pork chops with salt and pepper; place over bacon strips. Layer with onion, tomato and green pepper. Wrap the bacon strips over the vegetables and secure with a toothpick.

2. Coat grill rack with cooking spray before starting the grill for indirect heat, using a drip pan. Place the pork bundles over the drip pan. Grill, covered, over indirect medium heat for 20-25 minutes or until a meat thermometer reads 160°.

3. Place the cheese slices over bundles; cover and grill 1 minute longer or until cheese is melted. Discard toothpicks before serving. **Yield:** 2 servings.

Grilled Veggie Pork Bundles

Prep/Total Time: 30 min.

Linda Turner Ludwig, Columbiana, Ohio

Cherry-Glazed Roast Pork

Prep: 15 min. **Bake:** 1-3/4 hours

Beth Brandenburger, Rochester, Minnesota

This tender roast looks elegant yet is easy to prepare. I use it as a main dish when entertaining on holidays and other occasions. The cherry glaze makes a mouth-watering topping.

- 1 boneless rolled pork loin roast (3 to 4 pounds)
- 1/2 teaspoon salt, *divided*
- 1/4 teaspoon pepper
- 1 jar (12 ounces) cherry preserves
- 1/4 cup cranberry-raspberry juice
- 2 tablespoons corn syrup
- 1/4 teaspoon ground cinnamon
- 1/4 teaspoon ground nutmeg
- 1/4 teaspoon ground cloves

1. Place the roast fat side up on a rack in a shallow roasting pan. Sprinkle with 1/4 teaspoon salt and pepper. Bake, uncovered, at 350° for 1-1/4 hours.

2. In a small saucepan, combine the cherry preserves, juice, corn syrup, spices and remaining salt. Bring to a boil. Reduce the heat; simmer for 5 minutes. Pour 1/2 cup sauce over roast. Bake 30 minutes longer or

until a meat thermometer reads 160°. Cover and let stand for 15 minutes before slicing.

3. Scrape up browned bits and pan drippings; add to remaining sauce. Cook and stir until heated through. Serve with roast. **Yield:** 10-12 servings.

🎖️🎖️🎖️
Brined Roasting Chicken

Prep: 30 min. + marinating **Bake:** 1 hour 20 min.

Julie Noyes, Louisville, Kentucky

I discovered the art of brining turkey a few years ago and transferred the technique to roasting a whole chicken. The result is always a moist, delicious bird. I make a rich gravy from the pan drippings and a few additional ingredients.

    8 cups warm water
 1/2 cup kosher salt
 1/4 cup packed brown sugar
    3 tablespoons molasses
    1 tablespoon whole peppercorns, crushed
    1 tablespoon whole allspice, crushed
    2 teaspoons ground ginger
    1 roasting chicken
    4 cups cold water
    1 teaspoon canola oil
3/4 to 1 cup chicken broth
    1 tablespoon all-purpose flour

1. For brine, combine the first seven ingredients in a large kettle. Bring to a boil; cook and stir until the salt is dissolved. Remove from the heat. Cool to room temperature.

2. Remove the giblets from chicken; discard. Place cold water in a 2-gal. resealable plastic bag; add chicken. Place in a roasting pan. Carefully pour cooled brine into the bag. Squeeze out as much air as possible; seal bag and turn to coat. Refrigerate for 3-4 hours, turning several times.

3. Discard brine. Rinse chicken with water; pat dry. Skewer chicken openings; tie drumsticks together. Brush with oil. Place chicken in a roasting pan.

4. Bake, uncovered, at 350° for 80-90 minutes or until a meat thermometer reads 180°, basting occasionally with pan drippings (cover loosely with foil if chicken browns too quickly).

5. Remove chicken to a serving platter and keep warm. Pour drippings and loosened browned bits into a measuring cup; skim fat and discard. Add enough broth to measure 1 cup.

6. In a small saucepan, combine the flour and broth mixture until smooth. Bring to a boil; cook and stir for 2 minutes or until thickened. Serve gravy with chicken. **Yield:** 4-6 servings.

✿ ✿ ✿
Molasses-Glazed Baby Back Ribs

Prep: 20 min. + marinating **Grill:** 70 min.

Kim Braley, Dunedin, Florida

My husband grills these scrumptious ribs for our family at least once a month during summer. The sweet-and-sour barbecue sauce is the perfect condiment for the moist, tender meat.

4-1/2 **pounds pork baby back ribs**
   2 **liters cola**
 1/2 **teaspoon salt**

 1/2 **teaspoon pepper**
 1/4 **teaspoon garlic salt**
 1/4 **teaspoon dried oregano**
 1/4 **teaspoon onion powder**
 1/8 **teaspoon cayenne pepper**
BARBECUE SAUCE:
 1/4 **cup ketchup**
 1/4 **cup honey**
 1/4 **cup molasses**
   1 **tablespoon prepared mustard**
 1/2 **teaspoon cayenne pepper**
 1/2 **teaspoon salt**

1. Place the ribs in large resealable plastic bags; add the cola. Seal the bags and turn to coat; refrigerate for 8 hours or overnight.

2. Drain and discard cola. Pat ribs dry with paper towels. Combine the seasonings; rub over ribs.

3. Prepare grill for indirect heat, using a drip pan. Place ribs over pan; grill, covered, over indirect medium heat for 1 hour, turning occasionally.

4. In a small bowl, combine barbecue sauce ingredients. Brush over ribs; grill 10-20 minutes longer or until meat is tender. **Yield:** 4 servings.

Ole Polenta Casserole

Prep: 1 hour + chilling **Bake:** 40 min. + standing

 1 **cup yellow cornmeal**
 1 **teaspoon salt**
 4 **cups water,** *divided*
 1 **pound ground beef**
 1 **cup chopped onion**
1/2 **cup chopped green pepper**
 2 **garlic cloves, minced**
 1 **can (14-1/2 ounces) diced tomatoes, undrained**
 1 **can (8 ounces) tomato sauce**
1/2 **pound sliced fresh mushrooms**
 1 **teaspoon** *each* **dried basil, oregano and dill weed**
Dash hot pepper sauce
1-1/2 **cups (6 ounces) shredded part-skim mozzarella cheese**
1/4 **cup grated Parmesan cheese**

1. For polenta, in a small bowl, whisk cornmeal, salt and 1 cup water until smooth. In a large saucepan, bring remaining water to a boil. Add cornmeal mixture, stirring constantly. Bring to a boil; cook and stir for 3 minutes or until thickened.

2. Reduce heat to low; cover and cook for 15 minutes. Divide mixture between two greased 8-in. square baking dishes. Cover and refrigerate until firm, about 1-1/2 hours.

3. In a large skillet, cook beef, onion, green pepper and garlic over medium heat until meat is no longer pink; drain. Stir in the tomatoes, tomato sauce, mushrooms, herbs and hot pepper sauce; bring to a boil. Reduce heat; simmer, uncovered, for 20 minutes or until thickened.

4. Loosen one polenta from sides and bottom of dish; invert onto a waxed paper-lined baking sheet and set aside. Spoon half the meat mixture over remaining polenta. Sprinkle with half the mozzarella and half the Parmesan cheese. Top with the reserved polenta and remaining meat mixture.

5. Cover and bake at 350° for 40 minutes or until heated through. Uncover; sprinkle with remaining cheese. Bake 5 minutes longer or until cheese is melted. Let stand for 10 minutes before cutting. **Yield:** 6 servings.

ANGELA BIGGIN LYONS, ILLINOIS

With ground beef, two kinds of cheese and a dash of hot sauce, this Southwestern casserole has been a favorite in our family for more than 25 years. Servings are great with a dollop of sour cream on top and a salad on the side.

Grand
Prize
Winner

🎀🎀🎀
Chicken and Shrimp Satay

Prep: 20 min. + marinating **Grill:** 10 min.

Hannah Barringer, Loudon, Tennessee

I lightened up a recipe I discovered in a cookbook, and these grilled kabobs with chicken chunks and shrimp were the tasty result. The dipping sauce is the perfect accompaniment.

✓ This recipe includes Nutrition Facts and Diabetic Exchanges.

  3/4 **pound uncooked medium shrimp, peeled and deveined**
  3/4 **pound chicken tenderloins, cut into 1-inch cubes**
   4 **green onions, chopped**
   1 **tablespoon butter**
   2 **garlic cloves, minced**
   1 **tablespoon minced fresh parsley**
  1/2 **cup white wine *or* chicken broth**
   1 **tablespoon lemon juice**
   1 **tablespoon lime juice**
SAUCE:
  1/4 **cup chopped onion**
   1 **tablespoon butter**
  2/3 **cup reduced-sodium chicken broth**
  1/4 **cup reduced-fat chunky peanut butter**
2-1/4 **teaspoons brown sugar**
  3/4 **teaspoon lemon juice**
  3/4 **teaspoon lime juice**
  1/4 **teaspoon salt**
  1/4 **teaspoon *each* dried basil, thyme and rosemary, crushed**
  1/8 **teaspoon cayenne pepper**

1. Thread the shrimp and chicken onto 12 metal or soaked wooden skewers. Place in a large shallow dish; set aside.

2. In a small skillet, saute the green onions in butter until crisp-tender. Add garlic; cook 1 minute longer. Stir in the parsley, wine or broth, lemon juice and lime juice. Remove from the heat; cool slightly. Pour over the skewers and turn to coat. Cover and refrigerate for 4 hours, turning every 30 minutes.

3. In a small saucepan, saute onion in butter. Add the remaining sauce ingredients; cook and stir until blended. Remove from the heat; set aside.

4. Coat grill rack with cooking spray before starting the grill; prepare for indirect heat. Drain and discard the marinade. Grill skewers, covered, over indirect medium heat for 7-8 minutes, turning often. Brush with 1/4 cup sauce during the last minute of grilling. Serve with remaining sauce. **Yield:** 6 servings.

Nutrition Facts: 2 kabobs equals 190 calories, 7 g fat (3 g saturated fat), 126 mg cholesterol, 339 mg sodium, 7 g carbohydrate, 1 g fiber, 25 g protein. **Diabetic Exchanges:** 3 very lean meat, 1 fat, 1/2 starch.

Herbed Cranberry Chicken

Prep: 20 min. **Cook:** 15 min.

Margee Berry, Trout Lake, Washington

Sprinkled with pecans and coated with a homemade cranberry sauce, this main course is full of flavor—and no added salt is needed. Keep the recipe in mind for special dinners in fall and during the Christmas holiday season.

- 6 boneless skinless chicken breast halves (4 ounces *each*)
- 1 tablespoon salt-free herb seasoning blend
- 2 tablespoons olive oil, *divided*
- 2/3 cup chopped green onions
- 1/2 cup dried cranberries
- 1/2 cup reduced-sodium chicken broth
- 1/3 cup cranberry juice
- 4-1/2 teaspoons maple syrup
- 1 tablespoon balsamic vinegar
- 1/3 cup chopped pecans, toasted

1. Rub the chicken with the seasoning blend. In a large nonstick skillet, cook chicken in 1 tablespoon oil over medium heat for 4-5 minutes on each side or until a meat thermometer reaches 170°. Remove and keep warm.

2. In the same skillet, saute onions in remaining oil. Stir in the cranberries, broth, cranberry juice, syrup and vinegar; bring to a boil. Reduce heat; cook and stir for 2 minutes. Return the chicken to the pan; cook for 1 minute or until heated through. Sprinkle with pecans. **Yield:** 6 servings.

Mongolian Beef

Prep/Total Time: 25 min.

Heather Blum, Coleman, Wisconsin

This meal-in-one always goes over big with my husband, who is a true meat-and-potatoes man. The recipe makes use of inexpensive ingredients to deliver great taste.

- 1 tablespoon cornstarch
- 3/4 cup reduced-sodium chicken broth
- 2 tablespoons reduced-sodium soy sauce
- 1 tablespoon hoisin sauce
- 2 teaspoons sesame oil
- 1 pound beef top sirloin steak, cut into thin strips
- 1 tablespoon olive oil, *divided*
- 5 green onions, cut into 1-inch pieces
- 2 cups hot cooked rice

1. In a small bowl, combine the cornstarch and chicken broth until smooth. Stir in the soy sauce, hoisin sauce and sesame oil; set aside. In a large nonstick skillet or wok, stir-fry the beef strips in 1-1/2 teaspoons hot olive oil until meat is no longer pink. Remove and keep warm.

2. In the same skillet, stir-fry onions in remaining olive oil for 3-4 minutes or until crisp-tender. Stir cornstarch mixture and add to the pan. Bring to a boil; cook and stir for 2 minutes or until thickened. Reduce heat; add beef and heat through. Serve with rice. **Yield:** 4 servings.

1/2 teaspoon salt
1 cup milk
1 cup chicken broth
1 can (10-3/4 ounces) condensed cream of mushroom soup, undiluted
4 cups cubed cooked chicken

CRUST:
1-1/2 cups all-purpose flour
3/4 teaspoon baking powder
1 teaspoon salt
3 tablespoons cold butter
1/2 cup milk
2 cups (8 ounces) shredded cheddar cheese

1. In a large skillet, saute the celery, carrots and onion in butter until tender. Stir in the flour and salt until blended; gradually add milk and broth. Bring to a boil; cook and stir for 2 minutes or until thickened. Stir in soup and chicken. Spoon into a greased 13-in. x 9-in. baking dish; set aside.

2. For crust, combine flour, baking powder and salt. Cut in butter until crumbly. Add milk, tossing with a fork until mixture forms a soft dough; shape into a ball.

3. On a lightly floured surface, roll into a 12-in. x 10-in. rectangle. Sprinkle with cheese. Roll up jelly-roll style, starting from a long side. Cut into 12 slices. Place cut side down over chicken mixture. Bake, uncovered, at 350° for 35-40 minutes or until the crust is lightly browned. **Yield:** 6-8 servings.

🎗️🎗️🎗️

Chicken Pie in a Pan

Prep: 25 min. **Bake:** 35 min.

Kristine Conway, Alliance, Ohio

Comforting and filling, this potpie is the perfect way to use up leftover chicken or turkey. It also travels well, so it's a nice choice when you need something to take to a potluck.

2 celery ribs, diced
2 medium carrots, diced
1 small onion, chopped
3 tablespoons butter
1/4 cup all-purpose flour

🎗️🎗️🎗️

Pecan-Crusted Chicken

Prep/Total Time: 25 min.

Marjorie MacDonald, Huntsville, Ontario

With a crispy pecan coating and creamy mustard sauce, this easy-to-prepare chicken will perk up any meal. Cayenne pepper puts a little zip into each bite—but I think my husband likes this entree just for the sauce!

3/4 cup finely chopped pecans
2 tablespoons cornstarch
2 tablespoons minced fresh parsley
3/4 teaspoon dried thyme
1/2 teaspoon salt
1/4 teaspoon ground mustard
1/4 teaspoon cayenne pepper
1 egg
4 boneless skinless chicken breast halves (4 ounces *each*)
2 tablespoons canola oil

MUSTARD SAUCE:
1/2 cup sour cream

2 tablespoons Dijon mustard
1/2 teaspoon sugar
Pinch salt

1. In a shallow bowl, combine first seven ingredients. In another shallow bowl, beat the egg. Dip chicken in egg, then roll in pecan mixture.

2. In a large skillet, cook the chicken in oil for 15-20 minutes or until a meat thermometer reads 170°. In a small bowl, whisk the sauce ingredients. Serve with chicken. **Yield:** 4 servings.

✿✿✿
Louisiana Barbecue Brisket

Prep: 20 min. + marinating **Grill:** 4 hours

Allan Stackhouse Jr., Jennings, Louisiana

Turn to this lip-smacking brisket when you need a special entree to feed a crowd. Don't be deterred by the length of the recipe…it has many make-ahead steps.

- 3 tablespoons paprika
- 2 teaspoons *each* salt, garlic powder and pepper
- 1 teaspoon *each* cayenne pepper, dried oregano and ground mustard
- 1/2 teaspoon chili powder
- 1 fresh beef brisket (4 to 6 pounds)

BARBECUE SAUCE:
- 2 cups ketchup
- 1 cup packed brown sugar
- 1 cup unsweetened pineapple juice
- 2/3 cup light corn syrup
- 1/2 cup finely chopped onion
- 1/2 cup apple juice
- 1/4 cup chili powder
- 2 to 4 tablespoons hot pepper sauce
- 4 teaspoons Worcestershire sauce
- 1 to 4 teaspoons Liquid Smoke, optional

1. In a small bowl, combine the seasonings. Rub 2 teaspoons over the brisket. (Place the remaining seasoning mixture in an airtight container; save for up to 3 months for another use.)

2. In a large bowl, combine the sauce ingredients; stir until brown sugar is dissolved. Pour 2 cups into a large resealable plastic bag; add the brisket. Seal the bag and turn to coat; refrigerate for 8 hours or overnight, turning several times. Cover and refrigerate the remaining sauce.

3. Prepare grill for indirect heat, using a drip pan. Drain and discard marinade from brisket; pat dry with paper towels. Place the brisket over pan; grill, covered, over indirect low heat for 30-45 minutes on each side or until browned.

4. Transfer the brisket to a heavy-duty disposable roasting pan. Pour 1-1/4 cups of reserved sauce over brisket. Cover with a double layer of heavy-duty foil and seal tightly.

5. Grill, covered, over indirect low heat for 3-4 hours or until the meat is fork-tender. Slice the brisket across the grain. Serve with the remaining sauce. **Yield:** 12-16 servings.

Editor's Note: This is a fresh beef brisket, not corned beef. This recipe is best when the brisket is untrimmed.

Chicken with Mushroom Sauce

Prep/Total Time: 25 min.

Jennifer Pemberton, Muncie, Indiana

This mouth-watering main dish looks impressive yet comes together in no time. It's also on the lighter side, but I think the flavor rivals that of many full-fat entrees found in restaurants.

☑ This recipe includes Nutrition Facts and Diabetic Exchanges.

  2 teaspoons cornstarch
1/2 cup fat-free milk
  4 boneless skinless chicken breast halves (4 ounces *each*)
  1 tablespoon olive oil
1/2 pound fresh mushrooms, sliced
1/2 medium onion, sliced and separated into rings
  1 tablespoon reduced-fat butter
1/4 cup sherry *or* chicken broth
1/2 teaspoon salt
1/8 teaspoon pepper

1. In a small bowl, combine the cornstarch and milk until smooth; set aside. Flatten the chicken to 1/4-in. thickness. In a large nonstick skillet, cook chicken in oil over medium heat for 5-6 minutes on each side or until juices run clear. Remove and keep warm.

2. In the same skillet, saute mushrooms and onion in butter until tender. Stir in the sherry or chicken broth, salt and pepper; bring to a boil. Stir cornstarch mixture and add to the pan. Bring to a boil; cook and stir for 2 minutes or until thickened. Serve with the chicken. **Yield:** 4 servings.

Editor's Note: This recipe was tested with Land O'Lakes light stick butter.

Nutrition Facts: 1 chicken breast half with 1/3 cup sauce equals 212 calories, 8 g fat (2 g saturated fat), 68 mg cholesterol, 387 mg sodium, 7 g carbohydrate, 1 g fiber, 26 g protein. **Diabetic Exchanges:** 3 very lean meat, 1 vegetable, 1 fat, 1/2 starch.

No-Fuss Flattening

To flatten poultry, put it inside a heavy-duty resealable plastic bag or between two sheets of heavy plastic wrap to prevent messy splatters. Use the smooth side of a meat mallet to gently pound it to the desired thickness.

🎖🎖🎖 Chicken Pepper Stir-Fry

Prep/Total Time: 30 min.

Kelly Baumgardt, Seymour, Wisconsin

I challenged myself one day to create a sweet and spicy stir-fry using only the ingredients I had on hand. I've tweaked the recipe since then, and I think I've finally mastered it!

- 1 **each small green, sweet red and sweet yellow pepper, julienned**
- 1 **medium onion, quartered**
- 4 **tablespoons olive oil,** *divided*
- 2 **garlic cloves, minced**
- 3/4 **pound boneless skinless chicken breast halves, cubed**
- 3/4 **teaspoon Cajun seasoning**
- 1/3 **cup packed brown sugar**
- 2 **teaspoons cornstarch**
- 1 **tablespoon water**
- 1 **tablespoon lemon juice**
- 1 **tablespoon honey mustard**
- 1 **teaspoon soy sauce**
- 1 **teaspoon Worcestershire sauce**

Hot cooked rice, optional

1. In a large skillet, stir-fry the peppers and onion in 2 tablespoons oil until crisp-tender. Add the garlic; cook 1 minute longer. Remove and keep warm. In the same skillet, stir-fry chicken and Cajun seasoning in remaining oil until no longer pink.

2. In a small bowl, combine the brown sugar, cornstarch, water, lemon juice, mustard, soy sauce and Worcestershire sauce; pour over chicken. Return pepper mixture to the pan; cook and stir for 1 minute. Serve with rice if desired. **Yield:** 3-4 servings.

I took this crowd-pleasing main dish to the last church meal we had, and several people requested the recipe. The tomatoes with green chilies really add some zip. It's also easy to make—you just put all of the ingredients in the slow cooker, and dinner's ready before you know it.

- 3 **pounds beef stew meat, cut into 1-inch cubes**
- 2 **tablespoons brown sugar**
- 1-1/2 **teaspoons ground mustard**
- 1 **teaspoon salt**
- 1 **teaspoon paprika**
- 1/2 **teaspoon chili powder**
- 1/4 **teaspoon pepper**
- 1 **large onion, chopped**
- 2 **cans (10 ounces each) diced tomatoes and green chilies, undrained**
- 1 **can (16 ounces) ranch-style or chili beans, undrained**
- 1 **can (15-1/4 ounces) whole kernel corn, drained**

1. Place the beef in a 3-qt. slow cooker. Combine the brown sugar, mustard, salt, paprika, chili powder and pepper; sprinkle over beef and toss to coat. Top with onion, tomatoes, beans and corn.

2. Cover and cook on low for 6-8 hours or until meat is tender. **Yield:** 6-8 servings.

🎖🎖🎖 Beef 'n' Chili Beans

Prep: 15 min. **Cook:** 6 hours

Anita Hudson, Savoy, Texas

2 beef tenderloin steaks (4 ounces *each*)
1/2 cup dry red wine *or* reduced-sodium beef broth
1 teaspoon all-purpose flour
1/2 cup reduced-sodium beef broth
1 teaspoon *each* steak sauce, Worcestershire sauce and ketchup
1/2 teaspoon ground mustard
4 ounces fresh baby portobello mushrooms, sliced
1/4 teaspoon pepper
1/8 teaspoon salt
1 tablespoon minced chives, optional

1. In a large nonstick skillet coated with cooking spray, brown steaks on both sides over medium-high heat. Remove and keep warm.

2. Reduce heat to medium. Add wine or broth to pan, stirring to loosen browned bits; cook for 2-3 minutes or until liquid is reduced by half. Combine flour and broth until smooth; whisk into the pan juices. Add the steak sauce, Worcestershire sauce, ketchup and mustard. Bring to a boil.

3. Return the steaks to the skillet; add the mushrooms. Cook for 4-5 minutes on each side or until the meat reaches desired doneness (for medium-rare, a meat thermometer should read 145°; medium, 160°; well-done, 170°). Sprinkle with pepper, salt and chives if desired. **Yield:** 2 servings.

Nutrition Facts: 1 steak with 1/3 cup sauce equals 255 calories, 8 g fat (3 g saturated fat), 72 mg cholesterol, 422 mg sodium, 7 g carbohydrate, 1 g fiber, 26 g protein. **Diabetic Exchanges:** 3 lean meat, 1 starch.

Beef Fillets with Portobello Sauce

Prep/Total Time: 30 min.

Christel Stein, Tampa, Florida

These mouth-watering steaks may seem complicated, but they're actually fast enough for everyday dinners. We enjoy the mushroom-topped fillets with our favorite crusty French bread, a mixed salad and a light lemon dessert.

Southern Barbecued Chicken

Prep: 25 min. + marinating **Grill:** 40 min.

2 cups cider vinegar
1 cup canola oil
1 egg, lightly beaten
2 tablespoons hot pepper sauce
1 tablespoon garlic powder
1 tablespoon poultry seasoning
2 teaspoons salt
1 teaspoon pepper
1 broiler/fryer chicken (3 to 4 pounds), cut up

1. In a large saucepan, combine the first eight ingredients. Bring to a boil, stirring constantly. Reduce the heat; simmer, uncovered, for 10 minutes, stirring often. Cool.

2. Pour 1-2/3 cups marinade into a large resealable plastic bag; add the chicken. Seal bag and turn to coat; refrigerate overnight, turning occasionally. Cover; refrigerate remaining marinade for basting.

3. Prepare grill for indirect heat, using a drip pan. Drain and discard marinade from chicken. Place skin side down over pan. Grill, covered, over indirect medium heat for 20-25 minutes on each side or until juices run clear, basting occasionally with reserved marinade. **Yield:** 4 servings.

REVONDA STROUD FORT WORTH, TEXAS

Nothing says Texas like outdoor grilling, and summer is a prime time for picnics featuring this barbecued chicken. Guests are always surprised when I tell them the basis for my "mystery marinade" is simply vinegar and oil.

Grand Prize Winner

🎀🎀🎀
Mexican Pork Tenderloins

Prep: 10 min. **Grill:** 25 min.

Maria Chiarino, Concord, North Carolina

This recipe accents slices of grilled tenderloin with a homemade black bean salsa. To cut down on last-minute prep, make that condiment and the cumin-coriander pork rub ahead of time.

✓ This recipe includes Nutrition Facts and Diabetic Exchanges.

2 tablespoons ground cumin
1 tablespoon ground coriander
1 teaspoon *each* onion powder, garlic powder, dried oregano and pepper
1/2 teaspoon salt
1 teaspoon olive oil
2 pork tenderloins (1 pound *each*)

BLACK BEAN SALSA:
1 can (15 ounces) black beans, rinsed and drained
2 plum tomatoes, diced
1 can (11 ounces) Mexicorn, drained
2 tablespoons chopped red onion
1 jalapeno pepper, seeded and chopped
2 tablespoons olive oil
2 tablespoons minced fresh cilantro
1 tablespoon lime juice
1/2 teaspoon ground cumin
1/8 teaspoon salt
1/8 teaspoon pepper

1. Combine the seasonings. Rub oil and seasoning mixture over the meat; let stand for 10 minutes.

2. Coat grill rack with cooking spray before starting grill. Grill meat, covered, over medium heat for 10-12 minutes on each side or until a meat thermometer reads 160°. Remove from the grill. Cover and let stand for 5 minutes before slicing.

3. For the salsa, in a large bowl, combine the beans, tomatoes, corn, onion and pepper. Whisk together oil, cilantro, lime juice, cumin, salt and pepper. Drizzle over the bean mixture; toss to coat. Serve with the tenderloin. **Yield:** 8 servings.

Editor's Note: When cutting hot peppers, disposable gloves are recommended. Avoid touching your face.

Nutrition Facts: 3 ounces cooked pork with 1/2 cup salsa equals 257 calories, 8 g fat (2 g saturated fat), 63 mg cholesterol, 550 mg sodium, 18 g carbohydrate, 5 g fiber, 27 g protein. **Diabetic Exchanges:** 3 lean meat, 1 starch, 1/2 fat.

🏵️🏵️🏵️
Asian Chicken Thighs

Prep: 15 min. **Cook:** 50 min.

Dave Farrington, Midwest City, Oklahoma

A thick, tangy sauce coats golden chicken pieces in this savory skillet recipe. I like to serve them over long grain rice or with a helping of ramen noodle slaw.

- 5 bone-in chicken thighs (about 1-3/4 pounds), skin removed
- 5 teaspoons olive oil
- 1/3 cup warm water
- 1/4 cup packed brown sugar
- 2 tablespoons orange juice
- 2 tablespoons soy sauce
- 2 tablespoons ketchup
- 1 tablespoon white vinegar
- 4 garlic cloves, minced
- 1/2 teaspoon crushed red pepper flakes
- 1/4 teaspoon Chinese five-spice powder
- 2 teaspoons cornstarch
- 2 tablespoons cold water

Hot cooked rice
Sliced green onions

1. In a large skillet over medium heat, cook chicken in oil for 8-10 minutes on each side or until a meat thermometer reads 180°. In a small bowl, whisk warm water, brown sugar, orange juice, soy sauce, ketchup, vinegar, garlic, pepper flakes and five-spice powder.

2. Pour over chicken. Bring to a boil. Reduce heat; simmer, uncovered, for 30-35 minutes or until the chicken is tender, turning occasionally.

3. Combine cornstarch and cold water until smooth; gradually stir into the pan. Bring to a boil; cook and stir for 2 minutes or until thickened. Serve with rice. Garnish with green onions. **Yield:** 5 servings.

🏵️🏵️🏵️
Barbecued Chicken Legs

Prep: 10 min. **Bake:** 50 min.

Agnes Golian, Garfield Heights, Ohio

On a lazy summer's day when you need only a few servings, this easy chicken is a terrific choice. We often enjoy it with a side of baked beans and slices of watermelon. Try the zesty barbecue sauce on other grilled meats, too.

- 2 chicken leg quarters
- 1 tablespoon canola oil
- 1/4 cup ketchup
- 2 tablespoons Worcestershire sauce
- 1 tablespoon sugar
- 1 tablespoon cider vinegar
- 1 tablespoon steak sauce

Dash hot pepper sauce

1. In a large nonstick skillet, brown chicken in oil. Transfer to an 8-in. square baking dish coated with cooking spray. In a bowl, combine the ketchup, Worcestershire sauce, sugar, vinegar, steak sauce and hot pepper sauce; pour over chicken.

2. Bake, uncovered, at 350° for 55-60 minutes or until a meat thermometer reads 180°, basting the chicken every 15 minutes with sauce. **Yield:** 2 servings.

2/3 cup olive oil
1/2 cup beef broth
  3 tablespoons Dijon mustard
  2 tablespoons red wine vinegar
  2 tablespoons lemon juice
1/2 teaspoon sugar
  2 garlic cloves, minced
1/2 teaspoon salt
1/4 teaspoon *each* dried oregano, summer savory, tarragon and thyme
1/8 teaspoon pepper
  1 beef tenderloin roast (1-1/2 pounds)

1. In a small bowl, combine the oil, beef broth, mustard, vinegar, lemon juice, sugar and seasonings. Pour 3/4 cup into a large resealable plastic bag; add the beef. Seal the bag and turn to coat; refrigerate overnight, turning bag once or twice. Cover and refrigerate the remaining marinade for basting.

2. Drain and discard the marinade from beef. Grill, covered, over medium heat for 20-25 minutes or until meat reaches desired doneness (for medium-rare, a meat thermometer should read 145°; medium, 160°; well-done, 170°). Turn once and baste with 1/4 cup reserved marinade during the last 5 minutes.

3. Let the tenderloin stand for 10 minutes before slicing. Serve with remaining reserved marinade. **Yield:** 6 servings.

🎗🎗🎗
Mustard-Herb Grilled Tenderloin

Prep: 10 min. + marinating **Grill:** 20 min.

Phyllis Schmalz, Kansas City, Kansas

Our area is known for its beef, and we make this flavorful tenderloin on the grill often. The homemade marinade would also be good with grilled pork or chicken.

- -

🎗🎗🎗
Marinated Chuck Roast

Prep: 10 min. + marinating **Bake:** 3 hours + standing

Mary Lee Baker, Enon, Ohio

It's the simple marinade of orange juice, soy sauce, brown sugar and Worcestershire sauce that makes this beef roast so tasty and tender. If you like, thicken the juices to make a mouth-watering gravy and serve it with mashed potatoes.

1/2 cup orange juice
  3 tablespoons soy sauce
  3 tablespoons brown sugar
  1 teaspoon Worcestershire sauce
  1 boneless beef chuck roast (3 to 4 pounds)

1. In a large resealable plastic bag, combine the orange juice, soy sauce, brown sugar and Worcestershire sauce; add the roast. Seal bag and turn to coat; refrigerate for 8 hours or overnight.

2. Pour the marinade into a Dutch oven. Bring to a boil; boil for 2 minutes. Add roast to the pan. Cover

and bake at 325° for 3 to 3-1/2 hours or until meat is tender. Let stand for 10 minutes before slicing. Thicken juices for gravy if desired. **Yield:** 8-10 servings.

Brazilian-Style Turkey With Ham

Prep: 30 min. + marinating
Bake: 2 hours and 30 min. + standing

Carol Marriott, Centreville, Virginia

Looking for a different and fun way to prepare a whole turkey? Try the grilled recipe here. My mom served this poultry-and-ham main dish for fun events such as "Christmas in July" gatherings and weddings at her home.

    1 whole turkey (12 pounds)
4-1/2 teaspoons salt
    2 teaspoons pepper
    3 garlic cloves, minced
1-1/2 cups white vinegar
    1 cup olive oil
    4 medium tomatoes, seeded and chopped
    4 medium green peppers, seeded and chopped
1/2 cup minced fresh parsley
    2 pounds smoked ham, thinly sliced

1. Remove giblets from turkey and discard. Place a turkey-size oven roasting bag inside a second roasting bag; add turkey. Place in a roasting pan. Combine the salt, pepper and garlic; rub over turkey.

2. In a large bowl, combine the vinegar, oil, tomatoes, peppers and parsley. Pour over turkey and into cavity. Squeeze out as much air as possible from the bag; seal and turn to coat. Refrigerate for 12-24 hours, turning several times.

3. Drain and discard the marinade. Skewer turkey openings; tie drumsticks together. Prepare the grill for indirect heat, using a drip pan. Coat grill rack with cooking spray before starting the grill.

4. Grill turkey, covered, over indirect medium heat for 2 to 2-1/2 hours or until a meat thermometer reads 180°, tenting turkey with foil after about 1 hour. Let stand for 20 minutes before slicing. Meanwhile, warm the ham. Layer turkey and ham slices on a serving platter. **Yield:** 12 servings plus leftovers.

Indirect Advice

For grilling turkey and other large cuts of meat, indirect heat is recommended. When the recipe directs to grill the meat "covered," that means to place the cover on the grill during cooking.

Beef and Potato Moussaka

Prep: 25 min. **Bake:** 1 hour + standing

Jean Puffer, Chilliwack, British Columbia

When my son was in sixth grade, he brought home this recipe for moussaka—a classic Greek entree—for an assignment about Greece. It earned high marks when we made it for his class. The meat-and-potatoes combination has also gone over big with everyone else I've served it to.

  1 pound ground beef
  1 medium onion, chopped
  1 garlic clove, minced
3/4 cup water
  1 can (6 ounces) tomato paste
  3 tablespoons minced fresh parsley
  1 teaspoon salt
1/2 teaspoon dried mint, optional
1/4 teaspoon ground cinnamon
1/4 teaspoon pepper
PARMESAN SAUCE:
1/4 cup butter, cubed
1/4 cup all-purpose flour
  2 cups milk
  4 eggs, lightly beaten
1/2 cup grated Parmesan cheese
1/2 teaspoon salt
  5 medium potatoes, peeled and thinly sliced

1. In a large skillet, cook the beef and onion over medium heat until meat is no longer pink. Add the garlic; cook 1 minute longer. Drain. Stir in the water, tomato paste, parsley, salt, mint if desired, cinnamon and pepper. Set aside.

2. For sauce, melt butter in a saucepan over medium heat. Stir in flour until smooth; gradually add milk. Bring to a boil; cook and stir for 2 minutes or until thickened. Remove from the heat. Stir a small amount of hot mixture into eggs; return all to the pan, stirring constantly. Add cheese and salt.

3. Place half of the potato slices in a greased shallow 3-qt. baking dish. Top with half of the cheese sauce and all of the meat mixture. Arrange the remaining potatoes over meat mixture; top with the remaining cheese sauce.

4. Bake, uncovered, at 350° for 1 hour or until a meat thermometer reads 160°. Let stand for 10 minutes before serving. **Yield:** 8-10 servings.

Easy Crab Cakes

Prep/Total Time: 25 min.

Charlene Spelock, Apollo, Pennsylvania

Canned crabmeat makes these light, delicate patties simple enough for dinner on busy weeknights. For a change of pace, try forming the crab mixture into four thick cakes instead of eight.

✓ This recipe includes Nutrition Facts and Diabetic Exchanges.

2 cans (6 ounces *each*) crabmeat, drained,
  flaked and cartilage removed
1 cup seasoned bread crumbs, *divided*
1 egg, lightly beaten
1/4 cup finely chopped green onions
1/4 cup finely chopped sweet red pepper
1/4 cup reduced-fat mayonnaise
1 tablespoon lemon juice
1/2 teaspoon garlic powder
1/8 teaspoon cayenne pepper
1 tablespoon butter

1. In a large bowl, combine the crab, 1/3 cup bread crumbs, egg, onions, red pepper, mayonnaise, lemon juice, garlic powder and cayenne.

2. Divide the mixture into eight portions; shape into 2-in. balls. Roll in remaining bread crumbs. Flatten

to 1/2-in. thickness. In a large nonstick skillet, cook the crab cakes in butter for 3-4 minutes on each side or until golden brown. **Yield:** 4 servings.

Nutrition Facts: 2 crab cakes equals 295 calories, 12 g fat (3 g saturated fat), 142 mg cholesterol, 879 mg sodium, 23 g carbohydrate, 1 g fiber, 23 g protein. **Diabetic Exchanges:** 3 very lean meat, 1-1/2 starch, 1-1/2 fat.

Shrimp-Stuffed Chicken Breasts

Prep: 20 min. **Grill:** 15 min.

Wendy McGowan, Fontana, California

Filled with a flavorful combination of shrimp, mayonnaise, onions and tarragon, these golden chicken breasts are a special choice for a family celebration or dinner party.

6 boneless skinless chicken breast halves
  (6 ounces *each*)
2-1/2 cups frozen cooked salad shrimp, thawed
1/2 cup chopped green onions
1/2 cup mayonnaise
1 tablespoon dried tarragon
1 tablespoon lemon juice
1/2 teaspoon Liquid Smoke, optional
1 tablespoon canola oil
1/4 teaspoon salt
1/4 teaspoon pepper

1. Flatten chicken to 1/4-in. thickness. In a large bowl, combine the shrimp, onions, mayonnaise, tarragon, lemon juice and Liquid Smoke if desired. Place about 1/3 cup down the center of each chicken breast half; fold chicken over filling and secure with toothpicks.

2. Brush the chicken with oil; sprinkle with salt and pepper. Grill, covered, over medium heat for 6-8 minutes on each side or no longer pink. Discard the toothpicks. **Yield:** 6 servings.

🎗️🎗️🎗️
Eggplant Sausage Casserole

Prep: 45 min. **Bake:** 45 min. + standing

Carol Mieske, Red Bluff, California

If you want your children to happily eat a vegetable, try serving them eggplant in this cheesy pasta casserole.

- 1 package (16 ounces) penne pasta
- 2 pounds bulk Italian sausage
- 1 medium eggplant, peeled and cubed
- 1 large onion, chopped
- 2 tablespoons olive oil
- 2 garlic cloves, minced
- 1 can (28 ounces) diced tomatoes, undrained
- 1 can (6 ounces) tomato paste
- 1 teaspoon salt
- 1 teaspoon dried basil
- 1 teaspoon paprika
- 1 carton (15 ounces) ricotta cheese
- 4 cups (16 ounces) shredded part-skim mozzarella cheese, *divided*

1. Cook the pasta according to package directions. Meanwhile, in a large skillet, cook the sausage over medium heat until no longer pink; drain. Set the sausage aside.

2. In the same skillet, saute the eggplant and onion in oil. Add garlic; cook 1 minute longer. Stir in the tomatoes, tomato paste, salt, basil and paprika; simmer, partially covered, for 15 minutes. Remove from heat. Drain pasta; stir into eggplant mixture. Add sausage.

3. Spread half of sausage mixture in a greased 13-in. x 9-in. baking dish. Spread with ricotta cheese. Top with half of the cheese and remaining sausage mixture.

4. Cover and bake at 350° for 40 minutes. Uncover; sprinkle with remaining cheese. Bake 5 minutes longer or until the cheese is melted. Let stand for 10 minutes before serving. **Yield:** 12 servings.

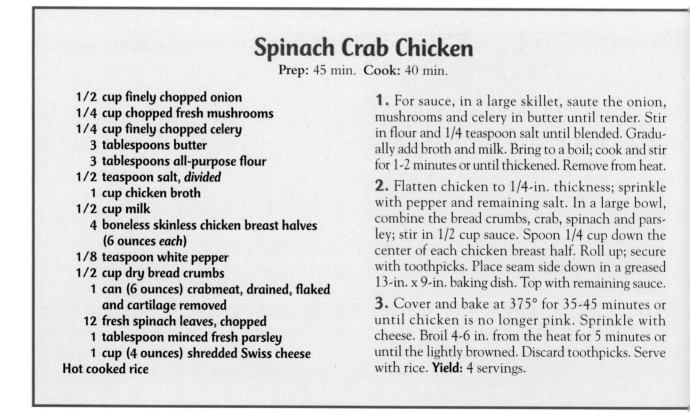

Spinach Crab Chicken

Prep: 45 min. **Cook:** 40 min.

- 1/2 cup finely chopped onion
- 1/4 cup chopped fresh mushrooms
- 1/4 cup finely chopped celery
- 3 tablespoons butter
- 3 tablespoons all-purpose flour
- 1/2 teaspoon salt, *divided*
- 1 cup chicken broth
- 1/2 cup milk
- 4 boneless skinless chicken breast halves (6 ounces *each*)
- 1/8 teaspoon white pepper
- 1/2 cup dry bread crumbs
- 1 can (6 ounces) crabmeat, drained, flaked and cartilage removed
- 12 fresh spinach leaves, chopped
- 1 tablespoon minced fresh parsley
- 1 cup (4 ounces) shredded Swiss cheese

Hot cooked rice

1. For sauce, in a large skillet, saute the onion, mushrooms and celery in butter until tender. Stir in flour and 1/4 teaspoon salt until blended. Gradually add broth and milk. Bring to a boil; cook and stir for 1-2 minutes or until thickened. Remove from heat.

2. Flatten chicken to 1/4-in. thickness; sprinkle with pepper and remaining salt. In a large bowl, combine the bread crumbs, crab, spinach and parsley; stir in 1/2 cup sauce. Spoon 1/4 cup down the center of each chicken breast half. Roll up; secure with toothpicks. Place seam side down in a greased 13-in. x 9-in. baking dish. Top with remaining sauce.

3. Cover and bake at 375° for 35-45 minutes or until chicken is no longer pink. Sprinkle with cheese. Broil 4-6 in. from the heat for 5 minutes or until the lightly browned. Discard toothpicks. Serve with rice. **Yield:** 4 servings.

VICKI MELIES ELKHORN, NEBRASKA

I changed a friend's recipe for crab-stuffed chicken to include one of my favorite vegetables—spinach. Now my husband requests this elegant entree all the time, and guests always enjoy it, too. Pair it with rice for a complete meal.

Grand Prize Winner

🏅🏅🏅
Grilled Veggie Sausage Pizza

Prep: 25 min. + rising **Grill:** 15 min.

Faith Sommers, Bangor, California

One summer, I did a little experimenting in the kitchen and came up with this crispy, thin-crust pizza. It met with such approval from my guests, they wanted the recipe so they could try it in their own backyards.

        1 tablespoon active dry yeast
1-1/3 cups warm water (110° to 115°)
        5 teaspoons sugar
        4 teaspoons canola oil
   1/4 teaspoon salt
   1/4 teaspoon garlic salt
   1/4 teaspoon dried oregano
3-1/4 to 3-1/2 cups all-purpose flour
TOPPINGS:
   1/2 pound bulk Italian sausage
1-1/2 cups pizza sauce
        2 cups (8 ounces) shredded part-skim
           mozzarella cheese
        1 cup sliced fresh mushrooms
   1/4 cup chopped sweet red pepper
   1/4 cup chopped green pepper

1. In a large bowl, dissolve yeast in water. Add sugar, oil, salt, garlic salt, oregano and 1-1/2 cups flour. Stir in enough of the remaining flour to form a soft dough.

2. Turn onto a floured surface; knead until smooth and elastic, about 6-8 minutes. Place in a greased bowl, turning once to grease top. Cover and let rise in a warm place for 30 minutes.

3. Wrap foil over outside bottom of two 12-in. pizza pans; grease pans and set aside. In a skillet, cook sausage over medium heat until no longer pink; drain and set aside.

4. Divide the dough in half. On a floured surface, roll each portion into a 13-in. circle. Transfer to prepared pans; build up edges slightly.

5. Spread the pizza sauce over the pizza crusts; sprinkle with the cooked sausage, mozzarella cheese, mushrooms and peppers. Grill, covered, over medium heat for 15-20 minutes or until the bottom of the crust is browned and the cheese is melted. **Yield:** 2 pizzas (8 slices each).

Pizza Pizzazz

Experiment with this recipe by changing or adding toppings to suit your family's tastes. For example, use chopped onion, pepperoni, ripe olives or different kinds of cheese.

🎗🎗🎗 Chicken Rice Bowl

Prep/Total Time: 10 min.

Tammy Daniels, Batavia, Ohio

This dinner is easy to toss together on a busy weeknight, so I usually keep the ingredients on hand. I start sauteing the onion and pepper first, then I prepare the instant rice. If you like, top it all with some shredded sharp cheddar cheese.

1 cup uncooked instant rice
1 cup chicken broth
1/2 cup chopped frozen green pepper, thawed
1/4 cup chopped onion
2 teaspoons olive oil
1 package (9 ounces) ready-to-use grilled chicken breast strips
1/2 cup frozen corn, thawed
1/2 cup frozen peas, thawed
1 teaspoon dried basil
1 teaspoon rubbed sage
1/8 teaspoon salt
1/8 teaspoon pepper

Cook the rice in broth according to package directions. Meanwhile, in a large skillet, saute the green pepper and onion in oil for 2-3 minutes or until crisp-tender. Stir in the chicken strips, corn, peas, basil and sage. Cook, uncovered, for 4-5 minutes over medium heat or until heated through. Stir in the rice, salt and pepper. **Yield:** 4 servings.

🎗🎗🎗 Roasted Pepper Ravioli Bake

Prep: 25 min. + standing Bake: 30 min.

Carol Poindexter, Norridge, Illinois

Convenient frozen cheese ravioli is dressed up with peppers, spaghetti sauce and mozzarella for this delicious casserole.

✓ This recipe includes Nutrition Facts and Diabetic Exchanges.

2 *each* medium green, sweet red and yellow peppers
1 package (25 ounces) frozen cheese ravioli
1 tablespoon olive oil
1 teaspoon sugar
1/4 teaspoon salt
2 cups meatless spaghetti sauce, *divided*
4 ounces sliced part-skim mozzarella cheese

1. Place peppers on a broiler pan. Broil 4 in. from heat until skins blister, about 6-8 minutes. With tongs, rotate peppers a quarter turn. Broil and rotate until all sides are blistered and blackened. Immediately place peppers in a bowl; cover and let stand for 15-20 minutes.

2. Meanwhile, cook the ravioli according to package directions; drain. Peel off and discard charred skin from peppers. Remove stems and seeds. Finely chop peppers; drain. In a large bowl, combine the peppers, oil, sugar and salt.

3. Spread 1-1/2 cups spaghetti sauce in a 13-in. x 9-in. baking dish coated with cooking spray. Layer with the ravioli, pepper mixture and cheese. Top with the remaining spaghetti sauce. Cover and bake at 350° for 15 minutes. Uncover; bake 15-20 minutes longer or until heated through. **Yield:** 8 servings.

Nutrition Facts: 1 serving equals 335 calories, 11 g fat (5 g saturated fat), 44 mg cholesterol, 415 mg sodium, 44 g carbohydrate, 5 g fiber, 16 g protein. **Diabetic Exchanges:** 2-1/2 starch, 1-1/2 fat, 1 lean meat, 1 vegetable.

★★★
Pork Tenderloin with Glazed Red Onions

Prep: 25 min. + marinating **Cook:** 1-1/4 hours

Patricia Schmidt, Sterling Heights, Michigan

This colorful main course has been a longtime family favorite. I like to pair it with rice pilaf or orzo to complement the thyme in the pork and the vinegar in the glazed onions.

☑ This recipe includes Nutrition Facts and Diabetic Exchanges.

1 tablespoon minced fresh thyme
1 tablespoon olive oil
3/4 teaspoon salt
1/2 teaspoon pepper
2 pork tenderloins (1 pound *each*)
RED ONION TOPPING:
4 large red onions, sliced
2 tablespoons olive oil
3/4 cup dry red wine *or* chicken broth
1/4 cup raisins
2 tablespoons sugar
1/4 teaspoon salt
1/4 cup balsamic vinegar
1-1/2 teaspoons minced fresh thyme

1. In a large resealable plastic bag, combine the thyme, oil, salt and pepper; add pork. Seal bag and turn to coat; marinate at room temperature for 30 minutes.

2. Meanwhile, saute onions in oil until tender; add the wine, raisins, sugar and salt. Bring to a boil. Reduce heat; cook, uncovered, for 45 minutes or until liquid is evaporated. Stir in vinegar and thyme; cook and stir 10 minutes longer to blend flavors. Set aside.

3. Drain and discard marinade. Place pork on a rack coated with cooking spray in a shallow roasting pan. Bake, uncovered, at 425° for 20-30 minutes or until a meat thermometer reads 160°. Let stand for 5-10 minutes before slicing. Serve with the warm red onion topping. **Yield:** 6 servings.

Nutrition Facts: 3-1/2 ounces cooked pork with 2/3 cup onion mixture equals 336 calories, 12 g fat (3 g saturated fat), 84 mg cholesterol, 461 mg sodium, 20 g carbohydrate, 2 g fiber, 32 g protein. **Diabetic Exchanges:** 4 lean meat, 1 vegetable, 1 fat, 1/2 starch.

★★★
Kitchen-Sink Soft Tacos

Prep/Total Time: 15 min.

Darlene King, Estevan, Saskatchewan

My children helped invent these when they tossed some taco seasoning on leftover sloppy joe meat we had in the fridge.

1/2 cup uncooked instant rice
1 can (15 ounces) chili with beans
1 teaspoon taco seasoning
12 flour tortillas (6 inches), warmed
1 cup (4 ounces) shredded cheddar cheese

1. Cook the rice according to package directions. In a microwave-safe bowl, combine the chili and taco seasoning. Cover and microwave on high for 2-3 minutes or until heated through.

2. Spoon rice and chili onto tortillas; sprinkle with cheese. Fold sides of tortilla over filling. **Yield:** 6 servings.

Editor's Note: This recipe was tested in a 1,100-watt microwave.

🎀🎀🎀
Honey-Citrus Chicken Kabobs

Prep: 15 min. + marinating **Grill:** 10 min.

Amanda Mills, Austin, Texas

When you want a quick, light and delicious summer meal, this one is hard to beat! You'll need only 30 minutes to marinate the chicken pieces for the tangy, fun-to-eat skewers. Then they go on the grill for just 10 minutes.

☑ This recipe includes Nutrition Facts and Diabetic Exchanges.

- 1/2 **cup lime juice**
- 1/2 **cup lemon juice**
- 1/2 **cup honey**
- 1 **garlic clove, minced**
- 1 **pound boneless skinless chicken breasts, cut into 1-inch cubes**
- 1 *each* **medium green, sweet red and yellow pepper, cut into 1-inch pieces**

1. In a small bowl, combine the lime juice, lemon juice, honey and garlic. Pour 1-1/4 cups into a large resealable plastic bag; add the chicken. Seal bag and turn to coat; refrigerate for at least 30 minutes. Cover and refrigerate remaining marinade for basting.

2. Coat grill rack with cooking spray before starting the grill. Drain and discard marinade from chicken. On eight metal or soaked wooden skewers, alternately thread chicken and peppers.

3. Grill, covered, over medium-hot heat for 8-10 minutes or until chicken is no longer pink, turning and basting frequently with the reserved marinade. **Yield:** 4 servings.

Nutrition Facts: 2 kabobs equals 194 calories, 3 g fat (1 g saturated fat), 63 mg cholesterol, 57 mg sodium, 19 g carbohydrate, 2 g fiber, 24 g protein. **Diabetic Exchanges:** 3 very lean meat, 1 starch, 1 vegetable.

Homemade Marinades

Marinating adds flavor to meat and tenderizes it. While many bottled marinades are available at grocery stores, some are high in fat and sodium. When you make your own marinade, you can control the amount of fat and sodium, plus use your favorite flavors.

🏅🏅🏅
Chicken-Stuffed Cubanelle Peppers

Prep: 20 min. **Bake:** 55 min.

Bev Burlingame, Canton, Ohio

Here's a deliciously different take on traditional stuffed peppers. I substituted shredded chicken for the usual ground beef and used Cubanelle peppers in place of the green peppers.

☑ This recipe includes Nutrition Facts and Diabetic Exchanges.

> 6 Cubanelle peppers *or mild banana peppers*
> 2 eggs
> 1 cup salsa
> 3 cups shredded cooked chicken breast
> 3/4 cup soft bread crumbs
> 1/2 cup cooked long grain rice
> 2 cups meatless spaghetti sauce, *divided*

1. Cut tops off peppers and remove seeds. In a large bowl, combine the eggs, salsa, chicken, bread crumbs and rice. Spoon into peppers.

2. Coat a 13-in. x 9-in. baking dish and an 8-in. square baking dish with cooking spray. Spread 1 cup spaghetti sauce in larger pan and 1/2 cup sauce in smaller pan. Place peppers over sauce. Spoon remaining spaghetti sauce over peppers.

3. Cover and bake at 350° for 55-60 minutes or until peppers are tender. **Yield:** 6 servings.

Nutrition Facts: 1 stuffed pepper equals 230 calories, 4 g fat (1 g saturated fat), 125 mg cholesterol, 661 mg sodium, 20 g carbohydrate, 5 g fiber, 26 g protein. **Diabetic Exchanges:** 3 very lean meat, 2 vegetable, 1 starch.

Crumb Clue

To make soft bread crumbs, tear several slices of fresh white, French or whole wheat bread into 1-inch pieces. Place them in a food processor or blender; cover it and push the pulse button several times to make coarse crumbs.

🎀🎀🎀
Peking Shrimp

Prep/Total Time: 25 min.

Janet Edwards, Beaverton, Oregon

During summer, we spend as much time as possible at our vacation home in a beach town. I serve a lot of seafood there because it's so fresh and readily available. This entree is always a top choice because it's a winner.

✓ This recipe includes Nutrition Facts and Diabetic Exchanges.

    1 tablespoon cornstarch
1/4 cup water
1/4 cup corn syrup
    2 tablespoons reduced-sodium soy sauce
    2 tablespoons sherry *or chicken broth*
    1 garlic clove, minced
1/4 teaspoon ground ginger
    1 small green pepper, cut into 1-inch pieces
    2 tablespoons canola oil
    1 pound uncooked medium shrimp, peeled and deveined
    1 medium tomato, cut into wedges
Hot cooked rice, optional

1. In a small bowl, combine cornstarch and water until smooth. Stir in the corn syrup, soy sauce, sherry or broth, garlic and ginger; set aside.

2. In a nonstick skillet or wok, stir-fry green pepper in hot oil for 3 minutes. Add shrimp; stir-fry 3 minutes longer or until shrimp turn pink. Stir the cornstarch mixture and add to the pan. Bring to a boil; cook and stir for 2 minutes or until sauce is thickened. Add tomato; heat through. Serve with rice if desired. **Yield:** 4 servings.

Nutrition Facts: 3/4 cup shrimp mixture (calculated without rice) equals 237 calories, 8 g fat (1 g saturated fat), 168 mg cholesterol, 532 mg sodium, 21 g carbohydrate, 1 g fiber, 19 g protein. **Diabetic Exchanges:** 2 lean meat, 1-1/2 fat, 1 starch, 1 vegetable.

🎀🎀🎀
Bean and Pork Chop Bake

Prep: 15 min. **Bake:** 45 min.

LaRita Lang, Lincoln, Nebraska

Having grown up on a pork-producing farm, I like to include that versatile meat in my cooking. This recipe featuring pork chops has apple-cinnamon flavor with a hint of sweet maple.

    4 boneless pork loin chops (1/2 inch thick and 4 ounces *each*)
    1 tablespoon canola oil
    1 large tart apple, peeled and chopped
    1 small onion, chopped
    1 can (28 ounces) baked beans
1/3 cup raisins
1/4 teaspoon ground cinnamon, *divided*
    1 tablespoon maple pancake syrup
1/4 teaspoon salt

1. In a large skillet, brown the pork chops on both sides in oil. Remove and keep warm. In the same pan, saute apple and onion until tender. Stir in the beans, raisins and 1/8 teaspoon cinnamon. Spoon into a greased 2-1/2-qt. baking dish; top with pork chops.

2. Cover and bake at 350° for 40 minutes. Brush the chops with syrup; sprinkle with the salt and remaining cinnamon. Bake, uncovered for 5-10 minutes longer or until a meat thermometer reads 160°. **Yield:** 4 servings.

1 teaspoon salt, *divided*
1/2 teaspoon pepper, *divided*
2 tablespoons olive oil
1 medium sweet red pepper, julienned
1 cup sliced fresh mushrooms
2 green onions, chopped
1/8 teaspoon ground nutmeg
1/8 teaspoon cayenne pepper
2/3 cup heavy whipping cream
1/2 cup chicken broth
8 ounces uncooked linguine
2/3 cup pine nuts, toasted
1/2 cup frozen peas, thawed
Shredded Parmesan cheese, optional

1. Sprinkle the chicken with 1/2 teaspoon salt and 1/4 teaspoon pepper. In a large skillet, cook chicken in oil over medium-high heat for 8-10 minutes or until no longer pink. Remove and keep warm.

2. In a same skillet, saute red pepper, mushrooms, onions, nutmeg and cayenne just until the vegetables are tender. Add cream and broth. Bring to a boil; cook until sauce is reduced by a third.

3. Cook the linguine according to package directions; drain. Add the chicken, linguine, pine nuts, peas and the remaining salt and pepper to sauce; heat through. Garnish with cheese if desired. **Yield:** 4 servings.

🎗🎗🎗
Primavera Chicken

Prep: 15 min. Cook: 25 min.

Vicky Root, Greenville, Ohio

You'll love the way the nutmeg blends with the cayenne pepper in this pretty pasta dish. It's especially good served with homemade pesto bread. I usually double the recipe because I like it the next day even better!

1-1/3 pounds boneless skinless chicken breast, cut into strips

🎗🎗🎗
Pizza Quesadillas

Prep/Total Time: 10 min.

Barbara Rupert, Edgefield, South Carolina

When my husband and I needed a quick dinner for the two of us, I fixed these using some leftover ingredients I had on hand. Unlike traditional Southwestern quesadillas, my recipe calls for Italian meats, cheeses and seasoning.

1 cup meatless spaghetti sauce
2 teaspoons butter, softened
4 flour tortillas (10 inches)
1 cup (4 ounces) shredded part-skim mozzarella cheese
8 thin slices hard salami
4 slices pepperoni
1/4 cup shredded Parmesan cheese
1/2 teaspoon dried oregano

1. In a small saucepan, cook the spaghetti sauce over medium-low heat for 3-4 minutes or until heated through.

2. Meanwhile, spread the butter over one side of each tortilla. Sprinkle unbuttered side of two tortillas with mozzarella cheese; top with salami and pepperoni.

Sprinkle with Parmesan cheese and oregano. Top with remaining tortillas, buttered side up.

3. Cook on a griddle over medium heat for 2-3 minutes on each side or until cheese is melted. Cut into wedges; serve with warmed spaghetti sauce. **Yield:** 2 servings.

🎗️🎗️🎗️

Sweet 'n' Sour Cashew Pork

Prep/Total Time: 30 min.

Janet Rodakowski, Wentzville, Missouri

A simple homemade sauce highlights this tangy pork stir-fry. Ginger, garlic and pineapple give it a traditional taste while snow peas, green onions and cashews add a little crunch.

- **2 tablespoons cornstarch,** *divided*
- **1 tablespoon sherry** *or* **chicken broth**
- **1 pork tenderloin (1 pound), cut into 1-inch pieces**
- **1/4 cup sugar**
- **1/3 cup water**
- **1/4 cup cider vinegar**
- **3 tablespoons reduced-sodium soy sauce**
- **3 tablespoons ketchup**
- **1 tablespoon canola oil**
- **1/3 cup unsalted cashews**
- **1/4 cup chopped green onions**
- **2 teaspoons minced fresh gingerroot**
- **2 garlic cloves, minced**
- **1/2 pound fresh snow peas (3 cups)**
- **1 can (8 ounces) unsweetened pineapple chunks, drained**

Hot cooked rice, optional

1. In a large bowl, combine 1 tablespoon cornstarch and sherry until smooth; add pork and toss to coat. In another bowl, combine the sugar and remaining cornstarch. Stir in the water, vinegar, soy sauce and ketchup until smooth; set aside.

2. In a large nonstick skillet or wok, stir-fry pork in hot oil until no longer pink. Add cashews, onions, ginger and garlic; stir-fry for 1 minute. Add the peas and pineapple; stir-fry 3 minutes longer or until peas are crisp-tender.

3. Stir the cornstarch mixture and add to the pan. Bring to a boil; cook and stir for 1-2 minutes or until the sauce is thickened. Serve over rice if desired. **Yield:** 4 servings.

Grilled Raspberry Chicken

Prep: 15 min. + marinating Grill: 30 min.

Gloria Warczak, Cedarburg, Wisconsin

Raspberry vinaigrette and raspberry jam lend tangy fruit flavor to this moist chicken dish prepared on the grill. Ever since I came up with the recipe, it's been a favorite on my dinner menus.

- 1 cup plus 4-1/2 teaspoons raspberry vinaigrette, *divided*
- 2 tablespoons minced fresh rosemary *or* 2 teaspoons dried rosemary, crushed, *divided*
- 6 bone-in chicken thighs
- 6 chicken drumsticks
- 1/2 cup seedless raspberry jam
- 1-1/2 teaspoons lime juice
- 1/2 teaspoon soy sauce
- 1/8 teaspoon garlic powder

1. In a large resealable plastic bag, combine 1 cup vinaigrette and half of the rosemary. Add chicken. Seal bag and turn to coat; refrigerate for 1 hour.

2. In a small bowl, combine the jam, lime juice, soy sauce, garlic powder, and remaining vinaigrette and rosemary; set aside.

3. Drain and discard the marinade. Place the chicken skin side down on grill rack. Grill, covered, over indirect medium heat for 20 minutes. Turn; grill 10-20 minutes longer or until juices run clear and a meat thermometer reads 180°, basting occasionally with raspberry sauce. **Yield:** 6 servings.

Creamy Prosciutto Pasta

Prep/Total Time: 10 min.

Christine Ward, Austin, Texas

I'm always looking for dinners that go together quickly. Here, I re-created a favorite pasta dish from an Italian restaurant using grocery store convenience products. Add crusty bread and a salad for a complete meal.

- 1 package (9 ounces) refrigerated fettuccine *or* refrigerated linguine
- 1/2 pound sliced fresh mushrooms
- 1 small onion, chopped
- 1 tablespoon butter
- 1 package (10 ounces) fresh baby spinach
- 1 jar (15 ounces) Alfredo sauce
- 1/3 pound thinly sliced prosciutto, chopped

1. Cook fettuccine according to package directions. Meanwhile, in a large saucepan, saute mushrooms and onion in butter until tender. Add spinach. Bring to a boil. Reduce heat; cook just until spinach is wilted.

2. Stir in Alfredo sauce and prosciutto; cook for 1-2 minutes or until heated through. Drain pasta; add to sauce and toss to coat. **Yield:** 4 servings.

🎖🎖🎖
Spinach-Stuffed Beef Tenderloin

Prep: 20 min. **Bake:** 30 min.

Deborah DeMers, Lakewood, Washington

This special tenderloin makes a wonderfully easy entree for company. Filled with spinach, garlic, blue cheese and fresh mushrooms, it gets rave reviews whenever I serve it.

✓ This recipe includes Nutrition Facts and Diabetic Exchanges.

- 1/2 pound sliced fresh mushrooms
- 4 garlic cloves, minced
- 1 package (6 ounces) fresh baby spinach, chopped
- 1 cup (4 ounces) crumbled blue cheese
- 1 beef tenderloin roast (2 pounds)
- 1/2 teaspoon salt, *divided*
- 1/2 teaspoon pepper, *divided*

1. In a small nonstick skillet coated with cooking spray, saute the mushrooms until tender. Add the garlic; cook for 1 minute. In a small bowl, combine the mushroom mixture, spinach and cheese; set aside.

2. Cut a lengthwise slit down center of the tenderloin to within 1/2 in. of bottom. Open the tenderloin so it lies flat; cover with plastic wrap. Flatten to 3/4-in. thickness. Remove the plastic wrap; sprinkle with 1/4 teaspoon salt and 1/4 teaspoon pepper. Spread stuffing over meat to within 1 in. of edges.

3. Close the tenderloin; tie at 2-in. intervals with kitchen string. Place on a rack in a shallow roasting pan. Sprinkle with remaining salt and pepper.

4. Bake, uncovered, at 425° for 30 minutes or until meat reaches desired doneness (for medium-rare, a meat thermometer should read 145°; medium, 160°; well-done, 170°). Let stand for 5-10 minutes before slicing. **Yield:** 8 servings.

Nutrition Facts: 5 ounces stuffed cooked beef equals 238 calories, 12 g fat (6 g saturated fat), 82 mg cholesterol, 417 mg sodium, 3 g carbohydrate, 1 g fiber, 28 g protein. **Diabetic Exchanges:** 3 lean meat, 1-1/2 fat.

· ·

🎖🎖🎖
Tilapia with Corn Salsa

Prep/Total Time: 10 min.

Brenda Coffey, Singer Island, Florida

My family loves fish, and this super-fast recipe is very popular. The fillets cook in just minutes. We like them garnished with lemon wedges and served with couscous on the side.

- 4 tilapia fillets (6 ounces *each*)
- 1 tablespoon olive oil
- 1/4 teaspoon salt
- 1/4 teaspoon pepper
- 1 can (15 ounces) black beans, rinsed and drained
- 1 can (11 ounces) whole kernel corn, drained
- 3/4 cup Italian salad dressing
- 2 tablespoons chopped green onion
- 2 tablespoons chopped sweet red pepper

1. Drizzle both sides of fillets with oil; sprinkle with salt and pepper.

2. Broil 4-6 in. from the heat for 5-7 minutes or until fish flakes easily with a fork. Meanwhile, in a small bowl, combine the remaining ingredients. Serve with fish. **Yield:** 4 servings.

Pretzel-Topped Sweet Potatoes, p. 127

Chili-Seasoned Potato Wedges, p. 131

Three-Pepper Chutney, p. 129

Side Dishes & Condiments

Rounding out menus for holiday celebrations, dinner parties and weeknight meals couldn't be easier when you have the rave-winning recipes here to choose from. Enjoy Golden Mashed Potato Bake, Glazed Carrot Coins and much more.

Spicy Asparagus Spears......................120
Swirled Potato Bake..........................120
Golden Diced Potatoes......................122
Skillet Sausage Stuffing.....................122
Bacon Mashed Potatoes....................123
Glazed Carrot Coins 123
Horseradish Creamed Carrots............124
Tomatoes with Horseradish Sauce......124
Spanish Squash Medley.....................126
Herbed Rice....................................126
Onion-Bacon Baby Carrots...............127
Pretzel-Topped Sweet Potatoes..........127

Golden Mashed Potato Bake..............128
Garden Vegetable Medley..................128
Three-Pepper Chutney......................129
Spiced Cranberry Ketchup................130
Ginger Garlic Linguine.....................130
Blue Cheese Green Beans..................131
Chili-Seasoned Potato Wedges..........131
Herbed Baked Spinach......................132
Party Carrots 132
Garbanzo Bean Medley.....................134
Cranberry Apple Saute......................134
Country Corn..................................135
Cheese Fries....................................135
Creamy Zucchini.............................136
Pickled Baby Carrots........................136
Dilly Stuffed Potatoes.......................137

Party Carrots, p. 132

Spicy Asparagus Spears

Prep/Total Time: 20 min.

Marlies Kinnell, Barrie, Ontario

This no-fuss dish gets its zippy taste from Cajun seasoning and crushed red pepper flakes. Even people who don't like other asparagus recipes will enjoy these buttery spears. Plus, they go well with many different main courses.

☑ This recipe includes Nutrition Facts and Diabetic Exchange.

    2 tablespoons butter
1/2 teaspoon onion powder
1/2 teaspoon seasoned salt
1/2 teaspoon Cajun seasoning
Crushed red pepper flakes to taste
1-3/4 pounds fresh asparagus, trimmed

1. In a large skillet, melt the butter. Stir in the onion powder, seasoned salt, Cajun seasoning and crushed red pepper flakes.

2. Add the asparagus spears, stir gently to coat. Cover and cook 5-7 minutes or until crisp-tender, stirring occasionally. **Yield:** 6 servings.

Nutrition Facts: 1 serving (prepared with reduced-fat butter) equals 26 calories, 2 g fat (1 g saturated fat), 7 mg cholesterol, 210 mg sodium, 2 g carbohydrate, 1 g fiber, 1 g protein. **Diabetic Exchange:** 1 vegetable.

Swirled Potato Bake

Prep: 35 min. Bake: 25 min.

2-1/2 pounds sweet potatoes, peeled and cubed
2-1/2 pounds Yukon Gold potatoes, peeled
       and cubed
1-1/2 cups milk, *divided*
    1 package (8 ounces) cream cheese, softened,
       divided
    2 tablespoons butter, *divided*
    2 green onions, finely chopped
1-1/2 teaspoons salt, *divided*
  1/4 teaspoon pepper
  1/2 teaspoon dried thyme

1. Place sweet potatoes in a large saucepan; cover with water. Bring to a boil. Reduce heat; cover and cook for 20-25 minutes or just until tender.

2. Meanwhile, place the Yukon Gold potatoes in another large saucepan; cover with water. Bring to a boil. Reduce heat; cover and cook for 15-20 minutes or until tender.

3. Drain Yukon Gold potatoes; mash with 3/4 cup milk, half of the cream cheese and 1 tablespoon butter. Add onions, 3/4 teaspoon salt and pepper; mix well. Spoon into a greased 13-in. x 9-in. baking dish.

4. Drain sweet potatoes; mash with the thyme and remaining milk, cream cheese, butter and salt. Spread over potato mixture. Cut through layers with a knife to swirl. Bake, uncovered, at 350° for 25-30 minutes or until heated through. **Yield:** 7 servings.

MARY ANN DELL PHOENIXVILLE, PENNSYLVANIA

Potato lovers dig right into this comforting, home-style bake from my mother-in-law. The creamy combination of Yukon Golds and sweet potatoes goes well with poultry or roasts. Leftovers taste great reheated, although they are rare!

Grand Prize Winner

🏅🏅🏅 Golden Diced Potatoes

Prep: 15 min. **Cook:** 30 min.

Angela Tiffany Wegerer, Colwich, Kansas

My aunt once prepared potatoes like these for us. When I couldn't remember her exact recipe, I experimented in the kitchen until I created this version. The lightly seasoned coating on the potatoes cooks to a pretty golden brown.

- 3/4 cup all-purpose flour
- 1 teaspoon seasoned salt
- 1/2 teaspoon onion powder
- 1/4 teaspoon garlic powder
- 1/4 teaspoon pepper
- 4 medium potatoes, peeled and cut into 1/2-inch pieces
- 1/2 cup butter

1. In a large resealable plastic bag, combine the first five ingredients. Add 1/2 cup potatoes at a time; shake to coat.

2. In two large skillets, melt butter. Add potatoes; cook and stir over medium heat for 25-30 minutes or until potatoes are tender. **Yield:** 6 servings.

🏅🏅🏅 Skillet Sausage Stuffing

Prep/Total Time: 25 min.

Jennifer Lynn Cullen, Taylor, Michigan

This recipe dresses up a package of stuffing mix with plenty of pork sausage, fresh mushrooms, celery and onion. It impressed my in-laws at a family gathering and has since become a popular side dish with my husband and children.

- 1 pound bulk pork sausage
- 1-1/4 cups chopped celery
- 1/2 cup chopped onion
- 1/2 cup sliced fresh mushrooms
- 1-1/2 teaspoons minced garlic
- 1-1/2 cups reduced-sodium chicken broth
- 1 teaspoon rubbed sage
- 1 package (6 ounces) stuffing mix

1. In a large skillet, cook the sausage, celery, onion and mushrooms over medium heat until meat is no longer pink. Add garlic; cook 1 minute longer; drain. Stir in broth and sage.

2. Bring to a boil. Stir in the stuffing mix. Cover and remove from the heat; let stand for 5 minutes. Fluff with a fork. **Yield:** 8 servings.

🎖🎖🎖
Bacon Mashed Potatoes
Prep/Total Time: 25 min.

Pat Mathison, Meadowlands, Minnesota

Featuring cheddar cheese, bacon bits and chives, these rich and hearty potatoes go well with just about anything. For a slightly different twist, add some chopped parsley.

2-1/2 cups cubed peeled potatoes (3/4 pound)
  1/4 cup milk
  1/4 cup mayonnaise
4-1/2 teaspoons minced chives
  1/8 teaspoon garlic powder
  1/8 teaspoon pepper
  1/2 cup shredded cheddar cheese
    3 bacon strips, cooked and crumbled

1. Place potatoes in a large saucepan and cover with water. Bring to a boil. Reduce heat; cover and cook for 10-15 minutes or until tender. Drain.

2. Transfer to a large bowl. Add the milk, mayonnaise, chives, garlic powder and pepper; mash potatoes. Stir in cheese and bacon. **Yield:** 3 servings.

🎖🎖🎖
Glazed Carrot Coins
Prep/Total Time: 25 min.

Helen Bethel, Maysville, North Carolina

Flavored with orange juice, cinnamon and ginger, these glossy sliced carrots are pretty enough for a holiday dinner or other special meal. To save time, you could substitute two 15-ounce cans of carrots for the fresh ones.

✓ This recipe includes Nutrition Facts and Diabetic Exchanges.

  2 tablespoons butter
  2 tablespoons brown sugar
  2 tablespoons orange juice
1/4 teaspoon salt
1/4 teaspoon ground ginger
1/8 teaspoon ground cinnamon
  6 medium carrots, cut into 1/2-inch slices

1. In a small saucepan, melt butter over medium heat. Stir in the brown sugar, orange juice, salt, ginger and cinnamon. Add the carrots; cover and cook for 20-25 minutes or until tender, stirring occasionally. **Yield:** 4 servings.

Nutrition Facts: 3/4 cup (prepared with reduced-fat butter) equals 94 calories, 3 g fat (2 g saturated fat), 10 mg cholesterol, 217 mg sodium, 17 g carbohydrate, 3 g fiber, 1 g protein. **Diabetic Exchanges:** 2 vegetable, 1/2 fruit.

Horseradish Creamed Carrots

Prep: 30 min. **Bake:** 20 min.

Meredith Sayre, Burlington, Kentucky

Jazzed up with a creamy horseradish sauce and buttery crumb topping, sliced carrots never tasted so good! My family is always happy to see this flavorful side dish on the table. And I love it because it's a snap to put together.

> 2 pounds carrots, cut into 1/2-inch slices
> 3/4 cup mayonnaise
> 1/3 cup half-and-half cream
> 1/4 cup prepared horseradish
> 2 tablespoons finely chopped onion
> 1 teaspoon salt
> 1/4 teaspoon pepper
> 1/2 cup crushed cornflakes
> 2 tablespoons butter, melted

1. Place 1 in. of water in a saucepan; add the carrots. Bring to a boil; reduce the heat. Cover and simmer for 8-10 minutes or until crisp-tender; drain.

2. In a large bowl, combine the mayonnaise, cream, horseradish, onion, salt and pepper; add carrots and toss to coat.

3. Transfer mixture to a greased 1-1/2-qt. baking dish. Combine cornflake crumbs and butter; sprinkle over the carrots.

4. Bake, uncovered, at 350° for 20-25 minutes or until bubbly. **Yield:** 6 servings.

Tomatoes with Horseradish Sauce

Prep/Total Time: 15 min.

✓ This recipe includes Nutrition Facts and Diabetic Exchange.

Refrigerated butter-flavored spray
> 4 large tomatoes, sliced
> 3 tablespoons mayonnaise
> 2 tablespoons half-and-half cream
> 1 tablespoon prepared horseradish

Minced fresh parsley

Coat a large skillet with refrigerated butter-flavored spray. Heat the skillet over medium heat. Add the tomato slices; cook for 2-3 minutes on each side or until the edges begin to brown. In a small bowl, whisk the mayonnaise, half-and-half cream and horseradish. Spoon over the tomatoes. Sprinkle with parsley. **Yield:** 4 servings.

Nutrition Facts: 1 serving (prepared with fat-free mayonnaise and half-and-half) equals 53 calories, 1 g fat (trace saturated fat), 1 mg cholesterol, 124 mg sodium, 11 g carbohydrate, 2 g fiber, 2 g protein.
Diabetic Exchange: 2 vegetable.

PHYLLIS SHAUGHNESSY LIVONIA, NEW YORK

This warm dish of lightly sautéed tomatoes in a tangy cream sauce is very tasty and quick to make. You'll need just 15 minutes and six everyday ingredients. I occasionally use both red and green tomatoes to add even more color.

Grand
Prize
Winner

Spanish Squash Medley

Prep/Total Time: 25 min.

Regina Gutierrez, San Antonio, Texas

Feel free to pair everything from chicken and pork to steak with this fresh-tasting medley of summer squash, zucchini, onion and tomato. But be warned—the side dish is so colorful and flavorful, it might steal the spotlight from your entree!

☑ This recipe includes Nutrition Facts and Diabetic Exchanges.

2 medium summer squash, halved and sliced
2 medium zucchini, halved and sliced
1/3 cup chopped onion

1-1/2 teaspoons olive oil
1 large plum tomato, diced
1 tablespoon butter
1/2 teaspoon lemon-pepper seasoning
1/4 teaspoon garlic powder
1/8 teaspoon salt
1/2 cup shredded Monterey Jack cheese

In a large skillet, saute the squash, zucchini and onion in oil for 8 minutes or until crisp-tender. Stir in the tomato, butter, lemon-pepper, garlic powder and salt. Cook for 2 minutes or until heated through. Remove from the heat; sprinkle with cheese. Cover for 1 minute or until cheese is melted. **Yield:** 8 servings.

Nutrition Facts: 3/4 cup (prepared with reduced-fat butter and cheese) equals 55 calories, 3 g fat (2 g saturated fat), 8 mg cholesterol, 123 mg sodium, 5 g carbohydrate, 2 g fiber, 3 g protein. **Diabetic Exchanges:** 1 vegetable, 1/2 fat.

Zippy Zucchini

Handle zucchini carefully; they're thin-skinned and easily damaged. To pick the freshest zucchini, look for a firm heavy squash that has a moist stem end and a shiny skin.

Herbed Rice

Prep/Total Time: 15 min.

Valerie Meldrum, Taylorsville, Utah

My mother gave me this 15-minute recipe, which is delicious with just about any main course. Try using beef bouillon instead of chicken bouillon if that's a better fit with your meal.

1-1/2 cups water
2 teaspoons chicken bouillon granules
1 teaspoon dried minced onion
1/2 teaspoon dried thyme
1/2 teaspoon dried marjoram
1/4 teaspoon dried rosemary, crushed
1-1/2 cups uncooked instant rice

In a large saucepan, bring water to a boil. Add the bouillon, onion, thyme, marjoram and rosemary; stir until the bouillon is dissolved. Stir in rice. Cover and remove from the heat; let stand for 5 minutes. Fluff with a fork. **Yield:** 3 servings.

2 large sweet onions, sliced
1 tablespoon olive oil
2 pounds fresh baby carrots, halved lengthwise
1 teaspoon salt
1/4 teaspoon coarsely ground pepper
1/4 cup maple syrup
2 tablespoons butter
1/2 cup french-fried onions
8 bacon strips, cooked and crumbled
1/4 cup chopped green onions

1. In a large skillet, cook onions in oil over medium heat for 15-20 minutes or until golden brown, stirring frequently.

2. In a large bowl, combine the onions, carrots, salt and pepper; toss to combine. Transfer to a greased shallow 3-qt. baking dish. Cover and bake at 400° for 40-45 minutes or until tender.

3. Stir in syrup and butter. Sprinkle with french-fried onions and bacon. Bake, uncovered, 5 minutes longer or until french-fried onions are browned. Sprinkle with the green onions. Serve with a slotted spoon. **Yield:** 8 servings.

🎗🎗🎗
Onion-Bacon Baby Carrots

Prep: 35 min. **Bake:** 45 min.

Diana Morrison Poole, Rock Hill, South Carolina

I came up with this side dish for Thanksgiving, and it was a big hit. Now it has a place not only on our holiday table, but also at impromptu get-togethers with family and friends.

🎗🎗🎗
Pretzel-Topped Sweet Potatoes

Prep: 20 min. **Bake:** 25 min.

Sue Mallory, Lancaster, Pennsylvania

Everyone with whom I've shared this recipe says it's the tastiest way to serve sweet potatoes. I like to make it for special dinners...and even for brunch as a colorful go-with dish. The mingled sweet, tart and salty flavors are an unusual treat.

2 cups chopped pretzel rods (about 13)
1 cup chopped pecans
1 cup fresh *or* frozen cranberries
1 cup packed brown sugar
1 cup butter, melted, *divided*
1 can (2-1/2 pounds) sweet potatoes, drained
1 can (5 ounces) evaporated milk
1/2 cup sugar
1 teaspoon vanilla extract

1. In a large bowl, combine the pretzels, pecans, cranberries, brown sugar and 1/2 cup butter; set aside.

2. In a large bowl, beat the sweet potatoes until smooth. Add the milk, sugar, vanilla and remaining butter; beat until well blended.

3. Spoon into a greased shallow 2-qt. baking dish; sprinkle with pretzel mixture. Bake, uncovered, at 350° for 25-30 minutes or until the edges are bubbly. **Yield:** 10-12 servings.

🎖🎖🎖
Golden Mashed Potato Bake

Prep: 30 min. **Bake:** 50 min.

Cathy Hanehan, Saratoga Springs, New York

My husband and his brother are partners in a dairy farm, so I use lots of dairy products in my cooking. These comforting, creamy potatoes complement many different main dishes.

> 8 medium potatoes, peeled and cubed
> 1 package (8 ounces) cream cheese, cubed
> 2 eggs
> 2 tablespoons all-purpose flour
> 2 tablespoons minced fresh parsley *or*
>   2 teaspoons dried parsley flakes
> 2 tablespoons minced chives
> 2 teaspoons salt
> 1/4 teaspoon pepper
> 1 can (2.8 ounces) french-fried onions

1. Place potatoes in a large saucepan and cover with water. Bring to a boil. Reduce heat; cover and simmer for 15-20 minutes or until tender. Drain.

2. In a large bowl, beat the potatoes and cream cheese until smooth. Beat in the eggs, flour, parsley, chives, salt and pepper; mix well.

3. Transfer to a greased 3-qt. baking dish. Bake, uncovered, at 350° for 45 minutes or until a thermometer reads 160°. Sprinkle with onions; bake 5-10 minutes longer or until golden brown. **Yield:** 12 servings.

🎖🎖🎖
Garden Vegetable Medley

Prep/Total Time: 20 min.

Betty Shepherd, Bear, Delaware

Colorful and summery, this side dish combines zucchini with tomatoes, onion and corn. Oregano gives the tender veggies great flavor, and the recipe takes just 20 minutes to fix.

> 1/2 cup sliced onion
> 1 teaspoon salt
> 1/4 teaspoon pepper
> 1/2 teaspoon dried oregano
> 1/4 cup butter
> 2 pounds zucchini, julienned
> 3 medium tomatoes, cut into thin wedges
> 1 cup whole kernel corn

In a large skillet, saute the onion, salt, pepper and oregano in butter until onion is crisp-tender. Add the zucchini, tomatoes and corn. Cook until vegetables are tender, about 8 minutes. **Yield:** 6 servings.

Three-Pepper Chutney

Prep: 30 min. **Cook:** 1-1/2 hours + chilling

Lisa Louw, Alachua, Florida

This sweet chutney is as good on pork, beef and poultry as it is on grilled hot dogs and hamburgers. We also like it as a substitute for high-fat mayonnaise on sandwiches.

1-1/2 cups packed brown sugar
1-1/2 cups cider vinegar
   3 medium green peppers, chopped
   3 medium sweet red peppers, chopped
   3 jalapeno peppers, seeded and chopped
   1 medium onion, chopped
   1 teaspoon salt

1. In a large saucepan, combine all ingredients. Bring to a boil. Reduce heat; simmer, uncovered, for 1-1/2 to 2 hours or until thickened. Cool.

2. Pour into a serving bowl. Cover and refrigerate for 1-2 hours or until chilled. **Yield:** 2 cups.

Editor's Note: When cutting hot peppers, disposable gloves are recommended. Avoid touching your face.

★★★ Spiced Cranberry Ketchup

Prep: 10 min. **Cook:** 30 min. + chilling

Gilda Lester, Wilmington, North Carolina

This special condiment may sound strange, but you'll be glad you gave it a try. It's absolutely fantastic on hamburgers and makes grilled chicken and turkey sing!

- 2-1/4 cups fresh or frozen cranberries
- 1/2 cup water
- 1/4 cup chopped green onions
- 2 bay leaves
- 3/4 cup plus 2 tablespoons sugar
- 1/4 cup white wine vinegar
- 1/4 cup balsamic vinegar
- 1-1/2 teaspoons Dijon mustard
- 1/2 teaspoon ground cinnamon
- 1/4 teaspoon salt
- 1/4 teaspoon ground allspice
- 1/4 teaspoon ground cloves
- 1/8 teaspoon ground cumin

1. In a small saucepan, combine the cranberries, water, onions and bay leaves. Cook over medium heat until berries pop, about 15 minutes. Cool slightly.

2. Discard bay leaves. Press cranberry mixture through a fine mesh strainer; discard cranberry skins. Return mixture to the pan.

3. Stir in remaining ingredients. Bring to a boil. Reduce heat; simmer, uncovered, for 8-10 minutes or until thickened. Cool. Cover and refrigerate (mixture will thicken more upon refrigeration). **Yield:** 1 cup.

★★★ Ginger Garlic Linguine

Prep/Total Time: 25 min.

Julie Miske, Acworth, Georgia

The ginger sauce in this recipe is great not only on pasta, but also over green beans, pierogies and salmon. I've often made a triple batch of it, then frozen the extra amount so I can whip up this linguine even faster on busy nights.

- 12 ounces uncooked linguine
- 4 green onions, finely chopped
- 2 tablespoons minced fresh gingerroot
- 2 teaspoons minced garlic
- 1 teaspoon dried basil
- 1/4 teaspoon cayenne pepper
- 1/2 cup butter
- 1/4 cup grated Parmesan cheese

Cook the linguine according to the package directions. Meanwhile, in a large skillet, saute onions, ginger, garlic, basil and cayenne in butter for 3-4 minutes or until the onions are tender. Drain the linguine; add to skillet and toss to coat. Sprinkle with the cheese. **Yield:** 6 servings.

Blue Cheese Green Beans

Prep/Total Time: 20 min.

Kate Hilts, Grand Rapids, Michigan

Bacon, blue cheese and chopped pecans make this my mom's favorite way to eat green beans. I always prepare this side dish when she's coming for dinner.

- 6 bacon strips, diced
- 1 pound fresh green beans, cut into 2-inch pieces
- 1/2 cup crumbled blue cheese
- 1/3 cup chopped pecans
- Pepper to taste

1. In a large skillet, cook the bacon over medium heat until crisp. Using a slotted spoon, remove to paper towels. Drain, reserving 2 tablespoons drippings.

2. In the reserved bacon drippings, cook and stir the green beans for 8-10 minutes or until beans are crisp-tender. Add the blue cheese, pecans, pepper and cooked bacon. Cook for 2 minutes or until heated through. **Yield:** 6 servings.

Chili-Seasoned Potato Wedges

Prep: 10 min. **Bake:** 35 min.

Irene Marshall, Nampa, Idaho

When I tried out these roasted potato wedges on my family, it was love at first taste! I generally have the onion soup mix and seasonings on hand, so the recipe couldn't be easier to fix. Feel free to alter the spice amounts to your liking.

- 1 tablespoon onion soup mix
- 1 tablespoon chili powder
- 1/4 teaspoon salt
- 1/4 teaspoon garlic powder
- 1/4 teaspoon pepper
- 4 large baking potatoes
- 2 tablespoons canola oil

1. In a large resealable plastic bag, combine the soup mix, chili powder, salt, garlic powder and pepper. Cut each potato into eight wedges; place in the bag and shake to coat.

2. Arrange in a single layer in a greased 15-in. x 10-in. x 1-in. baking pan. Drizzle with oil.

3. Bake, uncovered, at 425° for 12-20 minutes on each side or until crisp. **Yield:** 8 servings.

Herbed Baked Spinach

Prep: 10 min. **Bake:** 40 min.

Verna Hart, Seattle, Washington

Parmesan cheese and garlic really liven up this oven-baked spinach dish, which goes well with many different entrees and main-dish casseroles. Sometimes I use broccoli as a spinach substitute—the results are equally delicious.

- 1/2 cup chopped onion
- 2 tablespoons butter
- 1 garlic clove, minced
- 2 packages (10 ounces *each*) frozen chopped spinach, thawed and squeezed dry
- 1/2 cup heavy whipping cream
- 1/3 cup milk
- 5 tablespoons shredded Parmesan cheese, *divided*
- 1/4 cup dry bread crumbs
- 1/2 teaspoon salt
- 1/4 teaspoon dried marjoram
- 1/8 teaspoon pepper

1. In a large skillet, saute the onion in butter until onion is tender. Add garlic; cook 1 minute longer. Stir in the spinach, cream and milk. Remove from the heat; stir in 4 tablespoons cheese, bread crumbs, salt, marjoram and pepper.

2. Spoon into a greased 1-qt. baking dish. Sprinkle with remaining cheese. Bake, uncovered, at 350° for 40-45 minutes or until cheese is lightly browned. **Yield:** 6 servings.

Party Carrots

Prep: 15 min. **Bake:** 20 min.

- 2 pounds carrots, sliced
- 2 teaspoons chicken bouillon granules
- 8 ounces process cheese (Velveeta), cubed
- 2 tablespoons butter
- 1 package (8 ounces) cream cheese, cubed
- 4 green onions, sliced
- 1/4 teaspoon salt
- 1/4 teaspoon pepper

1. Place 1 in. of water in a large saucepan; add the carrots and bouillon. Bring to a boil. Reduce heat. Cover; simmer for 7-9 minutes or until crisp-tender.

2. Meanwhile, in another large saucepan, combine process cheese and butter. Cook and stir over low heat until melted. Add the cream cheese, onions, salt and pepper. Cook and stir until cream cheese is melted.

3. Drain carrots; stir into cheese sauce. Transfer to a greased shallow 2-qt. baking dish. Cover and bake at 350° for 20-25 minutes or until bubbly. **Yield:** 8 servings.

BERTHA JOHNSON INDIANAPOLIS, INDIANA

People who say they don't care for carrots often change their minds after sampling this cheesy, flavorful side. It's nice for potlucks because it's easy to fix and can be put together ahead of time. Be prepared to bring home an empty dish!

Grand Prize Winner

🎖🎖🎖
Garbanzo Bean Medley
Prep/Total Time: 10 min.

Denise Neal, Yorba Linda, California

I'm a vegetarian and am always on the lookout for tasty dishes without meat. This Italian bean recipe is fast, flavorful and filling. Sprinkle feta cheese on top for a change of pace.

✓ This recipe includes Nutrition Facts and Diabetic Exchanges.

- 1 small zucchini, cubed
- 1 teaspoon olive oil
- 2 teaspoons minced garlic
- 1 can (15 ounces) garbanzo beans or chickpeas, rinsed and drained
- 1 can (14-1/2 ounces) diced tomatoes, undrained
- 1 teaspoon Italian seasoning
- 1/4 teaspoon crushed red pepper flakes, optional
- 1/4 cup shredded Parmesan cheese

1. In a small skillet, saute zucchini in oil until tender. Add the garlic; saute 1 minute longer. Stir in the garbanzo beans, tomatoes, Italian seasoning and the pepper flakes if desired; heat through. Sprinkle with cheese. **Yield:** 4 servings.

Nutrition Facts: 3/4 cup equals 157 calories, 5 g fat (1 g saturated fat), 4 mg cholesterol, 354 mg sodium, 23 g carbohydrate, 6 g fiber, 7 g protein. **Diabetic Exchanges:** 1 starch, 1 lean meat, 1 vegetable.

🎖🎖🎖
Cranberry Apple Saute
Prep/Total Time: 30 min.

Rea Newell, Decatur, Illinois

My husband came up with this recipe when he added some cranberries to fried green apples. We thought the color combination was perfect for the Christmas season, and the tangy fruit flavor went well with our holiday ham.

- 1/2 cup sugar
- 1/4 cup butter, cubed
- 1/2 teaspoon ground cinnamon
- 1/8 teaspoon ground nutmeg
- Dash salt
- 4 medium unpeeled tart apples, thickly sliced
- 1 cup fresh or frozen cranberries

In a large saucepan, combine all ingredients. Cook over medium heat for 15-17 minutes or until the apples are tender and the sauce is slightly thickened, stirring occasionally. **Yield:** 6 servings.

🎀🎀🎀 Country Corn

Prep/Total Time: 20 min.

Kathleen Mancuso, Niskayuna, New York

I cook church dinners for over 100 people, so I'm interested in fast, inexpensive menu items. I've prepared this creamy corn several times, and there was never any left over.

- 6 green onions, chopped
- 3 tablespoons butter
- 1 package (16 ounces) frozen corn, thawed
- 2 teaspoons cornstarch
- 1/2 cup half-and-half cream
- 1/4 cup water
- 1/2 teaspoon salt
- 1/4 to 1/2 teaspoon pepper
- 1 cup grape tomatoes, halved

1. In a large skillet, saute the onions in butter for 2-3 minutes or until tender. Stir in the corn; cover and cook for 4-5 minutes or until heated through.

2. Meanwhile, in a small bowl, combine cornstarch, cream, water, salt and pepper until smooth. Gradually stir into the corn mixture. Bring to a boil. Cook, uncovered, for 2 minutes or until thickened. Stir in the tomatoes. **Yield:** 6 servings.

- 1 package (28 ounces) frozen steak fries
- 1 can (10-3/4 ounces) condensed cheddar cheese soup, undiluted
- 1/4 cup milk
- 1/2 teaspoon garlic powder
- 1/4 teaspoon onion powder

Paprika

1. Arrange the steak fries in a single layer in two greased 15-in. x 10-in. x 1-in. baking pans. Bake at 450° for 15-18 minutes or until fries are tender and golden brown.

2. Meanwhile, in a small saucepan, combine the soup, milk, garlic powder and onion powder; heat through. Drizzle over the fries and sprinkle with paprika. **Yield:** 8-10 servings.

🎀🎀🎀 Cheese Fries

Prep/Total Time: 20 min.

Melissa Tatum, Greensboro, North Carolina

I came up with this recipe when my daughter couldn't stop talking about the cheese fries she'd sampled at a restaurant. Now I can fix them quickly at home. Plus, the frozen fry packets can be refrigerated and reheated.

Smart Storage

Garlic powder and onion powder tend to absorb moisture from the air, especially during warm weather months. Store them in airtight spice jars to keep them as free from moisture and humidity as possible.

🎗️🎗️🎗️
Creamy Zucchini
Prep/Total Time: 20 min.

Marguerite Shaeffer, Sewell, New Jersey

Here's a deliciously different way to use up an abundance of garden-grown zucchini. Even though the creamy Parmesan sauce is homemade, the recipe's cooking time is short.

    4 **medium zucchini, julienned**
    2 **tablespoons olive oil**
1-1/2 **teaspoons minced garlic**
    2 **packages (3 ounces *each*) cream cheese, cubed**
    1 **cup half-and-half cream**
1/2 **cup shredded Parmesan cheese**
1/4 **teaspoon salt**
1/8 **teaspoon coarsely ground pepper**
Dash ground nutmeg
Shredded Swiss cheese

1. In a large skillet, saute the zucchini in oil for 3-5 minutes or until tender. Add garlic; cook 1 minute longer. Drain; remove zucchini mixture with a slotted spoon and keep warm.

2. In the same skillet, combine cream cheese and cream; cook and stir over low heat until smooth. Stir in the Parmesan cheese.

3. Return zucchini mixture to the pan. Cook and stir 1-2 minutes longer or until heated through. Sprinkle with the salt, pepper, nutmeg and Swiss cheese. **Yield:** 6 servings.

🎗️🎗️🎗️
Pickled Baby Carrots
Prep: 20 min. + chilling

Audrey Cremer, Harmony, Minnesota

With mild herb flavor and a crunchy texture, these baby carrots make a delightful addition to an appetizer tray or casual meal. You'll need just 20 minutes to prepare them before popping them in the refrigerator to chill.

    2 **pounds fresh baby carrots**
2/3 **cup white wine vinegar**
1/2 **cup honey**
    2 **tablespoons mustard seed**
    2 **tablespoons dill weed**
    1 **teaspoon salt**

1. Place 1 in. of water in a large saucepan; add carrots. Bring to a boil. Reduce heat; cover and simmer for 5-6 minutes or until crisp-tender. Drain.

2. In a large bowl, combine the remaining ingredients. Stir in carrots. Cover and refrigerate for 8 hours or overnight, stirring several times. Serve with a slotted spoon. **Yield:** 8-10 servings.

Dilly Stuffed Potatoes

Prep: 1 hour **Bake:** 30 min.

Koreen Ogg, Ste. Rose du Lac, Manitoba

Dill weed and cream cheese give these twice-baked potatoes a tangy taste. Want to get a head start on the prep work? You can stuff the potato shells beforehand and keep them in the fridge, then finish baking close to dinnertime.

- **4 large baking potatoes**
- **1/4 cup finely chopped onion**
- **1/4 cup butter, cubed**
- **1 cup (4 ounces) shredded cheddar cheese**
- **4 ounces cream cheese, cubed**
- **1 teaspoon dill weed**
- **4 bacon strips, cooked and crumbled**

1. Scrub and pierce potatoes. Bake at 400° for 1 hour or until tender. Meanwhile, in a small skillet, saute onion in butter until tender; set aside.

2. When potatoes are cool enough to handle, cut a thin slice off the top of each and discard. Scoop out pulp, leaving a thin shell. In a bowl, mash the pulp with cheddar cheese, cream cheese and dill. Stir in the bacon and reserved onion mixture. Spoon into the potato shells.

3. Place on a baking sheet. Bake at 400° for 30-35 minutes or until heated through. **Yield:** 4 servings.

Best Bacon

Always check the date stamp of vacuum-sealed bacon to make sure it's fresh. The date reflects the last date of sale. Once the package is opened, bacon should be used within a week. For long-term storage, freeze bacon for up to 1 month.

Marmalade Monkey Bread, p. 142

Sweet Potato Bread, p. 142

Lemon Blueberry Muffins, p. 144

Breads & Rolls

What makes eyes light up more than tender, golden baked goods fresh from the oven? You'll thrill everyone when you present any of the tempting treats here, from Orange Cranberry Gems to Corn Muffins with Honey Butter.

Spiced Walnut Loaf.............................140
Berry Bread with Spread......................140
Mini Italian Biscuits..........................141
Chocolate Chip Muffins.....................141
Sweet Potato Bread...........................142
Marmalade Monkey Bread.................142
Lemon Blueberry Muffins.................144
Berry Cream Muffins.......................144
Maple-Pecan Corn Bread................145
Christmas Bread..............................145
Quilt-Topped Corn Bread..................146
Pumpkin Chip Muffins....................146
Almond Berry Muffins.....................148

Oregano-Swiss Slices..........................149
Corn Muffins with Honey Butter......149
Maraschino Cherry Almond Bread......150
PB&J Spirals.....................................150
Easy Potato Rolls.............................152
Garlic Herb Twists...........................152
Apricot Banana Bread......................153
Lemon Ginger Muffins.....................153
Orange Cranberry Gems...................154
Dilly Bran Refrigerator Rolls............154
Cheery Cherry Loaf..........................155
Almond Peach Muffins......................155

Easy Potato Rolls, p. 152

🎀🎀🎀
Spiced Walnut Loaf

Prep: 15 min. **Bake:** 1 hour + cooling

Kristine Skinner, Marion, New York

I received the recipe for this delicious bread from a co-worker years ago. Many friends have asked for it since then. People especially like the topping that's slightly crunchy with brown sugar, cinnamon and walnuts.

2 cups all-purpose flour
1 teaspoon baking soda
1/2 teaspoon baking powder
1/2 teaspoon ground cinnamon
1/4 teaspoon salt
1/4 teaspoon ground allspice
1/4 teaspoon ground nutmeg
2 eggs, lightly beaten
1-1/4 cups unsweetened applesauce
1 cup sugar
1/2 cup canola oil
3 tablespoons milk
1/2 cup chopped walnuts
TOPPING:
1/4 cup chopped walnuts
1/4 cup packed brown sugar
1/2 teaspoon ground cinnamon

1. In a large bowl, combine the first seven ingredients. In a small bowl, combine the eggs, applesauce, sugar, oil and milk; add to dry ingredients just until moistened. Fold in the walnuts. Transfer to a greased and floured 9-in. x 5-in. loaf pan.

2. Combine the topping ingredients; sprinkle over the batter. Bake at 350° for 1 hour or until a toothpick inserted near the center comes out clean. Cool loaf for 10 minutes before removing to a wire rack. **Yield:** 1 loaf (12 slices).

🎀🎀🎀
Berry Bread with Spread

Prep: 20 min. **Bake:** 50 min. + cooling

Pat Stewart, Lee's Summit, Missouri

The recipe for these two loaves and the creamy strawberry spread came from my mother's collection. I added macadamia nuts to give the fruit bread a fun crunch.

1 package (8 ounces) cream cheese, softened
2 packages (10 ounces *each*) frozen sweetened sliced strawberries, thawed
3 cups all-purpose flour
2 cups sugar
1 teaspoon salt
1 teaspoon baking soda
4 eggs
1 cup canola oil
1 jar (3 ounces) macadamia nuts, chopped

1. For strawberry spread, in a small bowl, beat cream cheese until smooth. Drain strawberries, reserving 1/4 cup juice for the bread batter. Beat 6 tablespoons berries into the cream cheese. Set remaining berries aside. Chill spread until serving.

2. In a large bowl, combine the flour, sugar, salt and baking soda. Combine the eggs, oil, reserved berries and juice. Stir into the dry ingredients just until moistened. Fold in nuts (batter will be stiff). Transfer to two greased 8-in. x 4-in. loaf pans.

3. Bake at 350° for 50-55 minutes or until a toothpick inserted near the center comes out clean. Cool for 10 minutes before removing from pans to wire racks to cool completely. Serve with spread. **Yield:** 2 loaves (10 slices each) and about 1 cup spread.

🎖🎖🎖
Mini Italian Biscuits

Prep/Total Time: 20 min.

Elaine Whiting, Salt Lake City, Utah

I tasted biscuits like these at a seafood restaurant and really liked them. I experimented in my kitchen until I was able to get the same flavor in these fast little bites.

- 2 cups biscuit/baking mix
- 1/2 cup finely shredded cheddar cheese
- 1/2 teaspoon garlic powder
- 1/2 teaspoon dried oregano
- 1/2 teaspoon dried basil
- 2/3 cup milk

1. In a large bowl, combine the biscuit mix, cheese, garlic powder, oregano and basil. With a fork, stir in milk just until moistened.

2. Drop by rounded teaspoonfuls onto a lightly greased baking sheet. Bake at 450° for 7-8 minutes or until golden brown. Serve warm. **Yield:** about 3 dozen.

🎖🎖🎖
Chocolate Chip Muffins

Prep: 15 min. **Bake:** 25 min.

Kelly Kirby, Westville, Nova Scotia

Muffins are one of my favorite things to bake, and these are the best! I always keep some in the freezer for breakfast on the run. I can zap one in the microwave before heading out the door.

- 1/2 cup butter, softened
- 1 cup sugar
- 2 eggs
- 1 cup (8 ounces) plain yogurt
- 1 teaspoon vanilla extract
- 2 cups all-purpose flour
- 1 teaspoon baking soda
- 1/2 teaspoon baking powder
- 1/2 teaspoon salt
- 3/4 cup semisweet chocolate chips

TOPPING:
- 1/4 cup semisweet chocolate chips
- 2 tablespoons brown sugar
- 2 tablespoons chopped walnuts, optional
- 1 teaspoon ground cinnamon

1. In a large bowl, cream butter and sugar until light and fluffy. Add eggs, one at a time, beating well after each addition. Beat in yogurt and vanilla. Combine the flour, baking soda, baking powder and salt; add to the creamed mixture just until moistened. Fold in the chocolate chips. Fill paper-lined muffin cups two-thirds full.

2. Combine the topping ingredients and sprinkle over the batter. Bake at 350° for 25-30 minutes or until a toothpick inserted near the center comes out clean. Cool for 5 minutes before removing from pan to wire rack. Serve warm. **Yield:** 1 dozen.

1 teaspoon ground nutmeg
1/2 teaspoon salt
1/2 teaspoon ground cloves
2 cups mashed sweet potatoes
3 eggs
1 cup canola oil
3 cups sugar
1 cup chopped walnuts
1 cup raisins

GLAZE:
1-1/2 cups confectioners' sugar
4 to 5 teaspoons orange juice
1 teaspoon grated orange peel
1/3 cup chopped walnuts

1. In a large bowl, combine the first seven ingredients. Whisk together the sweet potatoes, eggs and oil. Add the sugar; whisk until smooth. Stir into dry ingredients just until combined. Fold in the walnuts and raisins (batter will be thick). Transfer to two greased 9-in. x 5-in. loaf pans.

2. Bake at 350° for 65-70 minutes or until a toothpick inserted near the center comes out clean. Cool in pans for 10 minutes before removing to wire racks.

3. Meanwhile, for glaze, combine the confectioners' sugar, orange juice and peel until blended. Spread over the loaves; sprinkle with the walnuts. **Yield:** 2 loaves (16 slices each).

Sweet Potato Bread

Prep: 20 min. **Bake:** 65 min. + cooling

Ann Jovanovic, Chicago, Illinois

I enjoy making this bread because it lets me use sweet potatoes in something besides pie. I discovered the recipe in an old Southern cookbook, then changed a few things. The orange juice in the glaze adds a pleasant citrus flavor.

3-1/2 cups all-purpose flour
2 teaspoons baking soda
1 teaspoon baking powder
1 teaspoon ground cinnamon

Whole Wheat Hint

Want to substitute fiber-rich whole wheat flour for some of the all-purpose flour in baked goods? For best results, use equal proportions of whole wheat flour and all-purpose flour.

Marmalade Monkey Bread

Prep: 15 min. **Bake:** 30 min.

2/3 cup orange marmalade
1/2 cup chopped pecans *or* walnuts
1/4 cup honey
2 tablespoons butter, melted
2 tubes (7-1/2 ounces *each*) refrigerated buttermilk biscuits

1. In a small bowl, combine the marmalade, pecans, honey and butter. Cut each biscuit into four pieces. Layer half of the pieces in a greased 10-in. tube pan; top with half of marmalade mixture. Repeat.

2. Bake at 375° for 27-30 minutes or until golden brown. Cool in pan for 5 minutes before inverting onto a serving plate. Serve warm. **Yield:** 8 servings.

DELIA KENNEDY DEER PARK, WASHINGTON

We love this pretty pull-apart bread, and guests just rave about it. Because the recipe calls for refrigerated buttermilk biscuits, it's so easy and quick to fix. Feel free to try whatever jam you have on hand in place of the marmalade.

Grand Prize Winner

🏅🏅🏅 Lemon Blueberry Muffins

Prep/Total Time: 30 min.

Kris Michels, Walled Lake, Michigan

When my sister and I spent the night at our grandmother's house as children, we often requested these berry-packed muffins for breakfast. Today, I bake them for my kids. The aroma itself is a trip down memory lane.

✓ This recipe includes Nutrition Facts and Diabetic Exchanges.

- 2 cups biscuit/baking mix
- 1/2 cup plus 2 tablespoons sugar, *divided*
- 1 egg
- 1 cup (8 ounces) sour cream
- 1 cup fresh *or* frozen blueberries
- 2 teaspoons grated lemon peel

1. In a large bowl, combine biscuit mix and 1/2 cup sugar. Whisk the egg and sour cream; stir into dry ingredients just until moistened. Fold in blueberries.

2. Fill greased or paper-lined muffin cups half full. Combine lemon peel and remaining sugar; sprinkle over batter.

3. Bake at 400° for 20-25 minutes or until a toothpick inserted near the center comes out clean. Cool for 5 minutes before removing from pan to a wire rack. Serve warm. **Yield:** 1 dozen.

Editor's Note: If using frozen blueberries, do not thaw before adding to batter.

Nutrition Facts: 1 muffin (prepared with reduced-fat baking mix and reduced-fat sour cream) equals 154 calories, 3 g fat (2 g saturated fat), 24 mg cholesterol, 251 mg sodium, 28 g carbohydrate, 1 g fiber, 3 g protein. **Diabetic Exchanges:** 1 starch, 1 fruit, 1/2 fat.

🏅🏅🏅 Berry Cream Muffins

Prep: 15 min. **Bake:** 20 min.

Linda Gilmore, Hampstead, Maryland

If you can't decide which kind of berries to use in these delightful muffins, try using half raspberries and half blueberries. Whatever you choose, you're in for a "berry" good treat!

- 4 cups all-purpose flour
- 2 cups sugar
- 1-1/4 teaspoons baking powder
- 1 teaspoon baking soda
- 1 teaspoon salt
- 3 cups fresh raspberries *or* frozen raspberries *or* blueberries
- 4 eggs, lightly beaten
- 2 cups (16 ounces) sour cream
- 1 cup canola oil
- 1 teaspoon vanilla extract

1. In a large bowl, combine the flour, sugar, baking powder, baking soda and salt; add berries and toss gently. Combine the eggs, sour cream, oil and vanilla; mix well. Stir into dry ingredients just until moistened.

2. Fill greased muffin cups two-thirds full. Bake at 400° for 20-25 minutes or until a toothpick inserted near the center comes out clean. Cool for 5 minutes before removing from pans to a wire rack. Serve warm. **Yield:** about 2 dozen.

🎖🎖🎖
Maple-Pecan Corn Bread

Prep: 10 min. **Bake:** 35 min. + cooling

Shirley Brownell, Amsterdam, New York

Our state trails only Vermont in the production of maple syrup in the United States. I have many childhood memories of tapping our maple trees in early spring and watching the sap come out. This nutty bread is a great way to enjoy that harvest.

- 1 cup all-purpose flour
- 1 cup yellow cornmeal
- 2 tablespoons brown sugar
- 1 teaspoon baking powder
- 1 teaspoon baking soda
- 1 teaspoon salt
- 2 eggs
- 3/4 cup buttermilk
- 1/3 cup maple syrup
- 3 tablespoons butter, melted
- 1/2 cup chopped pecans
- Additional maple syrup, optional

1. In a large bowl, combine the flour, cornmeal, brown sugar, baking powder, baking soda and salt. In a small bowl, whisk eggs, buttermilk, syrup and butter. Stir into dry ingredients just until moistened. Fold in nuts.

2. Pour into a greased 8-in. x 4-in. loaf pan. Bake at 350° for 35-40 minutes or until a toothpick inserted near the center comes out clean. Cool for 10 minutes in pan before removing to a wire rack. Serve warm with syrup if desired or allow to cool. **Yield:** 1 loaf (16 slices).

🎖🎖🎖
Christmas Bread

Prep: 15 min. + rising **Bake:** 30 min. + cooling

Betty Jean McLaughlin, La Vista, Nebraska

Fruitcake is a traditional Christmas treat, but my family and friends prefer this slightly sweet bread. It's so pretty drizzled with vanilla icing and dotted with festive red and green candied fruit. I like to sprinkle extra fruit on top for added appeal.

- 1 package (1/4 ounce) active dry yeast
- 3/4 cup warm water (110° to 115°)
- 3/4 cup evaporated milk
- 1/3 cup sugar
- 1/3 cup shortening
- 1/2 teaspoon salt
- 2 eggs
- 4 to 4-1/2 cups all-purpose flour, *divided*
- 1 cup chopped mixed candied fruit
- 1 cup confectioners' sugar
- 1/4 teaspoon vanilla extract
- 1 to 2 tablespoons milk
- Additional candied fruit, optional

1. In a large bowl, dissolve the yeast in water. Add the evaporated milk, sugar, shortening, salt, eggs and 2 cups of flour; beat until smooth. Stir in the mixed candied fruit and enough remaining flour to form a soft dough (do not knead).

2. Place in a greased bowl, turning once to grease the top. Cover and let rise in a warm place until doubled, about 1-1/4 hours.

3. Punch dough down. Turn onto a floured surface; knead 3-4 minutes. Pat evenly into a greased 10-in. tube pan. Cover and let rise in a warm place until nearly doubled, about 45 minutes.

4. Bake at 375° for 30-35 minutes or until golden brown. Remove from pan to cool on a wire rack.

5. Combine the confectioners' sugar, vanilla and enough milk to reach desired consistency; drizzle over bread. Garnish with additional candied fruit if desired. **Yield:** 1 loaf.

1 can (14-3/4 ounces) cream-style corn
1 can (11 ounces) Mexicorn, drained
1 cup (4 ounces) shredded reduced-fat cheddar cheese
2/3 cup water
1 egg, lightly beaten
1/4 cup egg substitute

1. Coat two 9-in. round baking pans with cooking spray. Slice green chilies in half lengthwise; pat dry. Place six chili halves skin side down in a star burst pattern in each pan. Cut the red pepper into twelve 1/4-in. slices and two 1-in. circles. Place slices between the chilies and circles in the center.

2. Place corn bread mix in a large bowl. Combine the cream-style corn, Mexicorn, cheese, water, egg and egg substitute; stir into corn bread mix just until moistened. Pour into prepared pans.

3. Bake at 425° for 30-35 minutes or until a toothpick inserted near the center comes out clean. Immediately invert onto serving plates. **Yield:** 16 servings.

Nutrition Facts: 1 wedge equals 187 calories, 5 g fat (2 g saturated fat), 25 mg cholesterol, 503 mg sodium, 31 g carbohydrate, 1 g fiber, 6 g protein. **Diabetic Exchanges:** 2 starch, 1/2 fat.

🎗️🎗️🎗️
Quilt-Topped Corn Bread
Prep: 20 min. **Bake:** 30 min.

Robyn Oro, Raytown, Missouri

We like to serve big slices of this colorful corn bread alongside a zippy salsa and light sour cream. It's great as a side for a Southwestern meal or your favorite chili.

☑ This recipe includes Nutrition Facts and Diabetic Exchanges.

2 cans (4 ounces *each*) whole green chilies
1 large sweet red pepper
2 packages (8-1/2 ounces *each*) corn bread/muffin mix

Savvy Serving

Corn breads and coffee cakes are best served warm. Serve quick breads (such as banana, zucchini and cranberry) a day after baking because that is when they slice and taste best.

Pumpkin Chip Muffins
Prep: 10 min. **Bake:** 15 min. + cooling

4 eggs
2 cups sugar
1 can (15 ounces) solid-pack pumpkin
1-1/2 cups canola oil
3 cups all-purpose flour
2 teaspoons baking soda
1 teaspoon baking powder
1 teaspoon ground cinnamon
1 teaspoon salt
2 cups (12 ounces) semisweet chocolate chips

1. In a large bowl, beat the eggs, sugar, pumpkin and oil until smooth. Combine the flour, baking soda, baking powder, cinnamon and salt; gradually add to pumpkin mixture and mix well. Fold in chocolate chips. Fill greased or paper-lined muffin cups three-fourths full.

2. Bake at 400° for 15-18 minutes or until a toothpick inserted near the center comes out clean. Cool in pan 10 minutes before removing to a wire rack. **Yield:** about 2 dozen muffins.

CINDY MIDDLETON CHAMPION, ALBERTA

I started cooking and baking at a young age—thanks to my mom, who was a great teacher. I love whipping up a batch of these chocolate-dotted muffins during fall.

Grand Prize Winner

🏅🏅🏅
Almond Berry Muffins

Prep: 20 min. **Bake:** 20 min.

Deborah Feinberg, East Setauket, New York

I made these moist muffins to take to the office, and they were a hit. Sugared almonds give them a crunchy topping. When strawberries aren't in season, I use individual frozen cut strawberries directly from the freezer.

1-1/4 **cups sliced almonds,** *divided*
    1 **egg white, lightly beaten**
1-1/2 **cups sugar,** *divided*
    1/4 **cup shortening**
    1/4 **cup butter, softened**
    2 **eggs**
    1 **teaspoon vanilla extract**
    1/2 **teaspoon almond extract**
    2 **cups all-purpose flour**
    1 **teaspoon baking powder**
    1/2 **teaspoon salt**
    1/4 **teaspoon baking soda**
    3/4 **cup buttermilk**
1-1/4 **cups fresh strawberries, chopped**

1. In a large bowl, combine 1 cup almonds and egg white. Add 1/2 cup sugar; toss to coat. Spoon into a greased 15-in. x 10-in. x 1-in. baking pan. Bake muffins at 350° for 9-11 minutes or until golden brown, stirring occasionally.

2. In a large bowl, cream the shortening, butter and remaining sugar until light and fluffy. Add eggs, one at a time, beating well after each addition. Beat in extracts. Combine flour, baking powder, salt and baking soda; add to creamed mixture alternately with buttermilk. Fold in strawberries and remaining almonds.

3. Fill greased or paper-lined muffin cups two-thirds full. Sprinkle with sugared almonds. Bake at 350° for 20-25 minutes or until a toothpick inserted near the center comes out clean. Cool for 5 minutes before removing from pans to wire racks. Serve warm. **Yield:** 1-1/2 dozen.

🎖🎖🎖
Oregano-Swiss Slices

Prep/Total Time: 30 min.

Laura Murphy, Ventura, California

I like to serve this dressed-up French bread with a chef's salad. The slices are also a great complement to a hot bowl of soup.

- 2 cups (8 ounces) shredded Swiss cheese
- 1/3 cup mayonnaise
- 1 tablespoon minced fresh oregano
- 1 tablespoon grated onion
- 1 tablespoon cider vinegar
- 1 loaf (1 pound) French bread, halved lengthwise

1. In a small bowl, combine the cheese, mayonnaise, oregano, onion and vinegar. Spread over the cut sides of bread.

2. Place on an ungreased baking sheet. Bake at 400° for 8-10 minutes or until cheese is melted and lightly browned. Serve warm. **Yield:** 16 slices.

🎖🎖🎖
Corn Muffins with Honey Butter

Prep: 25 min. **Bake:** 15 min.

Marilyn Platner, Marion, Iowa

A friend on our local Farm Bureau women's committee created this recipe to give people new ideas for using farm commodities. I especially like fixing these muffins for my family on a chilly night. Along with a pot of chili, they make for a hearty meal.

- 2 cups all-purpose flour
- 2 cups yellow cornmeal
- 1 cup nonfat dry milk powder
- 1/4 cup sugar
- 2 tablespoons baking powder
- 1 teaspoon salt
- 1/2 teaspoon baking soda
- 2-2/3 cups water
- 1/2 cup butter, melted
- 2 eggs, lightly beaten
- 1 tablespoon lemon juice

HONEY BUTTER:
- 2 tablespoons honey
- 1/2 cup butter, softened

1. In a large bowl, combine the flour, cornmeal, milk powder, sugar, baking powder, salt and baking soda. In a small bowl, combine water, butter, eggs and lemon juice; stir into dry ingredients just until moistened.

2. Fill greased muffin cups two-thirds full. Bake at 425° for 13-15 minutes or until a toothpick inserted near the center comes out clean. Cool for 5 minutes before removing from pans to wire racks.

3. In a small bowl, beat honey and softened butter until smooth. Serve with warm muffins. **Yield:** 2 dozen.

1 teaspoon vanilla extract
2 cups all-purpose flour
1 teaspoon baking powder
1/2 teaspoon salt
1/2 cup slivered almonds
ALMOND BUTTER:
1/2 cup butter, softened
1 tablespoon slivered almonds, finely chopped
1/2 teaspoon almond extract

1. Drain cherries, reserving juice; add enough water to juice to measure 1/2 cup. Cut cherries into quarters; blot dry and set aside.

2. In a large bowl, cream the butter and sugar until light and fluffy. Add eggs, one at a time, beating well after each addition. Beat in vanilla. Combine the flour, baking powder and salt; gradually add to the creamed mixture alternately with reserved juice. Fold in the cherries and almonds.

3. Pour into a greased 9-in. x 5-in. loaf pan. Bake at 350° for 50-60 minutes or until a toothpick inserted near the center comes out clean. Cool for 10 minutes before removing from the pan to a wire rack to cool completely.

4. In a small bowl, combine almond butter ingredients. Serve with bread. **Yield:** 1 loaf (12 slices, 1/2 cup almond butter).

🎀 🎀 🎀
Maraschino Cherry Almond Bread

Prep: 25 min. **Bake:** 50 min. + cooling

Gertrudis Miller, Evansville, Indiana

Pretty bits of maraschino cherries peek out of every piece of this bread, turning its moist interior bright pink. The recipe, which came from a special friend, makes such a lovely loaf. Spread on some almond butter and enjoy it morning, noon or night.

1 jar (10 ounces) maraschino cherries
1/2 cup butter, softened
3/4 cup sugar
2 eggs

Smart Storage

Store quick breads or muffins that have been wrapped in foil or plastic wrap at room temperature for up to 3 days. They should be refrigerated if made with cheese, cream cheese or other perishable foods.

PB&J Spirals

Prep/Total Time: 30 min.

1 tube (8 ounces) refrigerated crescent rolls
8 teaspoons creamy peanut butter
8 teaspoons grape jelly
1/4 cup chopped unsalted peanuts
2 tablespoons confectioners' sugar

1. Unroll crescent dough; separate into triangles. Spread 1 teaspoon each of peanut butter and jelly on the wide end of each triangle; sprinkle with peanuts. Roll up from the wide end and place point side down 2 in. apart on an ungreased baking sheet. Curve ends to form a crescent shape.

2. Bake at 375° for 11-13 minutes or until lightly browned. Dust with confectioners' sugar. Serve warm. **Yield:** 8 servings.

LISA RENSHAW KANSAS CITY, MISSOURI

Kids young and old love these peanut butter and jelly treats. They're easy to make using refrigerated crescent roll dough—and easy to vary using different jelly flavors or nuts to suit each person's taste. A dusting of confectioners' sugar is a sweet finishing touch.

Grand
Prize
Winner

🎗🎗🎗 Easy Potato Rolls

Prep: 15 min. + rising Bake: 20 min.

Jeanette McKinney, Belleview, Missouri

After I discovered this recipe, it became one of my menu mainstays. I prepare the dough ahead of time when company is coming, and I try to keep some in the refrigerator to make for the "hay hands" on our cattle ranch.

> 2 packages (1/4 ounce *each*) active dry yeast
> 1-1/3 cups warm water (110° to 115°), *divided*
> 2/3 cup sugar
> 2/3 cup shortening
> 2 eggs
> 1 cup mashed potatoes
> 2-1/2 teaspoons salt
> 6 to 6-1/2 cups all-purpose flour

1. In a small bowl, dissolve yeast in 2/3 cup warm water. In a large bowl, cream sugar and shortening until light and fluffy. Add the eggs, potatoes, salt, remaining water and 2 cups flour. Beat until smooth. Add enough remaining flour to form a soft dough.

2. Shape into a ball; do not knead. Place in a greased bowl, turning once to grease top. Cover and let rise in a warm place until doubled, about 1 hour.

3. Punch dough down; divide into thirds. Shape each portion into 15 balls and arrange in three greased 9-in. round baking pans. Cover; let rise until doubled, about 30 minutes.

4. Bake at 375° for 20-25 minutes or until golden brown. Remove from pans to cool on wire racks. **Yield:** 45 servings.

Using Yeast

Store unopened packages of dry yeast in a cool, dark, dry place and use them by the "best if used by" date on the package. Opened packages of bulk dry yeast should be stored in an airtight container in the refrigerator for about 6 weeks or frozen for up to 6 months.

🎗🎗🎗 Garlic Herb Twists

Prep/Total Time: 25 min.

Peggy Rosamond, Jacksonville, Texas

I'm a busy wife, mother and grandmother who also works full-time, so I need quick dinner ideas. These three-ingredient breadsticks are also good for church meetings and potlucks.

> 1 tube (8 ounces) refrigerated crescent rolls
> 1/3 cup sour cream
> 1 to 2 tablespoons herb with garlic soup mix

1. Unroll crescent dough into one long rectangle; seal seams and perforations. Combine sour cream and soup mix; spread over dough. Cut into 1-in. strips. Loosely twist strips and place on an ungreased baking sheet.

2. Bake at 375° for 11-13 minutes or until golden brown. Serve warm. **Yield:** 1 dozen.

🎖🎖🎖
Apricot Banana Bread

Prep: 15 min. **Bake:** 55 min.

Betty Hull, Stoughton, Wisconsin

Making this delightfully different twist on traditional banana bread is fun—but eating it is even better! Slices are wonderful spread with cream cheese or butter. I also prepare the recipe in small loaf pans to give as holiday gifts.

　1/3　cup butter, softened
　2/3　cup sugar
　　2　eggs
　　1　cup mashed ripe bananas (2 to 3 medium)
　1/4　cup buttermilk
1-1/4　cups all-purpose flour
　　1　teaspoon baking powder
　1/2　teaspoon baking soda
　1/2　teaspoon salt
　　1　cup 100% bran cereal (not flakes)
　3/4　cup chopped dried apricots (about 6 ounces)
　1/2　cup chopped walnuts

1. In a large bowl, cream the butter and sugar until light and fluffy. Beat in eggs. Combine the bananas and buttermilk. Combine the flour, baking powder, baking soda and salt; add to creamed mixture alternately with banana, beating well after each addition. Stir in bran, apricots and nuts.

2. Pour into a greased 9-in. x 5-in. loaf pan. Bake at 350° for 55-60 minutes or until a toothpick inserted near the center comes out clean. Cool 10 minutes before removing from the pan to a wire rack. **Yield:** 1 loaf (16 slices).

🎖🎖🎖
Lemon Ginger Muffins

Prep/Total Time: 30 min.

Joyce Baker-Mabry, Hamilton, Montana

These quick muffins are tender and have a lovely aroma while they're baking. Fat-free yogurt keeps them light but moist. If you like lemon and ginger, you're sure to enjoy these treats.

✓ This recipe includes Nutrition Facts and Diabetic Exchanges.

　1/3　cup butter, softened
　1/2　cup sugar
Sugar substitute equivalent to 1/2 cup sugar
　　4　egg whites
　　2　cups all-purpose flour
　　1　teaspoon baking soda
　　1　cup (8 ounces) fat-free plain yogurt
　　2　tablespoons minced fresh gingerroot
　　2　tablespoons grated lemon peel

1. In a large bowl, beat the butter, sugar and sugar substitute until crumbly. Add egg whites; beat well. Combine the flour and baking soda; add to the butter mixture alternately with yogurt. Stir in ginger and lemon peel.

2. Coat the muffin cups with cooking spray; fill three-fourths full with batter. Bake at 375° for 18-20 minutes or until a toothpick inserted near the center comes out clean. Cool for 5 minutes before removing from pan to a wire rack. Serve warm. **Yield:** 1 dozen.

Editor's Note: This recipe was tested with Splenda no-calorie sweetener.

Nutrition Facts: 1 muffin equals 171 calories, 5 g fat (3 g saturated fat), 14 mg cholesterol, 186 mg sodium, 27 g carbohydrate, 1 g fiber, 4 g protein. **Diabetic Exchanges:** 2 starch, 1/2 fat.

🏵🏵🏵
Orange Cranberry Gems

Prep: 15 min. **Bake:** 20 min. + cooling

Diane Jordan, Albemarle, North Carolina

I often make these muffins ahead of time so they can be quickly reheated for a breakfast treat. The orange flavor is delightful.

2 cups all-purpose flour
1/2 cup sugar
3/4 teaspoon baking soda
1/2 teaspoon salt
1 egg
2/3 cup buttermilk
1/3 cup orange juice
1/3 cup butter, melted
2 teaspoons grated orange peel
3/4 cup dried cranberries *or* raisins
1/2 cup chopped pecans

1. In a large bowl, combine the flour, sugar, baking soda and salt. In another bowl, combine the egg, buttermilk, orange juice, butter and orange peel; stir into dry ingredients just until moistened. Fold in the cranberries and pecans.

2. Fill greased muffin cups three-fourths full. Bake at 375° for 18-20 minutes or until a toothpick inserted near the center comes out clean. Cool for 5 minutes before removing from pan to wire rack. Serve warm. **Yield:** 1 dozen.

🏵🏵🏵
Dilly Bran Refrigerator Rolls

Prep: 40 min. + rising **Bake:** 20 min.

Dorothea Kampfe, Gothenburg, Nebraska

These rolls are perfect when you're expecting company for dinner or serving a holiday meal. The day before, mix and knead the dough, then refrigerate it. The next day, shape the rolls and let them rise, then pop them in the oven just before dinner. I've found leftovers will freeze well, too.

1-1/2 cups boiling water
1 cup All-Bran
2 packages (1/4 ounce *each*) active dry yeast
1/4 cup warm water (110° to 115°)
1/2 cup butter, melted
1/2 cup sugar
1-1/2 teaspoons salt
1 teaspoon dill seed
2 eggs
5-1/2 to 6 cups all-purpose flour

1. In a small bowl, combine boiling water and bran; set aside. In a large bowl, dissolve the yeast in warm water. Stir in the butter, sugar, salt, dill, eggs, 2 cups flour and bran mixture; beat until smooth. Stir in enough of the remaining flour to form a firm dough.

2. Turn onto a floured surface; knead until smooth and elastic, about 5-7 minutes. Place in a greased bowl,

turning once to grease top. Cover and refrigerate for 8 hours or overnight.

3. Punch dough down. Turn onto a lightly floured surface; divide into thirds. Shape each portion into 12 balls; place in three greased 9-in. round baking pans. Cover; let rise until doubled, about 1 to 1-1/2 hours.

4. Bake at 375° for 18-20 minutes or until lightly browned. Remove rolls from the pans to wire racks. **Yield:** 3 dozen.

★★★
Cheery Cherry Loaf

Prep: 20 min. **Bake:** 1 hour

Mina Dyck, Boissevain, Manitoba

You can serve this loaf year-round, but the cherries give it a pretty Christmasy look. In addition to being a lovely gift, it's something I often include in meals at home.

1 jar (6 ounces) red maraschino cherries
2-1/2 cups all-purpose flour
1 cup sugar
4 teaspoons baking powder
1/2 teaspoon salt
2 eggs
2/3 cup milk
1/3 cup butter, melted
1 jar (8 ounces) green maraschino cherries, drained and cut up
1/2 cup chopped pecans
1 tablespoon grated orange peel

1. Drain red cherries, reserving liquid; add water, if needed, to liquid to equal 1/3 cup. Cut up cherries; set cherries and liquid aside.

2. In a large bowl, combine the flour, sugar, baking powder and salt. In a small bowl, whisk the eggs, milk, butter and cherry liquid; stir into dry ingredients just until combined. Fold in the red and green cherries, pecans and orange peel.

3. Pour into a greased 9-in. x 5-in. loaf pan. Bake at 350° for 1 hour or until a toothpick inserted near the center comes out clean. Cool for 10 minutes before removing from pan to wire rack. **Yield:** 1 loaf (16 slices).

★★★
Almond Peach Muffins

Prep: 10 min. **Bake:** 20 min. + cooling

Robin Henry, Sugar Land, Texas

If you're looking for a good "brown bag" treat, try these. They're also nice for breakfast and as at-home snacks. Usually, I'll bake a double batch so we can eat some hot from the oven, and I pop the others in the fridge to heat later.

1-1/2 cups all-purpose flour
1 cup sugar
3/4 teaspoon salt
1/2 teaspoon baking soda
2 eggs
1/2 cup canola oil
1/2 teaspoon vanilla extract
1/8 teaspoon almond extract
1-1/4 cups chopped peeled fresh peaches
1/2 cup chopped almonds

1. In a large bowl, combine the flour, sugar, salt and baking soda. In another bowl, beat the eggs, oil and extracts; stir into dry ingredients just until moistened. Fold in peaches and almonds. Fill greased or paper-lined muffin cups three-fourths full.

2. Bake at 375° for 20-25 minutes or until a toothpick inserted near the center comes out clean. Cool for 10 minutes before removing from pan to a wire rack. Serve warm. **Yield:** 1 dozen.

Editor's Note: A 14-1/2-ounce can of peaches, drained and chopped, may be substituted for the fresh peaches.

Raspberry Coconut Bars, p. 177

Pistachio Cranberry Biscotti, p. 161

Hint-of-Berry Bonbons, p. 178

Cookies, Bars & Candy

Sweet tooths just won't be able to resist the tantalizing bites featured in this chapter, from luscious Meringue Coconut Brownies and Frosty Peanut Butter Cups to Pistachio Cranberry Biscotti and Elegant Dipped Cherries. Yum!

Peppermint Taffy.....................158
Chocolate Mint Wafers.....................158
Fudgy Oat Brownies.....................159
White Candy Bark.....................159
Nutty Chocolate Fudge.....................160
Caramel Truffles.....................160
Pistachio Cranberry Biscotti.............161
Irish Mint Brownies.....................162
Frosted Cookie Brownies.................163
Pecan Caramel Bars.....................163
Mocha Mousse Brownies.................164
Cookie Dough Truffles.....................164
Pecan Clusters.....................166
Chocolate Peanut Squares.................166
Berry-Cream Cookie Snaps.............167
Blondies with Chips.....................168
Noel Cookie Gems.....................168

Frosty Peanut Butter Cups.............169
Hazelnut Brownies.....................169
Coconut Snowmen.....................170
Meringue Coconut Brownies...........171
Butter Pecan Fudge.....................171
Raisin Pumpkin Bars.....................172
S'more Drops.....................172
Peanut Lover's Brownies.................173
Coffee 'n' Cream Brownies.............174
Blond Brownies a la Mode.............174
Almond Truffle Brownies.................176
Ribbon Crispies.....................176
Raspberry Coconut Bars.................177
Hint-of-Berry Bonbons.................178
Peanut Butter Blondies.................179
Butterscotch Hard Candy.............179
Creamy Cashew Brownies.............180
Hazelnut Toffee.....................180
Elegant Dipped Cherries.................181

Blond Brownies a la Mode, p. 174

🎀🎀🎀 Peppermint Taffy

Prep: 1-3/4 hours + cooling

Elaine Chichura, Kingsley, Pennsylvania

For a fun afternoon activity, get the kids or friends involved in an old-fashioned taffy pull. This soft, chewy candy has a minty taste, and it won't stick to the wrapper. Feel free to experiment with different colors and flavors.

 2-1/2 cups sugar
 1-1/2 cups light corn syrup
     4 teaspoons white vinegar
   1/4 teaspoon salt
   1/2 cup evaporated milk
   1/4 teaspoon peppermint oil
Red food coloring

1. Butter a 15-in. x 10-in. x 1-in. pan; set aside. In a heavy large saucepan, combine the sugar, corn syrup, vinegar and salt. Cook and stir over low heat until sugar is dissolved. Bring to a boil over medium heat. Slowly add the milk; cook and stir until a candy thermometer reads 248° (firm-ball stage).

2. Remove from the heat; stir in peppermint oil and food coloring, keeping face away from the mixture, as odor is very strong. Pour into prepared pan. Let stand for 8 minutes or until cool enough to handle.

3. With well-buttered fingers, quickly pull the candy until firm but pliable (color will become light pink).

Pull into a 1/2-in. rope; cut into 1-in. pieces. Wrap each in waxed paper. **Yield:** 1-3/4 pounds.

Editor's Note: We recommend that you test your candy thermometer before each use by bringing water to a boil; the thermometer should read 212°. Adjust your recipe temperature up or down based on your test.

🎀🎀🎀 Chocolate Mint Wafers

Prep: 20 min. + standing

Michelle Kester, Cleveland, Ohio

I created these melt-in-your-mouth thin mints for a cookie exchange, and everyone raved about them. To switch up the flavor, try using a different extract in place of peppermint.

   4 ounces dark chocolate candy coating
 1/8 to 1/4 teaspoon peppermint extract
  18 to 24 vanilla wafers

1. Place candy coating and extract in a microwave-safe bowl. Microwave, uncovered, on high for 30-60 seconds or until smooth, stirring every 15 seconds.

2. Dip vanilla wafers in coating; allow excess to drip off. Place on waxed paper; let stand until set. Store in an airtight container. **Yield:** about 1-1/2 dozen.

Editor's Note: This recipe was tested in a 1,100-watt microwave.

✿✿✿
Fudgy Oat Brownies
Prep: 30 min. **Bake:** 35 min. + cooling

Diana Otterson, Canandaigua, New York

These cake-like brownies have a rich, crunchy oat crust and a homemade chocolate frosting that canned varieties just can't beat. A packaged brownie mix makes the recipe easy to prepare.

- 1-1/2 cups quick-cooking oats
- 3/4 cup all-purpose flour
- 3/4 cup packed brown sugar
- 1/4 teaspoon baking soda
- 1/4 teaspoon salt
- 3/4 cup butter, melted
- 1 package fudge brownie mix (13-inch x 9-inch pan size)

FROSTING:
- 3 tablespoons butter
- 1-1/2 ounces unsweetened chocolate
- 2-1/4 cups confectioners' sugar
- 3 to 4 tablespoons hot water
- 1-1/2 teaspoons vanilla extract

1. In a large bowl, combine oats, flour, brown sugar, baking soda and salt. Stir in butter until combined. Press into an ungreased 13-in. x 9-in. baking pan. Bake at 350° for 10-11 minutes or until puffed and edges are lightly browned.

2. Meanwhile, prepare brownie mix according to package directions for cake-like brownies. Spread batter over crust. Bake 25-30 minutes longer or until a toothpick inserted near the center comes out clean.

3. For frosting, in a microwave-safe bowl, melt butter and chocolate; stir until smooth. Immediately stir in confectioners' sugar, 2 tablespoons hot water and vanilla until smooth. Add remaining water; stir until smooth. Immediately spread over brownies. Cool on a wire rack until firm. Cut into bars. **Yield:** 3 dozen.

✿✿✿
White Candy Bark
Prep: 20 min. + chilling

Marcia Snyder, Grand Junction, Colorado

Here's a speedy candy recipe that can be varied depending on the type of fruits or nuts you have on hand. Because we have a walnut tree, I use walnuts, but pecans could be substituted. You could also replace the cranberries with dried cherries.

- 1 tablespoon butter, melted
- 2 packages (10 to 12 ounces *each*) vanilla *or* white chips
- 1-1/2 cups walnut halves
- 1 cup dried cranberries
- 1/4 teaspoon ground nutmeg

1. Line a 15-in. x 10-in. x 1-in. pan with foil. Brush with butter; set aside. Place the chips in a microwave-safe bowl. Microwave, uncovered, at 70% power for 1 minute; stir. Microwave at additional 10- to 20-second intervals, stirring until smooth.

2. Stir in the walnuts, cranberries and nutmeg. Spread into prepared pan. Chill until firm. Break into pieces. **Yield:** 2 pounds.

Editor's Note: This recipe was tested in a 1,100-watt microwave.

☑ This recipe includes Nutrition Facts and Diabetic Exchanges.

1 jar (7 ounces) marshmallow creme
2/3 cup fat-free evaporated milk
1/2 cup butter, cubed
2 teaspoons vanilla extract
3 cups (18 ounces) semisweet chocolate chips
2 cups chopped pecans or walnuts, toasted

1. Line a 9-in. square pan with foil and coat foil with cooking spray; set aside.

2. In a large saucepan, combine the marshmallow creme, evaporated milk and butter. Cook and stir over medium heat until smooth. Bring to a boil; boil for 5 minutes, stirring constantly. Remove from the heat; add vanilla. Stir in chocolate chips until melted. Add pecans. Pour into prepared pan. Refrigerate for 2 hours or until firm.

3. Using foil, remove fudge from pan; carefully remove foil. Cut into 1-in. squares. Store in the refrigerator. **Yield:** 2-2/3 pounds (81 pieces).

Nutrition Facts: 1 piece equals 70 calories, 5 g fat (2 g saturated fat), 3 mg cholesterol, 16 mg sodium, 7 g carbohydrate, 1 g fiber, 1 g protein. **Diabetic Exchanges:** 1 fat, 1/2 starch.

🎗🎗🎗

Nutty Chocolate Fudge

Prep: 25 min. + chilling

A. J. Ristow, Tucson, Arizona

I've trimmed down the fat and calories in this recipe over the years, and now my family likes it more than ever. They don't even miss all of the sugar I used to add. Try replacing the chocolate chips with peanut butter or butterscotch ones.

🎗🎗🎗

Caramel Truffles

Prep: 1 hour + chilling

Charlotte Midthun, Granite Falls, Minnesota

These candies seem to disappear as fast as I can prepare them. It's a good thing the five-ingredient microwave recipe is easy! Drizzled with white almond bark and packaged with ribbon, the truffles can also make a pretty gift.

26 caramels
1 cup milk chocolate chips
1/4 cup heavy whipping cream
1-1/3 cups semisweet chocolate chips
1 tablespoon shortening

1. Line an 8-in. square dish with plastic wrap; set aside. In a microwave-safe bowl, combine caramels, milk chocolate chips and cream. Microwave, uncovered, on high for 1 minute; stir. Microwave 1 minute longer, stirring every 15 seconds or until caramels are melted and mixture is smooth. Spread into prepared dish; refrigerate for 1 hour or until firm.

2. Using plastic wrap, lift candy out of pan. Cut into 30 pieces; roll each piece into a 1-in. ball. Cover and refrigerate for 1 hour or until firm.

3. In a microwave-safe bowl, melt semisweet chips and shortening; stir until smooth. Dip caramels in chocolate; allow excess to drip off. Place on waxed paper; let stand until set. Refrigerate until firm. **Yield:** 2-1/2 dozen.

Editor's Note: This recipe was tested in a 1,100-watt microwave.

Pistachio Cranberry Biscotti

Prep: 30 min. **Bake:** 35 min. + cooling

Marta Perez-Stable, Westlake, Ohio

These Italian-style cookies are wonderful dipped into a cup of coffee…or even with a glass of sweet white wine for dessert. The sugary lemon drizzle makes them look special and festive.

☑ This recipe includes Nutrition Facts and Diabetic Exchanges.

1-1/2 cups dried cranberries
2 tablespoons orange juice
1/3 cup butter, softened
2/3 cup sugar
2 eggs
1 teaspoon vanilla extract
2 cups all-purpose flour
2 teaspoons baking powder
1/2 teaspoon salt
1 cup shelled pistachios
4 teaspoons grated lemon peel
ICING:
1 cup confectioners' sugar
1 teaspoon grated lemon peel
1 to 2 tablespoons fat-free milk

1. Place the cranberries in a small bowl; sprinkle with orange juice. In a large bowl, cream butter and sugar until light and fluffy. Add the eggs, one at a time, beating well after each addition. Beat in the vanilla. Combine the flour, baking powder and salt; gradually add to creamed mixture. Stir in pistachios and lemon peel. Drain cranberries; stir into dough.

2. On a lightly floured surface, divide dough into thirds. On a baking sheet coated with cooking spray, shape each portion into a 12-in. x 2-in. rectangle. Bake at 350° for 20-25 minutes or until golden brown. Cool for 5 minutes.

3. Transfer to a cutting board; with a serrated knife, cut each loaf into 20 slices. Place the cut side down on baking sheets coated with cooking spray. Bake for 12-15 minutes or until firm, turning once. Remove to wire racks to cool.

4. For icing, combine confectioners' sugar and lemon peel in a small bowl; stir in enough milk to achieve desired drizzling consistency. Drizzle over biscotti. Store in an airtight container. **Yield:** 5 dozen.

Nutrition Facts: 2 cookies equals 129 calories, 4 g fat (2 g saturated fat), 20 mg cholesterol, 109 mg sodium, 21 g carbohydrate, 1 g fiber, 2 g protein. **Diabetic Exchanges:** 1-1/2 starch, 1/2 fat.

🏅🏅🏅
Irish Mint Brownies

Prep: 45 min. **Bake:** 30 min. + chilling

Lori Risdal, Sioux City, Iowa

When I needed something for a church potluck, I created these. Topped with a minty mousse and chocolate icing, the brownies are great for St. Patrick's Day, too.

- 1 cup butter, cubed
- 4 ounces bittersweet chocolate, chopped
- 4 eggs
- 2 cups sugar
- 2 teaspoons vanilla extract
- 1-1/2 cups all-purpose flour
- 1 cup (6 ounces) double dark chocolate chips or semisweet chocolate chips
- 1/2 cup chopped walnuts

FILLING:
- 4 ounces white baking chocolate, chopped
- 1/4 cup refrigerated Irish creme nondairy creamer
- 1 cup heavy whipping cream
- 15 mint Andes candies, chopped

ICING:
- 12 ounces bittersweet chocolate, chopped
- 1 cup heavy whipping cream
- 2 tablespoons butter

Mint Andes candies, halved, optional

1. In a microwave, melt the butter and bittersweet chocolate; stir until smooth. Cool slightly. In a large bowl, beat the eggs, sugar and vanilla. Stir in the chocolate mixture. Gradually add flour until blended. Stir in chips and walnuts.

2. Spread into a greased 13-in. x 9-in. baking pan. Bake at 350° for 30-35 minutes or until a toothpick inserted near the center comes out clean (do not over-bake). Cool on a wire rack.

3. In a microwave, melt the white chocolate and creamer at 70% power for 1 minute; stir. Microwave at additional 10- to 20-second intervals, stirring until smooth. Transfer to a small bowl. Refrigerate for 30-40 minutes or until chilled.

4. In another small bowl, beat heavy whipping cream until soft peaks form; fold into the white chocolate mixture. Beat on medium speed until stiff peaks form, about 4 minutes. Fold in chopped candies. Spread over the brownies. Cover and refrigerate.

5. In a small saucepan, combine bittersweet chocolate and heavy whipping cream. Cook and stir over low heat until chocolate is melted and smooth; remove from the heat. Stir in butter until melted. Cool to room temperature. Carefully spread over filling. Cover and refrigerate for 1 hour or until icing is set. Cut into bars. Garnish with additional candies if desired. Store in refrigerator. **Yield:** 2-1/2 dozen.

🎗🎗🎗
Frosted Cookie Brownies

Prep: 30 min. **Bake:** 40 min. + cooling

Alicia French, Crestline, California

Years ago, my children and I came up with this recipe by combining two of their favorites. With a crisp cookie crust and fluffy frosting, these are the most-requested treats at our house.

- 1 tube (18 ounces) refrigerated chocolate chip cookie dough
- 3 cups miniature marshmallows
- 2 cups (12 ounces) semisweet chocolate chips
- 1 cup butter, cubed
- 4 eggs
- 2 teaspoons vanilla extract
- 1 cup all-purpose flour
- 1/2 teaspoon baking powder
- 1/4 teaspoon salt
- 1 cup chopped walnuts

FROSTING:
- 2 cups miniature marshmallows
- 6 tablespoons milk
- 1/4 cup butter, softened
- 2 ounces unsweetened chocolate
- 3 cups confectioners' sugar

1. Press the cookie dough into a greased 13-in. x 9-in. baking pan. Bake at 350° for 10 minutes.

2. Meanwhile, in a large saucepan, combine the marshmallows, chips and butter; cook and stir over low

heat until melted and smooth. Transfer to a large bowl; cool. Beat in the eggs and vanilla. Combine the flour, baking powder and salt; stir into the marshmallow mixture. Stir in nuts.

3. Spread over cookie crust. Bake for 30-35 minutes or until a toothpick inserted near the center comes out clean. Cool on a wire rack.

4. For frosting, in a small saucepan, combine the marshmallows, milk, butter and chocolate. Cook and stir over low heat until smooth. Remove from the heat; beat in confectioners' sugar until smooth. Frost the brownies. Cut into bars. **Yield:** 15 servings.

🎗🎗🎗
Pecan Caramel Bars

Prep: 20 min. **Bake:** 30 min. + cooling

Cheryl Guzman, Monroe, Georgia

My co-workers request these goodies all the time, so I make sure to bring some for our group lunches. The butterscotch chips make these different from most pecan bars.

- 1 package (12 ounces) vanilla wafers, crushed
- 2 tablespoons sugar
- 3/4 cup butter, melted
- 1 can (14 ounces) sweetened condensed milk
- 1 egg
- 1/2 teaspoon maple flavoring
- 1 cup butterscotch chips
- 1-1/2 cups coarsely chopped pecans

1. In a small bowl, combine the wafer crumbs, sugar and butter. Press into a greased 13-in. x 9-in. baking pan. Bake at 350° for 8-10 minutes or until lightly browned and set. Cool for 10 minutes on a wire rack.

2. In a small bowl, beat milk, egg and maple flavoring. Stir in the butterscotch chips. Spread over crust. Sprinkle with the pecans. Bake for 18-22 minutes or until golden brown. Cool on a wire rack. Cut into bars. **Yield:** 3 dozen.

🎀 🎀 🎀

Mocha Mousse Brownies

Prep: 40 min. **Bake:** 15 min. + chilling

Stacy Waller, Eagan, Minnesota

Chocolate is one of my favorite foods, and these doubly delightful goodies are the perfect pairing of coffee-flavored mousse and fudge brownie. My friends and family love them.

- 2/3 **cup semisweet chocolate chips**
- 1/2 **cup butter**
- 1 **cup plus 2 tablespoons sugar**
- 2 **eggs**
- 1/4 **cup hot water**
- 2 **tablespoons instant coffee granules**
- 1/2 **cup all-purpose flour**
- 1/2 **cup baking cocoa**
- 1 **teaspoon baking powder**

MOCHA MOUSSE:
- 1 **package (3 ounces) cream cheese, softened**
- 1/4 **cup sweetened condensed milk**
- 1/2 **cup semisweet chocolate chips, melted**
- 1 **envelope unflavored gelatin**
- 1/4 **cup cold water**
- 2 **tablespoons instant coffee granules**
- 1 **cup heavy whipping cream**

1. In a saucepan over low heat, melt chips and butter; pour into a large bowl. Beat in sugar until smooth. Add eggs, one at a time, beating well after each addition. Combine the hot water and coffee granules; add to the chocolate mixture. Combine the flour, cocoa and baking powder; gradually beat into chocolate mixture.

2. Spread into a greased 13-in. x 9-in. baking pan. Bake at 350° for 15-20 minutes or until a toothpick inserted near the center comes out clean (brownies will be thin). Cool on a wire rack.

3. For mousse, in a small bowl, beat cream cheese until smooth; beat in milk and melted chips. In a small saucepan, sprinkle gelatin over cold water; let stand for 1 minute. Cook and stir over low heat until gelatin is dissolved. Remove from heat; stir in coffee granules until dissolved. In a small bowl, beat whipping cream until slightly thickened. Beat in gelatin. Fold into cream cheese mixture. Spread over brownies. Cover and refrigerate for 3 hours or until set. Cut into squares. **Yield:** 2 dozen.

Cookie Dough Truffles

Prep: 1 hour + chilling

- 1/2 **cup butter, softened**
- 3/4 **cup packed brown sugar**
- 1 **teaspoon vanilla extract**
- 2 **cups all-purpose flour**
- 1 **can (14 ounces) sweetened condensed milk**
- 1/2 **cup miniature semisweet chocolate chips**
- 1/2 **cup chopped walnuts**
- 1-1/2 **pounds dark chocolate candy coating, coarsely chopped**

1. In a large bowl, cream the butter and brown sugar until light and fluffy. Beat in vanilla. Gradually add the flour alternately with the sweetened condensed milk, beating well after each addition. Stir in chips and walnuts. Shape into 1-in. balls; place on waxed paper-lined baking sheets. Loosely cover and refrigerate for 1-2 hours or until firm.

2. In a microwave-safe bowl, melt candy coating; stir until smooth. Dip balls in coating, allowing excess to drip off; place on waxed paper-lined baking sheets. Refrigerate until firm, about 15 minutes. If desired, remelt remaining candy coating and drizzle over candies. Store in the refrigerator. **Yield:** 5-1/2 dozen.

LANITA DEDON SLAUGHTER, LOUISIANA

The filling at the center of these yummy dipped candies tastes like homemade chocolate chip cookie dough…but you don't have the worry of raw eggs inside, as with real dough. Plus, the truffles are surprisingly easy to make.

Grand Prize Winner

2-1/4 cups packed brown sugar
1/8 teaspoon salt
1 can (14 ounces) sweetened condensed milk
1 teaspoon vanilla extract
1-1/2 pounds pecan halves, toasted
3/4 cup milk chocolate chips
3/4 cup semisweet chocolate chips
4 teaspoons shortening

1. Line baking sheets with waxed paper; lightly coat with cooking spray and set aside. Butter the sides of a heavy saucepan with 1 teaspoon butter. Cube the remaining butter; place in pan. Add corn syrup, brown sugar and salt. Cook and stir until the sugar is melted.

2. Gradually stir in sweetened condensed milk. Cook and stir over medium heat until the mixture comes to a boil. Cook and stir until a candy thermometer reads 248° (firm-ball stage), about 16 minutes. Remove from heat; stir in vanilla. Gently stir in pecans. Drop by rounded teaspoonfuls onto prepared baking sheets. Refrigerate until firm, about 12 minutes.

3. In a microwave, melt chips and shortening; stir until smooth. Drizzle over clusters. Chill until firm. Store in the refrigerator. **Yield:** about 6 dozen.

Editor's Note: We recommend that you test your candy thermometer before each use by bringing water to a boil; the thermometer should read 212°. Adjust your recipe temperature up or down based on your test.

❧ ❧ ❧
Pecan Clusters

Prep: 1-1/4 hours + chilling

Carrie Burke, Conway, Massachusetts

I made these turtle-like treats one Christmas for a cookie and candy exchange. My dad saw them on the counter waiting to be boxed up and said they looked like they came from a candy shop. It was the best compliment I've ever received!

1 teaspoon plus 1 cup butter, *divided*
1 cup light corn syrup

❧ ❧ ❧
Chocolate Peanut Squares

Prep: 20 min. + cooling

Nicole Trudell, Fort Lanley, British Columbia

It's hard for anyone to resist these rich, two-layer goodies. The no-bake recipe tops a slightly crunchy graham cracker and peanut butter layer with a smooth coating of melted chocolate chips and more peanut butter. They're heavenly!

2 cups confectioners' sugar
3/4 cup creamy peanut butter
2/3 cup graham cracker crumbs
1/2 cup butter, melted
TOPPING:
2/3 cup semisweet chocolate chips
4-1/2 teaspoons creamy peanut butter
1/2 teaspoon butter

1. Line a 9-in. square pan with foil and butter the foil; set aside. In a large bowl, combine confectioners' sugar, peanut butter, graham cracker crumbs and the butter. Spread into prepared pan.

2. Combine topping ingredients in a microwave-safe bowl; heat until melted. Spread over peanut butter layer. Refrigerate until cool. Using foil, lift out of pan. Cut into 1-in. squares. Store in an airtight container in the refrigerator. **Yield:** 1-1/2 pounds.

🎗🎗🎗
Berry-Cream Cookie Snaps

Prep: 40 min. + chilling **Bake:** 30 min. + cooling

Crystal Briddick, Colfax, Illinois

My mom and I combined two recipes to create this one. The cute snaps are crispy on the outside but have a light and fluffy strawberry cream on the inside. For a fun variation, bake the cookies flat and serve the filling as a dip.

    4 ounces cream cheese, softened
  1/4 cup sugar
    2 tablespoons seedless strawberry jam
  1/4 cup heavy whipping cream, whipped
    1 to 3 drops red food coloring, optional
BATTER:
  1/2 cup sugar
  1/3 cup all-purpose flour
    2 egg whites
  1/4 teaspoon vanilla extract
  1/8 teaspoon salt
  1/4 cup butter, melted and cooled
  1/2 cup chopped fresh strawberries
Additional sugar

1. For filling, in a small bowl, combine cream cheese, sugar and jam until blended. Fold in whipped cream and food coloring if desired. Chill.

2. In a small bowl, whisk the sugar, flour, egg whites, vanilla and salt until smooth. Whisk in butter until blended. Line baking sheets with parchment paper. Preparing four cookies at a time, drop batter by 1-1/2 teaspoonfuls 4 in. apart onto prepared pan. Bake at 400° for 5-8 minutes or until edges are lightly browned.

3. Immediately remove one cookie at a time from parchment and form into a tube around a greased clean round wooden clothespin. Press lightly to seal; hold until set, about 20 seconds.

4. Remove cookie from clothespin; place on waxed paper to cool. Continue with remaining cookies. If cookies become too cool to shape, return to oven for 1 minute to soften. Repeat with remaining batter.

5. Just before serving, pipe or spoon the filling into cookie shells. Dip the ends of cookies into chopped strawberries and additional sugar. Refrigerate leftovers. **Yield:** about 2 dozen.

Paper Pointer

Parchment paper is excellent for lining baking sheets when making cookies because it makes cleanup a snap. There is no right or wrong side to parchment paper, so either side can be used. For the best baking results, use a fresh sheet of parchment paper for each pan of cookies.

1/3 cup all-purpose flour
1/3 cup whole wheat flour
1/4 cup packed brown sugar
1/2 teaspoon baking powder
1/4 teaspoon salt
1 egg
1/4 cup canola oil
2 tablespoons honey
1 teaspoon vanilla extract
1/2 cup semisweet chocolate chips

1. In a small bowl, combine the first five ingredients. In another bowl, whisk the egg, oil, honey and vanilla; stir into dry ingredients just until combined. Stir in chocolate chips (batter will be thick).

2. Spread into an 8-in. square baking dish coated with cooking spray. Bake at 350° for 20-22 minutes or until a toothpick inserted near the center comes out clean. Cool on a wire rack. Cut into bars. **Yield:** 1 dozen.

Nutrition Facts: 1 bar equals 133 calories, 7 g fat (2 g saturated fat), 18 mg cholesterol, 67 mg sodium, 17 g carbohydrate, 1 g fiber, 2 g protein. **Diabetic Exchanges:** 1 starch, 1 fat.

🏵 🏵 🏵
Blondies with Chips

Prep: 5 min. **Bake:** 20 min. + cooling

Kai Skupinski, Canton, Michigan

My friends and family encouraged me to enter this recipe for a contest. They love the lightened-up blonde brownies...and never suspect that one of the ingredients is whole wheat flour.

✓ This recipe includes Nutrition Facts and Diabetic Exchanges.

🏵 🏵 🏵
Noel Cookie Gems

Prep: 35 min. **Bake:** 10 min./batch

Patsy Noel, Exeter, California

I found this recipe when my husband and I were dating. Now that we share the last name of Noel, I like to whip up a batch of "our" cookies every Christmas. They're a cinch to assemble and freeze. If you like, replace the strawberry jam with a different flavor, such as raspberry or cherry.

1/4 cup butter, softened
1/4 cup shortening
3/4 cup sugar
1 egg
1 teaspoon vanilla extract
2-2/3 cups all-purpose flour
1/2 teaspoon salt
1/4 teaspoon baking powder
1/4 teaspoon baking soda
1/2 cup sour cream
3/4 cup finely chopped nuts
1/3 cup seedless strawberry jam

1. In a large bowl, cream the butter, shortening and sugar until light and fluffy. Beat in egg and vanilla. Combine the flour, salt, baking powder and baking soda; gradually add to creamed mixture alternately with sour cream, beating well after each addition. Shape into 1-1/4-in. balls; roll in nuts.

2. Place 2 in. apart on greased baking sheets. Using the end of a wooden spoon handle, make a 3/8- to 1/2-in.-deep indentation in the center of each ball. Fill with jam.

3. Bake at 350° for 10-12 minutes or until lightly browned. Remove to wire racks. **Yield:** 3 dozen.

Frosty Peanut Butter Cups

Prep: 15 min. + freezing

Kimberly Rendino, Cicero, New York

With a creamy texture, graham-cracker crust and peanut butter flavor, these lightened-up treats are downright addictive! They freeze well in muffin cups for cute individual servings.

1 cup reduced-fat graham cracker crumbs (about 5 whole crackers)
2 tablespoons butter, softened
1 cup cold 1% milk
1/2 cup reduced-fat creamy peanut butter
1 package (3.4 ounces) instant vanilla pudding mix
2 cups fat-free whipped topping

1. In a small bowl, combine the cracker crumbs and butter. Press about 1 tablespoon each into 12 paper-lined muffin cups.

2. In a large bowl, whisk the milk and peanut butter until blended. Whisk in vanilla pudding mix until smooth. Fold in the whipped topping. Spoon into muffin cups. Freeze until firm. Remove the liners and let stand at room temperature for 5 minutes before serving. **Yield:** 1 dozen.

Nutrition Facts: 1 peanut butter cup equals 154 calories, 6 g fat (1 g saturated fat), 1 mg cholesterol, 277 mg sodium, 23 g carbohydrate, 1 g fiber, 4 g protein. **Diabetic Exchanges:** 1-1/2 starch, 1 fat.

Hazelnut Brownies

Prep: 25 min. **Bake:** 30 min. + chilling

Becki Strader, Kennewick, Washington

After these baked brownies cool, I divide them up and put some in the freezer—otherwise, we'll eat the entire pan instantly!

1 cup butter, melted
2 cups sugar
4 eggs
2 teaspoons vanilla extract
1 cup all-purpose flour
3/4 cup baking cocoa
1/2 teaspoon baking powder
1/4 teaspoon salt
1/2 cup chopped hazelnuts
FROSTING:
2 cups (12 ounces) semisweet chocolate chips
1 cup heavy whipping cream or refrigerated hazelnut nondairy creamer
2 tablespoons butter
1/2 cup coarsely chopped hazelnuts

1. In a large bowl, combine the butter and sugar until light and fluffy. Add eggs, one at a time, beating well after each addition. Beat in vanilla. Combine the flour, cocoa, baking powder and salt; gradually add to the butter mixture. Fold in hazelnuts.

2. Spread into a greased 13-in. x 9-in. baking pan. Bake at 350° for 30-35 minutes or until a toothpick inserted near the center comes out clean. Cool on a wire rack.

3. For frosting, in a microwave, melt the chips and cream until the chips are melted; stir until smooth. Stir in the butter until melted. Cover and refrigerate for 30 minutes or until the frosting achieves spreading consistency, stirring several times. Frost brownies. Sprinkle with hazelnuts. **Yield:** 2 dozen.

🎖🎖🎖

Coconut Snowmen

Prep: 4 hours + chilling

Donell Mayfield, Rio Rancho, Minnesota

My mom made a basic coconut candy recipe for years, but I took it a step further and created jolly snowman heads.

    4 cups flaked coconut, coarsely chopped
3-3/4 cups confectioners' sugar
    2/3 cup sweetened condensed milk
    1/4 cup butter, softened
1-1/2 cups vanilla or white chips
      2 packages (11-1/2 ounces each) milk chocolate chips
      1 package (10 ounces) large marshmallows
Black, orange and red decorator icing
Green leaf-shaped decorator candies

1. In a large bowl, combine coconut, confectioners' sugar, milk and butter. Shape into 1-1/4-in. balls; place on waxed paper-lined baking sheets. Loosely cover and chill for 1-1/4 hours or until firm.

2. In a microwave, melt the vanilla chips at 70% power for 1 minute; stir. Microwave at additional 10- to 20-second intervals, stirring until smooth.

3. Dip the coconut balls in melted vanilla chips; place on waxed paper-lined baking sheets. Chill until firm, about 15 minutes. Set aside the remaining melted vanilla chips.

4. In a microwave, melt milk chocolate chips on high for about 1 minute; stir. Microwave at additional 10- to 20-second intervals, stirring until smooth.

5. For hats, dip each marshmallow in chocolate; place on a waxed paper-lined baking sheet, allowing excess to drip down. Swirl the marshmallows in chocolate on waxed paper to create hat brims. Chill until firm, about 15 minutes.

6. Level the top of coated coconut balls. Attach the marshmallows hats, using reserved melted vanilla chips. With black icing, add the eyes and a mouth to each face; with orange icing, add a nose. Use the red icing and leaf candies for holly on hats. Store in an airtight container. **Yield:** 4 dozen.

Cool Creativity

Have fun decorating these cute snowmen with different colors of icing or different candies, such as red-hot candies or colored sprinkles.

🎗🎗🎗
Meringue Coconut Brownies
Prep: 30 min. **Bake:** 30 min. + cooling

Diane Bridge, Clymer, Pennsylvania

Looking for an ooey-gooey brownie that's a little different? This recipe combines a shortbread-like crust and a brown sugar meringue with chocolate, coconut and walnuts.

- 3/4 cup butter, softened
- 1-1/2 cups packed brown sugar, *divided*
- 1/2 cup sugar
- 3 eggs, *separated*
- 1 teaspoon vanilla extract
- 2 cups all-purpose flour
- 1 teaspoon baking powder
- 1/4 teaspoon baking soda
- 1/4 teaspoon salt
- 2 cups (12 ounces) semisweet chocolate chips
- 1 cup flaked coconut
- 3/4 cup chopped walnuts

1. In a large bowl, cream the butter, 1/2 cup brown sugar and sugar until light and fluffy. Beat in egg yolks and vanilla until well blended. Combine flour, baking powder, baking soda and salt; add to creamed mixture until blended (batter will be thick). Spread into a greased 13-in. x 9-in. baking pan. Sprinkle with the chocolate chips, coconut and walnuts.

2. In another large bowl, beat egg whites until soft peaks form. Gradually beat in remaining brown sugar,

1 tablespoon at a time. Beat until stiff peaks form. Spread over the top.

3. Bake at 350° for 30-35 minutes or until a toothpick inserted near the center comes out clean. Cool on a wire rack. Cut into bars. Store in the refrigerator. **Yield:** 3 to 3-1/2 dozen.

🎗🎗🎗
Butter Pecan Fudge
Prep: 20 min. + cooling

Pam Smith, Alta Loma, California

Toasted pecans add a nutty crunch to these creamy, buttery squares. I've given the fudge as a gift during the Christmas holiday season many times, and people always rave about it.

- 1/2 cup butter
- 1/2 cup sugar
- 1/2 cup packed brown sugar
- 1/2 cup heavy whipping cream
- 1/8 teaspoon salt
- 1 teaspoon vanilla extract
- 2 cups confectioners' sugar
- 1 cup pecan halves, toasted and coarsely chopped

1. In a large heavy saucepan, combine the butter, sugars, cream and salt. Bring to a boil over medium heat, stirring occasionally. Boil for 5 minutes, stirring constantly. Remove from the heat; stir in vanilla. Stir in confectioners' sugar until smooth. Fold in pecans.

2. Spread into a buttered 8-in. square dish. Cool to room temperature. Cut into 1-in. squares. Store the fudge in an airtight container in the refrigerator. **Yield:** 1-1/4 pounds.

❧❧❧ Raisin Pumpkin Bars

Prep: 20 min. **Bake:** 25 min.

Mrs. J. B. Hendrix, Ganado, Texas

These moist, frosted treats will keep well—if your family doesn't snatch them all up right away! Rely on this recipe when you need something to take to a potluck supper…or when you want a snack or dessert at home anytime.

    2 cups sugar
    1 can (15 ounces) solid-pack pumpkin
    1 cup canola oil
    4 eggs
    2 cups all-purpose flour
    2 teaspoons baking powder
    1 teaspoon baking soda
    1 teaspoon ground cinnamon
    1 teaspoon ground nutmeg
    1/2 teaspoon salt
    1/8 teaspoon ground cloves
    1/2 cup raisins
    1/3 cup chopped pecans *or* walnuts
FROSTING:
    1/3 cup butter, softened
    1 package (3 ounces) cream cheese, softened
    1 tablespoon milk
    1 teaspoon vanilla extract
    2 cups confectioners' sugar

1. In a large bowl, beat the sugar, pumpkin, oil and eggs. Combine the flour, baking powder, baking soda, cinnamon, nutmeg, salt and cloves; gradually add to pumpkin mixture and mix well. Stir in raisins and nuts.

2. Pour into a greased 15-in. x 10-in. x 1-in. baking pan. Bake at 350° for 25-30 minutes or until a toothpick inserted near the center comes out clean. Cool bars on a wire rack.

3. For frosting, combine the butter, cream cheese, milk and vanilla in a bowl; beat until smooth. Gradually beat in confectioners' sugar. Spread over bars. Store in the refrigerator. **Yield:** about 2 dozen.

❧❧❧ S'more Drops

Prep: 20 min. + cooling

Diane Angell, Rockford, Illinois

I first tried these gooey morsels in a sixth-grade home economics class. My friends and I would eat the mouth-watering drops so fast, they didn't even have time to chill! We still reminisce about making and munching these indoor s'mores.

    4 cups Golden Grahams
1-1/2 cups miniature marshmallows
    1 cup (6 ounces) semisweet chocolate chips
    1/3 cup light corn syrup
    1 tablespoon butter
    1/2 teaspoon vanilla extract

1. In a large bowl, combine cereal and marshmallows; set aside. Place the chocolate chips, corn syrup and butter in a 1-qt. microwave-safe dish.

2. Microwave, uncovered, on high for 1-2 minutes or until smooth, stirring every 30 seconds. Stir in the vanilla. Pour over cereal mixture and mix well. Drop

by tablespoonfuls onto waxed paper-lined baking sheets. Cool. **Yield:** 2-1/2 dozen.

Editor's Note: This recipe was tested in a 1,100-watt microwave.

🎗🎗🎗

Peanut Lover's Brownies

Prep: 30 min. + cooling **Bake:** 30 min. + chilling

April Phillips, Lafayette, Indiana

Peanut butter lovers won't be able to eat just one of these tantalizing treats. The chocolaty brownies are sandwiched between a graham cracker crust and creamy nut-flavored mousse.

1/2 cup butter, softened
3/4 cup all-purpose flour
1/2 cup graham cracker crumbs
1/4 cup sugar
1/2 cup salted peanuts, chopped
BROWNIE LAYER:
3/4 cup butter, cubed
4 ounces unsweetened chocolate, chopped
4 eggs
2 cups sugar
2 teaspoons vanilla extract
1 cup all-purpose flour
PEANUT CREAM TOPPING:
1 cup creamy peanut butter
1 carton (12 ounces) frozen whipped topping, thawed
12 miniature peanut butter cups, coarsely chopped

1. Line a 13-in. x 9-in. baking pan with foil; grease the foil. In a small bowl, combine the butter, flour, cracker crumbs and sugar; press into prepared pan. Bake at 350° for 10-12 minutes or until set. Cool on a wire rack. Sprinkle peanuts over crust.

2. In a microwave, melt the butter and chocolate; stir until smooth. In a large bowl, combine the eggs, sugar, vanilla and chocolate mixture. Gradually add flour. Spread over the crust. Bake for 30-40 minutes or until a toothpick inserted near the center comes out clean. Cool on a wire rack.

3. For peanut cream topping, warm peanut butter for 30 seconds in a microwave. Gradually fold in whipped topping; spread over the brownies. Refrigerate for 1 hour. Sprinkle with the chopped peanut butter cups. Using the foil, lift brownies out of the pan; remove the foil. Cut into bars. Store in the refrigerator. **Yield:** 2 dozen.

1 cup sugar
1 teaspoon vanilla extract
2/3 cup all-purpose flour
1/4 teaspoon baking soda
FILLING:
1 tablespoon heavy whipping cream
1 teaspoon instant coffee granules
2 tablespoons butter, softened
1 cup confectioners' sugar
GLAZE:
1 cup (6 ounces) semisweet chocolate chips
1/3 cup heavy whipping cream

1. In a microwave, melt butter and chocolate; stir until smooth. Cool slightly. In a small bowl, beat the eggs, sugar and vanilla; stir in the chocolate mixture. Combine flour and baking soda; gradually add to chocolate mixture.

2. Spread into a greased 8-in. square baking pan. Bake at 350° for 25-30 minutes or until a toothpick inserted near the center comes out clean (do not over-bake). Cool on a wire rack.

3. For filling, combine cream and coffee granules in a small bowl; stir until coffee is dissolved. In a small bowl, cream butter and confectioners' sugar until light and fluffy. Beat in coffee mixture; spread over brownies.

4. In a small saucepan, combine chips and cream. Cook and stir over low heat until chocolate is melted and mixture is thickened. Cool slightly. Carefully spread over filling. Let stand for 30 minutes or until glaze is set. Cut into squares. Store in the refrigerator. **Yield:** 16 servings.

🎖🎖🎖

Coffee 'n' Cream Brownies

Prep: 25 min. **Bake:** 25 min. + cooling

Michelle Tiemstra, Lacombe, Alberta

A friend gave me the recipe for these rich, cake-like squares topped with a creamy mocha filling and chocolate glaze. For an added touch, I like to top each brownie with a coffee bean.

1/2 cup butter, cubed
3 ounces unsweetened chocolate, chopped
2 eggs

Blond Brownies a la Mode

Prep: 25 min. **Bake:** 25 min. + cooling

3/4 cup butter, softened
2 cups packed brown sugar
4 eggs
2 teaspoons vanilla extract
2 cups all-purpose flour
2 teaspoons baking powder
1 teaspoon salt
1-1/2 cups chopped pecans
MAPLE CREAM SAUCE:
1 cup maple syrup
2 tablespoons butter
1/4 cup evaporated milk
Vanilla ice cream and chopped pecans

1. In a large bowl, cream butter and brown sugar until light and fluffy. Add the eggs, one at a time,

beating well after each addition. Beat in vanilla. Combine flour, baking powder and salt; gradually add to creamed mixture. Stir in pecans.

2. Spread into a greased 13-in. x 9-in. baking pan. Bake at 350° for 25-30 minutes or until a toothpick inserted near the center comes out clean. Cool on a wire rack.

3. For the sauce, combine the syrup and butter in a saucepan. Bring to a boil; cook and stir for 3 minutes. Remove from the heat; stir in evaporated milk. Cut brownies into squares; cut in half if desired.

4. Place on dessert plates with a scoop of ice cream. Top with the sauce; sprinkle with the pecans. **Yield:** 20 servings.

PAT PARKER CHESTER, SOUTH CAROLINA

We have a lot of church socials, and I'm always looking for something new and different to prepare. Drizzled with a sweet maple sauce and sprinkled with chopped pecans, these brownies are a sure hit...with or without the ice cream.

Grand
Prize
Winner

🎀🎀🎀
Almond Truffle Brownies

Prep: 15 min. **Bake:** 25 min. + chilling

Lynn Snow, Taylors, South Carolina

This wonderful recipe is one my mom just had to share with me after she made it—and I'm glad she did! The fudgy nut brownies sprinkled with toasted almonds are prepared in several steps, but the effort is well worth it.

> 1 package fudge brownie mix (13-inch x 9-inch pan size)
> 1/2 cup water
> 1/2 cup canola oil
> 1 egg
> 3/4 cup chopped almonds
> 1 teaspoon almond extract
> **FILLING:**
> 1 cup (6 ounces) semisweet chocolate chips
> 1 package (8 ounces) cream cheese, softened
> 1/4 cup confectioners' sugar
> 2 tablespoons milk
> 1/2 teaspoon almond extract
> **TOPPING:**
> 1/2 cup semisweet chocolate chips
> 1/4 cup heavy whipping cream
> 1/2 cup sliced almonds, toasted

1. In a large bowl, combine the first six ingredients. Pour into a greased 13-in. x 9-in. baking pan. Bake at 350° for 23-25 minutes or until a toothpick inserted near the center comes out clean (do not overbake). Cool on a wire rack.

2. In a microwave, melt chocolate chips; stir until smooth. In a large bowl, beat cream cheese and confectioners' sugar until smooth. Beat in the milk, extract and melted chips. Spread over brownies. Refrigerate for 1 hour or until firm.

3. For topping, in a small saucepan, melt chips and cream over low heat, stirring occasionally. Spread over filling. Sprinkle with almonds. Refrigerate at least 1 hour longer before cutting. **Yield:** 1-1/2 dozen.

🎀🎀🎀
Ribbon Crispies

Prep: 10 min. **Cook:** 10 min. + cooling

Nancy Baker, Boonville, Missouri

These dressed-up rice cereal treats are a yummy twist on a long-time favorite, and they're always a big hit no matter where I share them. Children from age 1 to 101 can't get enough!

> 1/2 cup butter, cubed
> 2 jars (7 ounces *each*) marshmallow creme
> 11 cups crisp rice cereal
> 1 to 1-1/2 cups peanut butter
> 1 to 1-1/2 cups hot fudge ice cream topping, warmed

1. In a large saucepan, melt butter over medium-low heat. Stir in the marshmallow creme until smooth. Remove from the heat; stir in cereal until blended.

2. Press half of the cereal mixture into a greased 15-in. x 10-in. x 1-in. pan; spread with the peanut butter. Carefully spread with the hot fudge ice cream topping. Press the remaining cereal mixture over the fudge layer (the pan will be full). Cool for 10 minutes before cutting. **Yield:** 3 dozen.

Raspberry Coconut Bars

Prep: 20 min. **Bake:** 20 min. + chilling

Barb Bovberg, Fort Collins, Colorado

I make a batch of these every Christmas. The drizzle of melted chocolate and vanilla chips creates such a pretty, lacy effect.

- 1-2/3 cups graham cracker crumbs
- 1/2 cup butter, melted
- 2-2/3 cups flaked coconut
- 1 can (14 ounces) sweetened condensed milk
- 1 cup seedless raspberry preserves
- 1/3 cup chopped walnuts, toasted
- 1/2 cup semisweet chocolate chips
- 1/4 cup white baking chips

1. In a small bowl, combine the cracker crumbs and butter. Press into a 13-in. x 9-in. baking dish coated with cooking spray. Sprinkle with coconut; drizzle with sweetened condensed milk.

2. Bake at 350° for 20-25 minutes or until lightly browned. Cool completely on a wire rack.

3. Spread the preserves over crust. Sprinkle with walnuts. In a microwave, melt the chocolate chips; stir until smooth. Drizzle over walnuts. Repeat with the vanilla chips. Cut into bars. Refrigerate for 30 minutes or until chocolate is set. **Yield:** 3 dozen.

Toasty Technique

To toast nuts, spread them in a 15-in. x 10-in. x 1-in. baking pan and then bake them at 350° for 5-10 minutes or until lightly browned, stirring occasionally. Or, spread the nuts in a dry non-stick skillet and heat them over low heat until lightly browned, stirring occasionally.

🎗🎗🎗
Hint-of-Berry Bonbons

Prep: 1-1/2 hours + chilling

Brenda Hoffman, Stanton, Michigan

You'll have a hard time eating just one of these heavenly sweets. Underneath the rich milk chocolate coating is a fudgy center with a hint of strawberry. The white chocolate drizzle makes these bonbons even more special.

- 1 package (8 ounces) cream cheese, softened
- 1 cup milk chocolate chips, melted and cooled
- 3/4 cup crushed vanilla wafers (about 25 wafers)
- 1/4 cup strawberry preserves
- 15 ounces milk chocolate candy coating, chopped
- 2 ounces white baking chocolate

1. In a large bowl, beat cream cheese until fluffy. Beat in melted chocolate chips. Stir in wafer crumbs and preserves. Cover and refrigerate for 2 hours or until easy to handle.

2. Divide the mixture in half. Return one portion to refrigerator. Shape remaining mixture into 1-in. balls. Place on a waxed paper-lined pan; refrigerate. Repeat with remaining mixture.

3. In a microwave, melt the milk chocolate chips at 70% power for 1 minute; stir. Microwave at additional 10- to 20-second intervals, stirring until smooth. Dip balls in coating; allow excess to drip off. Place on waxed paper-lined baking sheets. Refrigerate until set.

4. In a microwave, melt the white chocolate at 70% power for 1 minute; stir. Microwave at additional 10- to 20-second intervals, stirring until smooth. Transfer to a heavy-duty resealable plastic bag; cut a small hole in a corner of bag. Decorate candies with white chocolate. Store in an airtight container in the refrigerator. **Yield:** about 4-1/2 dozen.

🎖🎖🎖
Peanut Butter Blondies

Prep: 30 min. **Bake:** 35 min. + cooling

Karla Johnson, Tyler, Minnesota

The children I baby-sit for love these moist and chewy bars. The blondies have lots of peanut butter flavor, yummy home-made chocolate frosting and a sprinkling of peanut butter chips.

3/4 cup creamy peanut butter
2/3 cup butter, softened
1 cup packed brown sugar
1/2 cup sugar
2 eggs
1 teaspoon vanilla extract
1-3/4 cups all-purpose flour
1 teaspoon baking powder
1/3 cup milk
1 cup peanut butter chips
FROSTING:
1/4 cup butter, softened
1/4 cup baking cocoa
2 tablespoons milk
1 tablespoon light corn syrup
1 teaspoon vanilla extract
1-1/2 cups confectioners' sugar
1/3 cup peanut butter chips

1. In a large bowl, cream the peanut butter, butter and sugars until light and fluffy. Beat in eggs and vanilla. Combine the flour and baking powder; add to creamed mixture alternately with milk, beating well after each addition. Stir in chips.

2. Spread into a greased 13-in. x 9-in. baking pan. Bake at 325° for 35-40 minutes or until a toothpick inserted near the center comes out clean (do not over-bake). Cool on a wire rack.

3. For frosting, in a small bowl, combine the butter, cocoa, milk, corn syrup and vanilla. Gradually add confectioners' sugar; beat until smooth. Frost the brownies. Sprinkle with the chips. Cut into bars. **Yield:** 2 dozen.

🎖🎖🎖
Butterscotch Hard Candy

Prep: 10 min. **Cook:** 30 min. + cooling

Darlene Smithers, Elkhart, Indiana

I love making this classic butterscotch recipe for special occasions or anytime. We think the homemade candy is even better than the kind found in stores. And it sure doesn't last long!

1 teaspoon plus 1 cup butter, *divided*
2-1/2 cups sugar
3/4 cup water
1/2 cup light corn syrup
1/4 cup honey
1/2 teaspoon salt
1/2 teaspoon rum extract

1. Butter a 15-in. x 10-in. x 1-in. pan with 1 teaspoon butter; set aside. Cube remaining butter and set aside.

2. In a heavy saucepan, combine the sugar, water and corn syrup. Cover and bring to a boil over medium heat without stirring. Cook, uncovered, until a candy thermometer reads 270° (soft-crack stage). Add the honey, salt and remaining butter; stir constantly until the mixture reaches 300° (hard-crack stage).

3. Remove from the heat. Stir in the rum extract. Pour into prepared pan without scraping; do not spread. Cool for 1-2 minutes or until the candy is almost set. Score candy into 1-in. squares; cool completely. Break squares apart. Store in an airtight container. **Yield:** 1-1/2 pounds.

Editor's Note: We recommend that you test your candy thermometer before each use by bringing water to a boil; the thermometer should read 212°. Adjust your recipe temperature up or down based on your test.

🎗🎗🎗
Creamy Cashew Brownies

Prep: 15 min. **Bake:** 25 min. + chilling

Karen Wagner, Danville, Illinois

My sister-in-law dubbed me the "dessert queen" because I bring treats like this to our family get-togethers. The brownies have a fudge-like texture and rich cream cheese topping. Cashews and a hot fudge swirl make them even more tempting.

1 package fudge brownie mix (13-inch x 9-inch pan size)
1/3 cup water
1/4 cup canola oil
1 egg
1 cup (6 ounces) semisweet chocolate chips
TOPPING:
   2 packages (8 ounces *each*) cream cheese, softened
1-1/2 cups confectioners' sugar
1 teaspoon vanilla extract
1 cup salted cashews, coarsely chopped
1/2 cup hot fudge ice cream topping, warmed

1. In a large bowl, combine the brownie mix, water, oil and egg. Stir in chips. Spread into a greased 13-in. x 9-in. baking pan.

2. Bake at 350° for 25-27 minutes or until a toothpick inserted near the center comes out clean (do not over-bake). Cool on a wire rack.

3. For topping, in a large bowl, beat the cream cheese, confectioners' sugar and vanilla until smooth. Spread over brownies. Sprinkle with cashews; drizzle with hot fudge topping. Refrigerate before cutting. Store in the refrigerator. **Yield:** 2 dozen.

🎗🎗🎗
Hazelnut Toffee

Prep: 45 min. + cooling

Joanne Simpson, Portland, Oregon

This is one of my most-requested recipes. The toffee is sweet and buttery, with plenty of crunch. If you wish, you could substitute almonds for the hazelnuts…or use dark, milk or white chocolate in place of the semisweet.

2 teaspoons plus 1 cup butter, *divided*
1 cup sugar
3 tablespoons water
1 tablespoon light corn syrup
1/3 cup chopped hazelnuts
TOPPING:
   2 cups (12 ounces *each*) semisweet chocolate chips
1/2 cup finely chopped hazelnuts

1. Line a 13-in. x 9-in. pan with foil; coat the foil with cooking spray and set aside. Butter the sides of a large heavy saucepan with 2 teaspoons butter. Cube the remaining butter; place in pan. Add the sugar, water and corn syrup. Cook and stir until the mixture turns golden brown and a candy thermometer reads 300° (hard crack stage).

2. Remove from the heat; stir in hazelnuts. Pour into prepared pan without scraping; spread evenly. Let stand at room temperature until cool, about 1 hour.

3. In a microwave-safe bowl, melt the chocolate chips. Spread evenly over toffee. Sprinkle with nuts, pressing down gently. Let stand for 1 hour. Break into bite-sized pieces. Store in refrigerator. **Yield:** 1-3/4 pounds.

Editor's Note: We recommend that you test your candy thermometer before each use by bringing water to a boil; the thermometer should read 212°. Adjust your recipe temperature up or down based on your test.

Elegant Dipped Cherries

Prep: 1-1/4 hours + freezing

Sedora Brown, Waynesboro, Virginia

Here's a sure way to impress your holiday guests. The sweet maraschino cherries are wrapped in unsweetened chocolate, then dipped in melted vanilla chips. A chocolate drizzle is the finishing touch to dress them up for your dessert tray.

   1 jar (10 ounces) maraschino cherries with
     stems, well drained
   3 tablespoons butter, melted
   2 tablespoons light corn syrup
   1 ounce unsweetened chocolate, melted
   2 teaspoons half-and-half cream
   2 cups confectioners' sugar
   1 cup vanilla *or* white chips
2-1/2 teaspoons shortening, *divided*
   1/2 cup semisweet chocolate chips

1. Pat cherries dry with paper towels and set aside. In a large bowl, combine butter, corn syrup, unsweetened chocolate and cream. Stir in the confectioners' sugar.

2. Knead until smooth. Roll into 18 balls; flatten each into a 2-in. circle. Wrap each circle around a cherry and lightly roll in hands. Place cherries, stem side up, in a shallow paper-lined container. Cover and freeze for at least 2 hours.

3. The day before serving, remove the cherries from freezer. In a microwave, melt vanilla chips and 1-1/2 teaspoons shortening at 70% power for 1 minute; stir. Microwave at additional 10- to 20-second intervals, stirring until smooth. Holding onto the stem, dip each cherry into the vanilla mixture; allowing excess to drip off. Place on waxed paper; let stand until set.

4. In a microwave, melt the chocolate chips and the remaining shortening; stir until smooth. Drizzle over the candies. Refrigerate until firm. Store candies in an airtight container. **Yield:** 1-1/2 dozen.

Cranberry Pear Pie, p. 202

White Chocolate Mousse Cherry Pie, p. 196

Chocolate Carrot Cake, p. 192

Cakes & Pies

From cool and creamy confections for warm summer days to favorites that come fresh from the oven, the tempting treats in this chapter are guaranteed to please everyone at the dinner table. Just remind them to save room for dessert!

Sweet Potato Mini Cakes.................184

Butter Pecan Pumpkin Pie...............184

German Chocolate Pie.....................186

Pumpkin Cheesecake Pie.................187

Pecan Angel Food Cake..................187

Triple Layer Brownie Cake...............188

Frosty Lemon Pie.............................188

Cranberry Bundt Cake.....................189

Popover Apple Pie..........................189

Buttermilk Banana Cake.................190

Martha Washington Pies..................190

Chocolate Carrot Cake....................192

Grapefruit Pie................................192

Upside-Down Apple Pie...................193

Sunflower Potluck Cake 194

Ricotta Nut Pie..............................194

Peanut Butter Pie 195

Caramel Apple Cake........................195

Lemon Pie in Meringue Shell...........196

White Chocolate Mousse Cherry Pie....196

Chocolate Potato Cake....................198

Mud Pie..198

Eggnog Cranberry Pie.....................199

Layered Carrot Cake...........................199

Triple-Layer Lemon Cake...............200

Grasshopper Pie............................201

Chock-full of Fruit Snackin' Cake......201

Berry Pinwheel Cake 202

Cranberry Pear Pie..........................202

Caramel Apple Cream Pie...............204

Frozen Strawberry Pie.....................204

Chocolate Raspberry Pie.................205

Peachy Rhubarb Pie........................205

Berry Pinwheel Cake, p. 202

🎀🎀🎀
Sweet Potato Mini Cakes

Prep: 40 min. **Bake:** 25 min. + cooling

Joyce Larson, New Market, Iowa

Whenever I make these cute desserts, I think of my grandmother. She always used the extra sweet potatoes from her vegetable garden in pies, breads and cakes…and added black walnuts from her trees for good measure.

- 2 **cups all-purpose flour**
- 1 **cup sugar**
- 1 **cup packed brown sugar**
- 1 **teaspoon salt**
- 1 **teaspoon baking soda**
- 1 **teaspoon baking powder**
- 1 **teaspoon ground cinnamon**
- 1 **teaspoon pumpkin pie spice**
- 4 **eggs**
- 1-1/4 **cups canola oil**
- 3 **cups shredded peeled sweet potatoes**
- 1 **teaspoon rum extract**
- 1 **can (8 ounces) crushed pineapple, drained**
- 1 **cup golden raisins**
- 1 **cup chopped walnuts**

FROSTING:
- 1 **package (8 ounces) cream cheese, softened**
- 1 **cup butter, softened**
- 5 **cups confectioners' sugar**
- 4 **teaspoons brown sugar**
- 1 **teaspoon vanilla extract**
- 1/2 **teaspoon rum extract**
- 1-1/2 **cups ground walnuts**

1. In a large bowl, combine the first eight ingredients. Add eggs, oil, potatoes and extract; beat until combined. Stir in pineapple, raisins and walnuts.

2. Fill 12 greased or paper-lined jumbo muffin cups three-fourths full. Bake at 350° for 25-30 minutes or until a toothpick inserted in the center comes out clean. Cool for 10 minutes before removing from pans to wire racks to cool completely.

3. For frosting, in a large bowl, beat cream cheese and butter until fluffy. Beat in the sugars and extracts until smooth. Frost sides of cakes; roll in walnuts. Place cakes upside down and frost tops with the remaining frosting. **Yield:** 1 dozen.

Butter Pecan Pumpkin Pie

Prep: 20 min. + freezing

- 1 **quart butter pecan ice cream, softened**
- 1 **pastry shell (9 inches), baked**
- 1 **cup canned pumpkin**
- 1/2 **cup sugar**
- 1/4 **teaspoon** *each* **ground cinnamon, ginger and nutmeg**
- 1 **cup heavy whipping cream, whipped**
- 1/2 **cup caramel ice cream topping**
- 1/2 **cup chocolate ice cream topping, optional**
Additional whipped cream

1. Spread ice cream into the crust; freeze for 2 hours or until firm. In a small bowl, combine the pumpkin, sugar, cinnamon, ginger and nutmeg; fold in the whipped cream. Spread over ice cream. Cover and freeze for 2 hours or until firm. May be frozen for up to 2 months.

2. Remove from freezer 15 minutes before slicing. Drizzle with caramel ice cream topping. Drizzle with chocolate ice cream topping if desired. Dollop with whipped cream. **Yield:** 6-8 servings.

ARLETTA SLOCUM VENICE, FLORIDA

This refreshing ice cream pie has always been a family favorite for holidays. It's also nice to have in the freezer when unexpected company stops in for coffee and dessert.

Grand Prize Winner

🏅🏅🏅
German Chocolate Pie

Prep: 45 min. + chilling

Debbie Clay, Farmington, New Mexico

Thanksgiving dinner at our house includes an average of 25 guests and a dozen different pies. With chocolate, coconut and pecans, this one has all the luscious flavor of classic German chocolate cake...and is always popular.

- 4 **ounces German sweet chocolate, chopped**
- 1 **tablespoon butter**
- 1 **teaspoon vanilla extract**
- 1/3 **cup sugar**
- 3 **tablespoons cornstarch**
- 1-1/2 **cups milk**
- 2 **egg yolks, lightly beaten**
- 1 **pastry shell (9 inches), baked**

TOPPING:
- 2/3 **cup evaporated milk**
- 1/2 **cup sugar**
- 1/4 **cup butter, cubed**
- 1 **egg, lightly beaten**
- 1-1/3 **cups flaked coconut, toasted**
- 1/2 **cup chopped pecans, toasted**

1. In a microwave, melt the chocolate and butter; stir until smooth. Stir in vanilla; set aside.

2. In a small saucepan, combine sugar, cornstarch and milk until smooth. Cook and stir over medium-high heat until thickened and bubbly. Reduce heat; cook and stir 2 minutes longer. Remove from the heat. Stir a small amount of hot filling into egg yolks; return all to the pan, stirring constantly. Bring to a gentle boil; cook and stir 2 minutes longer. Remove from the heat. Gently stir in the chocolate mixture. Spoon into pastry shell.

3. In a small saucepan, combine the evaporated milk, sugar and butter. Cook and stir until butter is melted and mixture just comes to a boil. Remove from the heat. Stir a small amount of hot liquid into egg; return all to the pan, stirring constantly. Bring to a gentle boil; cook and stir 2 minutes longer.

4. Remove from the heat. Stir in the coconut and pecans. Pour over filling. Cool on a wire rack. Cover and chill for at least 3 hours. Refrigerate leftovers. **Yield:** 8 servings.

🎀🎀🎀
Pumpkin Cheesecake Pie

Prep: 30 min. **Bake:** 45 min. + chilling

Sharon Crockett, La Palma, California

If you're looking for a classic autumn dessert everyone will love, try this pumpkin cheesecake in a gingersnap cookie pie crust. It's a winner at potlucks and on the Thanksgiving table, too.

```
1-1/2  cups crushed gingersnap cookies
    1  tablespoon sugar
  1/4  cup butter, melted
FILLING:
    2  packages (8 ounces each) cream cheese,
         softened
  3/4  cup sugar
    2  eggs, lightly beaten
    1  can (15 ounces) solid-pack pumpkin
    1  teaspoon ground cinnamon
  1/4  teaspoon ground ginger
  1/4  teaspoon ground nutmeg
  1/8  teaspoon salt
TOPPING:
    1  cup (8 ounces) sour cream
  1/4  cup sugar
    1  teaspoon vanilla extract
Ground cinnamon, optional
```

1. In a small bowl, combine the gingersnap crumbs and sugar. Stir in butter. Press onto the bottom and up the sides of a greased 9-in. deep-dish pie plate. Bake at 350° for 8-10 minutes or until lightly browned.

2. In a large bowl, beat cream cheese and sugar until smooth. Add the eggs; beat on low speed just until combined. Stir in the pumpkin, cinnamon, ginger, nutmeg and salt. Pour into the crust. Bake for 35-40 minutes or until center is almost set.

3. In a small bowl, combine sour cream, sugar and vanilla. Spread over pie. Bake 8-12 minutes longer or until set. Cool on a wire rack. Cover and refrigerate for at least 4 hours. Sprinkle with cinnamon if desired. **Yield:** 8-10 servings.

🎀🎀🎀
Pecan Angel Food Cake

Prep: 30 min. **Bake:** 40 min.

Margaret Wampler, Butler, Pennsylvania

Chopped pecans add a wonderfully nutty flavor and texture to this made-from-scratch angel food cake, which is a nice change of pace from the plain variety.

```
1-1/2  cups egg whites (about 10)
    1  cup all-purpose flour
    1  teaspoon cream of tartar
    2  teaspoons vanilla extract
1-1/2  cups sugar
1-1/2  cups finely chopped pecans
Whipped cream, optional
```

1. Place egg whites in a large bowl; let stand at room temperature for 30 minutes. Sift flour twice; set aside. Add cream of tartar and vanilla to egg whites; beat on medium speed until soft peaks form. Gradually beat in sugar, about 2 tablespoons at a time, on high until stiff glossy peaks form. Gradually fold in flour, about 1/4 cup at a time. Fold in pecans.

2. Gently spoon into an ungreased 10-in. tube pan. Cut through the batter with a knife to remove the air pockets. Bake on lowest oven rack at 350° for 35-40 minutes or until lightly browned and the entire top appears dry.

3. Immediately invert pan; cool completely, about 1 hour. Run a knife around side and center tube of pan; remove cake. Serve with whipped cream if desired. **Yield:** 12-16 servings.

Triple Layer Brownie Cake

Prep: 30 min. + chilling **Bake:** 25 min. + cooling

Barbara Dean, Littleton, Colorado

A little of this rich brownie cake goes a long way, so you're sure to have plenty to share with family and friends. Chocolate lovers will be especially thrilled with this decadent treat.

1-1/2 **cups butter**
   6 **ounces unsweetened chocolate, chopped**
   3 **cups sugar**
   5 **eggs**
1-1/2 **teaspoons vanilla extract**
1-1/2 **cups all-purpose flour**
  3/4 **teaspoon salt**
FROSTING:
   16 **ounces semisweet chocolate, chopped**
    3 **cups heavy whipping cream**
  1/2 **cup sugar, optional**
    2 **milk chocolate candy bars (1.55 ounces *each*), shaved**

1. In a large microwave-safe bowl, melt butter and chocolate; stir until smooth. Stir in sugar. Add eggs, one at a time, beating well after each addition. Stir in vanilla, flour and salt.

2. Pour mixture into three greased and floured 9-in. round baking pans. Bake at 350° for 23-25 minutes or until a toothpick inserted near the center comes out clean. Cool for 10 minutes; remove from pan to a wire rack to cool completely.

3. For frosting, melt chocolate in a heavy saucepan over medium heat. Gradually stir in cream and sugar, if desired, until well blended. Heat to a gentle boil; boil and stir for 1 minute. Remove from the heat; transfer to a large bowl. Refrigerate for 2-3 hours or until the mixture reaches a pudding-like consistency, stirring a few times.

4. Beat frosting until soft peaks form. Immediately spread between layers and over top and sides of the cake. Sprinkle with the shaved chocolate. Store in the refrigerator. **Yield:** 16-20 servings.

Frosty Lemon Pie

Prep: 30 min. + freezing

Judith Wilke, Dousman, Wisconsin

When you want a light and refreshing finish to a summer picnic or patio supper, try this make-ahead dessert.

  3/4 **cup sugar**
  1/3 **cup lemon juice**
  1/4 **cup butter, cubed**
Dash salt
   3 **eggs, lightly beaten**
   2 **pints vanilla ice cream, softened, *divided***
   1 **graham cracker crust (9 inches)**
Whipped topping, fresh mint and lemon peel, optional

1. In a small saucepan, combine the sugar, lemon juice, butter and salt; cook and stir over medium heat until sugar is dissolved and the butter is melted. Whisk a small amount of the sugar mixture into eggs; return all to the pan. Cook and stir over medium heat until mixture reaches 160° or is thick enough to coat back of a metal spoon. Refrigerate until completely cooled.

2. Spread half of the ice cream into the crust; freeze for 1 hour or until firm. Cover with half of the lemon mixture; freeze for 1 hour or until firm. Repeat layers. Cover and freeze for several hours or overnight.

3. Remove from the freezer 10 minutes before serving. Garnish with whipped topping, mint and lemon peel if desired. **Yield:** 8 servings.

🎗🎗🎗
Cranberry Bundt Cake

Prep: 10 min. **Bake:** 2-1/2 hours + standing

Esther McCoy, Dillonvale, Ohio

I first served this nutty, sugar-dusted treat several years ago as one of the desserts for Thanksgiving dinner. Now, the cake is a must-have alongside the pumpkin pies at our holiday feast.

> 2/3 cup butter, softened
> 1 cup sugar
> 3 eggs
> 1-1/2 teaspoons vanilla extract
> 2 cups all-purpose flour
> 1 teaspoon baking powder
> 3/4 teaspoon baking soda
> 1/2 teaspoon salt
> 1 cup (8 ounces) sour cream
> 3/4 cup chopped dried cranberries
> 1/3 cup chopped pecans
> Confectioners' sugar

1. In a large bowl, cream butter and sugar until light and fluffy. Add the eggs, one at a time, beating well after each addition. Beat in vanilla. Combine the flour, baking powder, baking soda and salt; add to creamed mixture alternately with sour cream and mix well. Fold in cranberries and pecans.

2. Pour into a greased and floured 8-in. fluted tube pan. Bake at 350° for 45-50 minutes or until a toothpick inserted near the center comes out clean. Cool for 10 minutes; remove from pan to a wire rack. Dust with confectioners' sugar. **Yield:** 8-10 servings.

Editor's Note: Cake can be baked in a 9-in. square baking pan at the same time and temperature.

🎗🎗🎗
Popover Apple Pie

Prep: 20 min. **Bake:** 30 min.

Beki Kosydar-Krantz, Clarks Summit, Pennsylvania

My family loves this comforting dessert, especially on chilly autumn and winter days. The golden brown crust bakes in the oven, and the apple and cranberry filling cooks in the microwave.

> 3/4 cup all-purpose flour
> 1/2 teaspoon salt
> 2 eggs
> 2 egg whites
> 3/4 cup 1% milk
> 1 cup cold orange juice
> 1 package (.8 ounce) sugar-free cook-and-serve vanilla pudding mix
> 3/4 teaspoon apple pie spice
> 6 large peeled tart apples, sliced
> 1/2 cup dried cranberries
> 1/4 cup chopped walnuts
> 1 teaspoon confectioners' sugar

1. In a large bowl, combine flour and salt. Combine the eggs, egg whites and milk; whisk into the dry ingredients just until blended. Pour into a 10-in. ovenproof skillet coated with butter-flavored cooking spray.

2. Bake at 450° for 20 minutes. Reduce heat to 350° (do not open oven door). Bake 10-15 minutes longer or until deep golden brown (do not underbake).

3. In a microwave-safe bowl, whisk the orange juice, pudding mix and apple pie spice. Stir in the apples and cranberries. Cover and microwave on high for 5 minutes, stirring once. Cover and cook 3-4 minutes longer or until apples are tender, stirring once.

4. Spoon hot apple mixture into crust. Sprinkle with walnuts. Dust with the confectioners' sugar and serve immediately. **Yield:** 8 servings.

★★★
Buttermilk Banana Cake

Prep: 35 min. **Bake:** 25 min. + cooling

Arlene Grenz, Linton, North Dakota

Frosted with sweetened whipped cream, this impressive dessert is so tempting. And the taste doesn't disappoint! The banana cake is layered with a yummy pecan filling.

- 3/4 cup butter, softened
- 1 cup sugar
- 1/2 cup packed brown sugar
- 2 eggs
- 1 cup mashed ripe bananas (about 2 medium)
- 1 teaspoon vanilla extract
- 2 cups cake flour
- 1 teaspoon baking powder
- 1 teaspoon baking soda
- 1/2 teaspoon salt
- 1/2 cup buttermilk

FILLING:
- 1/2 cup sugar
- 2 tablespoons all-purpose flour
- 1/4 teaspoon salt
- 1/2 cup half-and-half cream
- 2 tablespoons butter
- 1 teaspoon vanilla extract
- 1/2 cup chopped pecans

FROSTING:
- 2 cups heavy whipping cream
- 1/4 cup confectioners' sugar

1. In a large bowl, cream butter and sugars until light and fluffy. Beat in the eggs, bananas and vanilla; beat for 2 minutes. Combine flour, baking powder, baking soda and salt; add to creamed mixture alternately with buttermilk, beating well after each addition.

2. Pour mixture into two greased and floured 9-in. round baking pans. Bake at 375° for 25-30 minutes or until a toothpick inserted near the center comes out clean. Cool for 10 minutes before removing from pans to wire racks to cool completely.

3. For filling, combine the sugar, flour and salt in a small saucepan. Stir in half-and-half until smooth; add butter. Bring to a boil; cook and stir for 2 minutes or until thickened. Remove from heat; stir in vanilla and pecans. Cool. Spread between cake layers.

4. In a chilled large bowl, beat whipping cream until soft peaks form. Gradually beat in the confectioners' sugar, a tablespoon at a time, until stiff peaks form. Spread over the top and sides of the cake. Store in the refrigerator. **Yield:** 12-16 servings.

Martha Washington Pies

Prep: 30 min. **Bake:** 25 min. + standing

- 4 egg whites
- 1/4 teaspoon cream of tartar
- 1 cup plus 1 tablespoon sugar, *divided*
- 1 cup finely chopped pecans
- 1/2 cup crushed saltines (about 12 crackers)
- 1 teaspoon vanilla extract
- 6 cups sliced fresh strawberries
- 2/3 cup reduced-fat whipped topping

1. In a large bowl, beat the egg whites and cream of tartar on medium speed until soft peaks form. Gradually beat in 1 cup sugar, 2 tablespoons at a time, on high until stiff glossy peaks form and the sugar is dissolved.

2. Fold in the nuts, crackers and vanilla. Drop by rounded 1/3 cupfuls onto parchment-lined baking sheets. Shape into 3-1/2-in. rounds with the back of a spoon.

3. Bake at 300° for 25-30 minutes or until set. Turn oven off; leave in oven with door closed for 2 hours. Toss strawberries with the remaining sugar; spoon 2/3 cup into each shell. Dollop each with whipped topping. **Yield:** 18 servings.

GINGER CLARK HINESVILLE, GEORGIA

My mother handed down this fun recipe for individual miniature pies. It calls for topping the nutty meringues with strawberries, but I often use peaches during the summer. A dollop of whipped topping is the perfect finishing touch.

Grand Prize Winner

2 cups all-purpose flour
2 cups sugar
1/2 cup baking cocoa
1 teaspoon baking soda
1/2 teaspoon salt
4 eggs
1-1/4 cups canola oil
3 cups finely shredded carrots
FROSTING:
1 package (8 ounces) cream cheese, softened
1/2 cup butter, softened
3-3/4 cups confectioners' sugar
1/4 cup baking cocoa
3 teaspoons vanilla extract
1/4 cup chopped walnuts
1/4 cup semisweet chocolate chips

🎀 🎀 🎀
Chocolate Carrot Cake

Prep: 35 min. **Bake:** 25 min. + cooling

Pamela Brown, Williamsburg, Michigan

Finely shredding the carrots gives this rich layer cake an especially nice texture. It's topped with a homemade cream-cheese frosting, then sprinkled with walnuts and chocolate chips.

1. Line two 9-in. round baking pans with waxed paper; grease the paper and set aside. In a large bowl, combine the flour, sugar, cocoa, baking soda and salt. Add the eggs, oil and carrots; beat until combined. Pour into prepared pans.

2. Bake at 350° for 25-30 minutes or until a toothpick inserted near the center comes out clean. Cool for 10 minutes before removing from pans to wire racks to cool completely.

3. For frosting, in a large bowl, beat cream cheese and butter until fluffy. Beat in confectioners' sugar, cocoa and vanilla until smooth.

4. Place the bottom layer on a serving plate; top with half of the frosting. Repeat with the remaining cake layer. Sprinkle with nuts and chocolate chips. **Yield:** 12-16 servings.

🎀 🎀 🎀
Grapefruit Pie

Prep: 25 min. + cooling

Debbie Phillips, Pittsburg, Texas

Grapefruit may be an unusual filling for a pie, but this surprising dessert has been a hit at our house for years. The sweet marshmallows and coconut balance out the fruit's tartness.

32 large marshmallows
1/2 cup grapefruit juice, *divided*
3 large red grapefruit
1 cup heavy whipping cream, whipped
1 pastry shell (9 inches), baked
1/4 cup flaked coconut, toasted

1. In a heavy saucepan, combine the marshmallows and 1/4 cup grapefruit juice. Cook and stir over low heat until marshmallows are melted. Cool to room temperature.

2. Peel the grapefruit and cut into sections (about 2-1/2 cups). Stir the grapefruit, whipped cream and remaining grapefruit juice into the marshmallow mixture. Pour into crust. Sprinkle with the coconut. Refrigerate for 3 hours or until set. **Yield:** 6-8 servings.

Upside-Down Apple Pie

Prep: 30 min. + chilling **Bake:** 50 min. + cooling

Susan Frisch, Germansville, Pennsylvania

This drizzled pie has won eight ribbons at area fairs. People say it looks and tastes like a giant apple-cinnamon bun! I take time off from work during the holiday season to fill requests for it from family and friends.

    2 cups all-purpose flour
1/2 teaspoon salt
    6 tablespoons shortening
    2 tablespoons cold butter
    5 to 7 tablespoons orange juice
FILLING:
    6 tablespoons butter, melted, *divided*
1/2 cup packed brown sugar
1/2 cup chopped pecans
    1 cup sugar
1/3 cup all-purpose flour
3/4 teaspoon ground cinnamon
1/4 teaspoon ground nutmeg
    8 cups thinly sliced peeled Golden Delicious
        apples (about 1/8 inch thick)
GLAZE:
1/2 cup confectioners' sugar
    2 to 3 teaspoons orange juice

1. In a large bowl, combine the flour and salt; cut in shortening and butter until crumbly. Gradually add the orange juice, tossing with a fork until dough forms a ball. Divide dough into two balls. Wrap in plastic wrap; refrigerate for at least 30 minutes.

2. Line a 9-in. deep-dish pie plate with heavy-duty foil, leaving 1-1/2 in. beyond edge; coat the foil with cooking spray. Combine 4 tablespoons butter, brown sugar and pecans; spoon into prepared pie plate.

3. In a large bowl, combine the sugar, flour, cinnamon, nutmeg, apples and the remaining butter; toss gently.

4. On waxed paper, roll out one ball of pastry to fit the pie plate. Place the pastry over the nut mixture, pressing firmly against the mixture and sides of plate; trim to 1 in. beyond the plate edge. Fill with the apple mixture.

5. Roll out the remaining pastry to fit top of pie; place over filling. Trim to 1/4 in. beyond plate edge. Fold bottom pastry over top pastry; seal and flute edges. Cut four 1-in. slits in top pastry.

6. Bake at 375° for 20 minutes. Cover edges loosely with foil. Bake 30 minutes longer or until apples are tender and crust is golden brown.

7. Cool for 15 minutes on a wire rack. Invert onto a serving platter; carefully remove foil. Combine glaze ingredients; drizzle over pie. **Yield:** 6-8 servings.

❀❀❀
Sunflower Potluck Cake

Prep: 25 min. **Bake:** 25 min. + cooling

Lola Horton Wiemer, Clarklake, Michigan

I first saw a cake like this at a picnic…and never found out who made it. Afterward, I created my own variation at home. I love seeing people's eyes light up when I serve it.

- 3/4 cup butter, softened
- 1-2/3 cups sugar
- 3 eggs
- 1 teaspoon vanilla extract
- 2 cups all-purpose flour
- 2/3 cups baking cocoa
- 1-1/4 teaspoons baking soda
- 1 teaspoon salt
- 1/4 teaspoon baking powder
- 1-1/3 cups water
- 1 cup prepared chocolate frosting, *divided*
- 1 cup (6 ounces) semisweet chocolate chips
- 22 individual cream-filled sponge cakes
- 1 teaspoon milk
- 2 craft decorating bees, optional

1. In a large bowl, cream butter and sugar until light and fluffy. Add eggs, one at a time, beating well after each addition. Beat in vanilla. Combine dry ingredients; gradually add to the creamed mixture alternately with water, beating well after each addition. Pour into two greased and floured 9-in. round baking pans.

2. Bake at 350° for 25-30 minutes or until a toothpick inserted near the center comes out clean. Cool in pans for 10 minutes before removing to wire racks to cool completely.

3. Freeze one layer for future use. Set aside 1 tablespoon frosting. Frost top and sides of remaining cake.

4. Place cake in the center of a large round tray (about 18 in.) Arrange chocolate chips on top of cake. Place sponge cakes around cake. Mix reserved frosting with milk; drizzle over sponge cakes. Decorate with bees if desired. **Yield:** 22 servings.

❀❀❀
Ricotta Nut Pie

Prep: 20 min. + chilling **Bake:** 10 min. + cooling

Renee Bennett, Manlius, New York

I'm always proud to serve this to family and guests. It's similar to a traditional Italian ricotta pie but has a few fun twists.

- 1-1/2 cups crushed vanilla wafers (about 45 wafers)
- 1/2 cup butter, softened
- 1/4 cup apricot preserves
- 1 carton (15 ounces) ricotta cheese
- 1/2 cup sugar
- 1 teaspoon vanilla extract
- 3 ounces semisweet chocolate, chopped
- 1/2 cup finely chopped toasted almonds
- 1/4 cup chopped dried apricots
- 1 cup heavy whipping cream, whipped
- 1/4 cup slivered almonds, toasted

1. In a small bowl, combine wafer crumbs and butter; press onto the bottom and up the sides of an ungreased 9-in. pie plate.

2. Bake at 375° for 6-8 minutes or until the crust is lightly browned; cool on a wire rack. Spread the preserves over crust.

3. In a large bowl, beat the ricotta, sugar and vanilla until smooth. Stir in the chocolate, chopped almonds and apricots. Fold in whipped cream. Spoon into the crust. Sprinkle with the slivered almonds. Cover and refrigerate overnight. **Yield:** 6-8 servings.

🎀🎀🎀
Peanut Butter Pie

Prep: 25 min. + chilling

Lillibell Welter, Rainier, Oregon

Although I make this fudgy peanut butter pie regularly for luncheons at our church, I have yet to eat a full piece. There's usually nothing left for me to take home but crumbs!

- 1 package (8 ounces) cream cheese, softened
- 1 cup plus 2 tablespoons creamy peanut butter, *divided*
- 1/2 cup sugar
- 1 carton (12 ounces) frozen whipped topping, thawed, *divided*
- 1 chocolate crumb crust (8 inches)
- 2/3 cup plus 2 tablespoons hot fudge ice cream topping, *divided*

1. In a large bowl, beat cream cheese until smooth. Beat in 1 cup peanut butter and sugar. Fold in 3 cups whipped topping; spoon into crust.

2. In a microwave-safe bowl, heat 2/3 cup hot fudge topping for 30 seconds. Pour over peanut butter layer and spread to edges of crust. Refrigerate for 2 hours.

3. Spread remaining whipped topping over pie. Cut into slices. Place the remaining hot fudge topping and peanut butter in two separate plastic bags. Cut a small hole in corner of each bag; pipe topping and peanut butter over each slice of pie. **Yield:** 8 servings.

🎀🎀🎀
Caramel Apple Cake

Prep: 25 min. **Bake:** 45 min. + cooling

Paulette Reyenga, Brantford, Ontario

The bounty of apples we got at a local orchard one year inspired me to adjust a recipe I'd seen and create this dessert. The topping adds yummy caramel flavor to the moist cake.

- 1/2 cup chopped walnuts
- 1/3 cup packed brown sugar
- 1 cup flaked coconut
- 2-1/2 cups all-purpose flour
- 1-1/2 cups sugar
- 1-1/2 teaspoons baking soda
- 1 teaspoon salt
- 1/2 teaspoon baking powder
- 1/4 teaspoon ground cinnamon
- 2 eggs
- 1/2 cup evaporated milk
- 1/2 cup water
- 2 cups finely shredded peeled apples
- CARAMEL TOPPING:
- 1/3 cup packed brown sugar
- 1/4 cup evaporated milk
- 2 tablespoons butter

1. In a small bowl, combine the walnuts, brown sugar and coconut; set aside. In another bowl, combine the next six ingredients.

2. In a small bowl, whisk the eggs, milk, water and apples. Stir into dry ingredients just until moistened.

3. Pour into a greased 13-in. x 9-in. baking dish. Sprinkle with nut mixture. Bake at 325° for 45-50 minutes or until a toothpick inserted near the center comes out clean.

4. Meanwhile, in a heavy saucepan, combine the topping ingredients; cook over medium heat until the sugar is dissolved and the mixture has thickened slightly, about 8 minutes, stirring constantly.

5. Poke holes with a fork in the top of the hot cake; immediately spoon the topping over cake. Cool completely on a wire rack. **Yield:** 12-15 servings.

3 egg whites
1/4 teaspoon cream of tartar
1-1/2 cups sugar, *divided*
4 egg yolks
3 tablespoons lemon juice
1 tablespoon grated lemon peel
1/8 teaspoon salt
2 cups heavy whipping cream, whipped

1. Place egg whites in a small bowl; let stand at room temperature for 30 minutes. Add cream of tartar; beat until soft peaks form. Gradually add 1 cup of sugar, 1 tablespoon at a time, beating until stiff peaks form. Spread onto the bottom and up the sides of a greased 9-in. pie plate. Bake at 350° for 25-30 minutes. Cool on a wire rack.

2. In a large saucepan, combine egg yolks, lemon juice, peel, salt and remaining sugar. Cook and stir over medium heat until mixture reaches 160° or is thick enough to coat the back of a metal spoon. Reduce heat; cook and stir 2 minutes longer. Remove from the heat. Cool to room temperature without stirring.

3. Fold half of the whipped cream into lemon filling; spread into meringue shell. Top with remaining whipped cream. Refrigerate leftovers. **Yield:** 6-8 servings.

🎀 🎀 🎀
Lemon Pie in Meringue Shell

Prep: 25 min. + standing
Bake: 25 min. + cooling

Carol Mumford, Casstown, Ohio

This delightful pie is a part of all of our family's get-togethers. I usually prepare it the day before and refrigerate it overnight.

White Chocolate Mousse Cherry Pie

Prep: 1 hour   **Bake:** 15 min. + chilling

14 cream-filled chocolate sandwich cookies
3/4 cup chopped macadamia nuts
2 tablespoons butter, melted
FILLING:
1 tablespoon cornstarch
2 tablespoons water
1 can (21 ounces) cherry pie filling
1/2 teaspoon almond extract
WHITE CHOCOLATE MOUSSE:
1 cup cold milk
1 package (3.3 ounces) instant white chocolate pudding mix
1 envelope unflavored gelatin
3 cups heavy whipping cream, *divided*
1/4 cup sugar
1/4 teaspoon almond extract
Chocolate curls and chocolate ice cream topping, optional

1. In a food processor, combine cookies and nuts; cover and process until cookies are finely chopped. Add butter; cover and pulse until mixture resembles coarse crumbs. Press onto the bottom and up the sides of an ungreased 9-in. deep-dish pie plate.

Bake at 350° for 8-10 minutes or until set. Cool on a wire rack.

2. For filling, combine cornstarch and water in a small saucepan until smooth. Stir in pie filling. Bring to a boil; cook and stir for 1 minute or until slightly thickened. Remove from the heat; stir in extract. Cool completely.

3. For mousse, in a large bowl, whisk milk and pudding mix for 2 minutes. Let stand for 2 minutes or until soft-set; set aside. In a small saucepan, sprinkle gelatin over 1/2 cup cream; let stand for 1 minute. Heat over low heat, stirring until gelatin is completely dissolved. Remove from the heat.

4. In a large bowl, beat remaining cream until it begins to thicken. Add the sugar and extract; beat until soft peaks form. Gradually beat in gelatin mixture. Fold into the pudding. Refrigerate until slightly firm, about 30 minutes.

5. Spread cooled filling into crust; top with mousse. Refrigerate for 2 hours or until firm. Garnish with chocolate curls and chocolate topping if desired. **Yield:** 8-10 servings.

BERNICE JANOWSKI STEVENS POINT, WISCONSIN

A homemade cookie crust is topped with a cherry-almond filling and light-as-air mousse in this delectable dessert. It makes any dinner extra special. For an elegant finish, garnish the pie with chocolate curls and a chocolate drizzle.

Grand Prize Winner

★★★
Chocolate Potato Cake

Prep: 40 min. **Bake:** 25 min. + cooling

Catherine Hahn, Winamac, Indiana

I was thrilled when I won grand champion honors in a potato festival baking contest with this moist chocolate cake.

- 1 **cup butter, softened**
- 2 **cups sugar**
- 2 **eggs**
- 1 **cup cold mashed potatoes (without added milk and butter)**
- 1 **teaspoon vanilla extract**

- 2 **cups all-purpose flour**
- 1/2 **cup baking cocoa**
- 1 **teaspoon baking soda**
- 1 **cup milk**
- 1 **cup chopped walnuts** *or* **pecans**

CARAMEL ICING:
- 1/2 **cup butter, cubed**
- 1 **cup packed brown sugar**
- 1/4 **cup evaporated milk**
- 2 **cups confectioners' sugar**
- 1/2 **teaspoon vanilla extract**

1. In a large bowl, cream butter and sugar until light and fluffy. Add eggs, one at a time, beating well after each addition. Add potatoes and vanilla. Combine the flour, cocoa and baking soda; gradually add to creamed mixture alternately with milk, beating well after each addition. Stir in nuts.

2. Pour mixture into two greased and floured 9-in. round baking pans. Bake at 350° for 25-30 minutes or until a toothpick inserted near the center comes out clean. Cool for 10 minutes before removing from pans to wire racks to cool completely.

3. For icing, in a saucepan over low heat, cook butter and brown sugar until butter is melted and mixture is smooth. Stir in the evaporated milk; bring to a boil, stirring constantly. Remove from the heat; cool to room temperature. Stir in confectioners' sugar and vanilla until smooth. Spread between layers and over top of cake. **Yield:** 10-12 servings.

★★★
Mud Pie

Prep: 15 min. + chilling

Deboraha Woolard, Las Vegas, Nevada

I fell in love when I tasted this layered chocolate pie filled with chopped pecans. It's not only scrumptious, but it also takes only 15 minutes to assemble using basic ingredients. Then you just pop it in the refrigerator until serving time.

- 3 **ounces semisweet chocolate, chopped**
- 1/4 **cup sweetened condensed milk**
- 1 **chocolate crumb crust (8 inches)**
- 1/2 **cup chopped pecans**
- 2 **cups cold milk**
- 2 **packages (3.9 ounces** *each***) instant chocolate pudding mix**
- 1 **carton (8 ounces) frozen whipped topping, thawed,** *divided*

1. In a microwave, melt chocolate; stir in sweetened condensed milk until smooth. Pour into the crust and sprinkle with pecans.

2. In a small bowl, whisk milk and pudding mixes for 2 minutes. Let stand for 2 minutes or until soft-set. Carefully spread 1-1/2 cups of pudding mixture over the pecans.

3. Fold 1/2 cup whipped topping into the remaining pudding mixture; spoon over the pudding layer. Top with the remaining whipped topping. Chill until set. Refrigerate leftovers. **Yield:** 8 servings.

🎀🎀🎀 Eggnog Cranberry Pie

Prep: 40 min. + chilling

Mrs. Ruth White, Bedford, Ohio

With a creamy eggnog layer on top of tangy cranberries, this elegant pie "says" the Christmas holiday season in every bite.

- 1/2 cup sugar
- 1 tablespoon cornstarch
- 6 tablespoons cold water, *divided*
- 2 cups fresh *or* frozen cranberries
- 1 pastry shell (9 inches), baked
- 1 tablespoon unflavored gelatin
- 1-3/4 cups eggnog
- 2 tablespoons rum *or* 1 teaspoon rum extract
- 1/2 cup heavy whipping cream, whipped
- 1/8 teaspoon ground nutmeg

1. In a large saucepan, combine the sugar, cornstarch and 2 tablespoons cold water until smooth; stir in the cranberries. Cook over medium heat for 5 minutes or until thickened, stirring occasionally. Cool for 15 minutes. Pour into pastry shell; set aside.

2. In a small saucepan, sprinkle gelatin over remaining water; let stand for 5 minutes. Cook and stir over low heat, stirring until gelatin is completely dissolved. Gradually stir in eggnog and rum.

3. Refrigerate for 5 minutes or until slightly thickened, stirring occasionally. Fold in whipped cream; pour over cranberry layer. Refrigerate for 2 hours or until set. Sprinkle with nutmeg. **Yield:** 6-8 servings.

Editor's Note: This recipe was tested with commercially prepared eggnog.

🎀🎀🎀 Layered Carrot Cake

Prep: 50 min. **Bake:** 30 min. + cooling

Anna Morgan, Eatonville, Washington

I never liked carrot cake until I tried this one. Rich and moist with an orange-flavored frosting, it's now a family tradition.

- 1 package (18-1/4 ounces) yellow cake mix
- 1 package (3.4 ounces) instant vanilla pudding mix
- 2 teaspoons ground cinnamon
- 4 eggs
- 2/3 cup orange juice
- 1/2 cup canola oil
- 3 cups grated carrots
- 1/2 cup raisins
- 1/2 cup chopped walnuts

ORANGE CREAM CHEESE FROSTING:

- 1 package (8 ounces) cream cheese, softened
- 1/2 cup butter, softened
- 3 cups confectioners' sugar
- 1 to 2 tablespoons orange juice
- 1 tablespoon grated orange peel

1. In a large bowl, combine the cake mix, pudding mix and cinnamon. Whisk the eggs, orange juice and oil; add to dry ingredients. Beat until well blended. Stir in the carrots, raisins and nuts (batter will be thick).

2. Pour batter into two greased and floured 9-in. round baking pans. Bake at 350° for 30-35 minutes or until a toothpick inserted near the center comes out clean. Cool for 10 minutes before removing from pans to wire racks to cool completely.

3. For frosting, in a large bowl, beat cream cheese and butter until fluffy. Add confectioners' sugar, orange juice and peel; beat until smooth. Spread the frosting between layers and over top and sides of cake. Store in the refrigerator. **Yield:** 12-14 servings.

🎀🎀🎀
Triple-Layer Lemon Cake

Prep: 30 min. + chilling **Bake:** 20 min. + cooling

Connie Jurjevich, Atmore, Alabama

A smooth, silky citrus filling separates the three layers of this lemon cake. It's a homemade favorite my friends and family never tire of. Serve it after a special spring or summer dinner.

2 cups sugar
3/4 cup canola oil
4 eggs, *separated*
1 teaspoon vanilla extract
3 cups all-purpose flour
3 teaspoons baking powder
1/4 teaspoon salt
1 cup milk
FILLING:
3/4 cup sugar
2 tablespoons cornstarch
1/8 teaspoon salt
1/2 cup water
1 egg, lightly beaten
1/3 cup lemon juice
1-1/2 teaspoons grated lemon peel
1 tablespoon butter, softened
FROSTING:
1 cup butter, softened
6 cups confectioners' sugar
2 tablespoons lemon juice
1 teaspoon grated lemon peel
4 to 6 tablespoons heavy whipping cream

1. In a large bowl, beat sugar and oil. Add egg yolks and vanilla; beat well. Combine dry ingredients; add to sugar mixture alternately with milk. In a large bowl, beat egg whites until stiff peaks form; fold into batter.

2. Pour batter into three greased and waxed paper-lined 9-in. round baking pans. Bake at 350° for 20-25 minutes or until a toothpick comes out clean. Cool for 10 minutes; remove to wire racks to cool.

3. For filling, in a large saucepan, combine the sugar, cornstarch and salt. Stir in water until smooth. Cook and stir over medium-high heat until thickened and bubbly. Reduce heat; cook and stir 2 minutes longer. Remove from heat. Stir a small amount of hot filling into the egg; return all to the pan, stirring constantly. Bring to a gentle boil; cook and stir 2 minutes longer. Remove from the heat. Gently stir in lemon juice, peel and butter. Cool to room temperature without stirring. Cover and refrigerate.

4. In a large bowl, combine the butter, confectioners' sugar, lemon juice, peel and enough cream to achieve desired spreading consistency. Spread filling between the cake layers. Frost top and sides of cake. Store in the refrigerator. **Yield:** 12-14 servings.

🎀🎀🎀
Grasshopper Pie

Prep: 45 min. + chilling

Sally Vandermus, Rochester, Minnesota

After a hearty dinner, this refreshing chocolate-and-mint pie always hits the spot. I make it at Christmastime and whenever my son comes to visit. He loves it with sweet cherries on top.

- 2/3 cup semisweet chocolate chips
- 2 tablespoons heavy whipping cream
- 2 teaspoons shortening
- 1 cup finely chopped walnuts

FILLING:
- 35 large marshmallows
- 1/4 cup milk
- 1/4 teaspoon salt
- 3 tablespoons green creme de menthe
- 3 tablespoons clear creme de cacao
- 1-1/2 cups heavy whipping cream, whipped
- Chocolate curls, optional

1. Line a 9-in. pie plate with foil; set aside. In a large heavy saucepan, combine the chocolate chips, cream and shortening; cook over low heat until chips are melted. Stir in walnuts. Pour into the prepared pie plate; spread evenly over the bottom and sides of plate. Refrigerate for 1 hour or until set.

2. In a large heavy saucepan, combine the marshmallows, milk and salt; cook over low heat until marshmallows are melted, stirring occasionally. Remove from the heat; stir in the creme de menthe and creme de cacao. Refrigerate for 1 hour or until slightly thickened.

3. Carefully remove the foil from chocolate crust and return crust to pie plate. Fold whipped cream into filling; pour into crust. Refrigerate overnight. Garnish with chocolate curls if desired. **Yield:** 6-8 servings.

🎀🎀🎀
Chock-full of Fruit Snackin' Cake

Prep: 15 min. **Bake:** 40 min. + cooling

Sami Taylor, Hermiston, Oregon

This yummy snack cake is loaded with wholesome ingredients, including apples, carrots, raisins, dried cranberries and walnuts.

- 2 cups all-purpose flour
- 2 cups quick-cooking oats
- Sugar substitute equivalent to 1-1/2 cups sugar
- 2-3/4 teaspoons baking powder
- 1/4 teaspoon baking soda
- 1/8 teaspoon salt
- 3 eggs
- 1 cup orange juice
- 1/3 cup canola oil
- 2 large carrots, shredded
- 2 medium apples, peeled and shredded
- 1 cup raisins
- 1 cup dried cranberries
- 1 cup chopped walnuts

1. In a large bowl, combine the first six ingredients. Whisk the eggs, orange juice and oil and stir into the dry ingredients just until moistened. Fold in the remaining ingredients.

2. Pour into a 13-in. x 9-in. baking dish coated with cooking spray. Bake at 350° for 40-45 minutes or until a toothpick inserted near the center comes out clean. Cool on a wire rack. Cut the cake into squares. **Yield:** 18 servings.

Editor's Note: This recipe was tested with Splenda No Calorie Sweetener. Look for it in the baking aisle of your grocery store.

FILLING:
  1 **cup heavy whipping cream**
  1 **tablespoon sugar**
  3 **tablespoons lemon curd**
  2 **cups chopped fresh strawberries**

1. In a large bowl, beat the egg yolks, eggs and sugar until thick and lemon-colored. Beat in the water, oil and vanilla. Combine flour, baking powder and salt; gradually add to egg mixture. Grease a 15-in. x 10-in. x 1-in. baking pan and line with waxed paper; grease and flour the paper. Spread batter into pan.

2. Bake at 375° for 10-12 minutes or until cake springs back when lightly touched. Cool for 5 minutes. Turn onto a kitchen towel dusted with confectioners' sugar. Peel off waxed paper. Roll up cake in towel jelly-roll style, starting with a short side. Cool on a wire rack.

3. In a large bowl, beat cream until soft peaks form; gradually add sugar, beating until stiff peaks form. Fold in lemon curd; gradually fold in strawberries.

4. Unroll cake; spread filling evenly to within 1/2 in. of edges. Roll up again; dust with confectioners' sugar. Cover and chill cake for 1 hour before serving. Refrigerate leftovers. **Yield:** 8 servings.

🎗🎗🎗
Berry Pinwheel Cake

Prep: 30 min. **Bake:** 10 min. + chilling

Becky Ruff, McGregor, Iowa

When you want to use fresh strawberries for something other than pie or shortcake, try this lovely chiffon cake. Even if you've never made a jelly-roll-style dessert before, it's easy to make.

  4 **egg yolks**
  2 **eggs**
  1/2 **cup sugar**
4-1/2 **teaspoons water**
  2 **teaspoons canola oil**
  1 **teaspoon vanilla extract**
  1 **cup cake flour**
  1 **teaspoon baking powder**
  1/2 **teaspoon salt**
Confectioners' sugar

Tangy Tip

Lemon curd adds a twist of citrus to this yummy cake. Commercially prepared lemon curd is available in larger grocery stores alongside the jams and jellies or with the baking supplies.

Cranberry Pear Pie

Prep: 20 min. **Bake:** 50 min. + cooling

Pastry for single-crust pie (9 inches)
  2 **tablespoons all-purpose flour**
  1/2 **cup maple syrup**
  2 **tablespoons butter, melted**
  5 **cups sliced peeled fresh pears**
  1 **cup fresh or frozen cranberries**
TOPPING:
  1/2 **cup all-purpose flour**
  1/4 **cup packed brown sugar**
  1 **teaspoon ground cinnamon**
  1/3 **cup cold butter, cubed**
  1/2 **cup chopped walnuts**

1. Line a 9-in. pie plate with pastry; trim and flute edges. Set aside. In a large bowl, combine the flour, syrup and butter until smooth. Add the pears and cranberries; toss to coat. Spoon into crust.

2. For topping, combine the flour, brown sugar and cinnamon; cut in butter until crumbly. Stir in the walnuts. Sprinkle over filling.

3. Cover the edges of the crust loosely with foil to prevent overbrowning. Bake at 400° for 15 minutes. Reduce heat to 350°. Remove foil; bake 35-40 minutes longer or until crust is golden brown and filling is bubbly. Cool on a wire rack. **Yield:** 6-8 servings.

HELEN TOULANTIS WANTAGH, NEW YORK

When our family is invited to holiday gatherings, this scrumptious pie usually comes with us. The recipe is very versatile—you can make it with a double crust or replace the pears with baking apples. Serve oven-warmed slices with vanilla ice cream.

Grand
Prize
Winner

Caramel Apple Cream Pie

Prep: 30 min. + chilling **Bake:** 35 min. + cooling

Lisa DiNuccio, Boxford, Massachusetts

When I first made this pie for my family, their reactions were "Ooh!" and "Mmm!" I created the recipe to enter at a local fair. My goal was to come up with an apple pie like no other, and it ended up winning third prize.

- 1 pastry shell (9 inches)
- 1/4 cup butter, cubed
- 1/2 cup packed brown sugar
- 4 medium tart apples, peeled and cut into 1/2-inch chunks
- 1-1/2 teaspoons pumpkin pie spice, *divided*
- 1 to 2 tablespoons all-purpose flour
- 1/2 cup caramel ice cream topping
- 1/2 cup chopped pecans
- 1 package (8 ounces) cream cheese, softened
- 1/4 cup sugar
- 1 egg
- 1 tablespoon lemon juice
- 1 teaspoon vanilla extract
- Whipped topping

1. Line unpricked pastry shell with a double thickness of heavy-duty foil. Bake at 450° for 8 minutes. Remove foil; bake 5 minutes longer. Cool on a wire rack.

2. In a large skillet over medium heat, melt butter and brown sugar. Stir in apples and 1 teaspoon pumpkin pie spice; simmer for 12-15 minutes, stirring frequently, or until tender.

3. Stir in flour; cook and stir for 1 minute. Drizzle caramel topping over pastry shell; sprinkle with pecans. Spoon apple mixture over pecans; set aside.

4. In a large bowl, beat cream cheese, sugar, egg, lemon juice and vanilla until smooth. Pour over the apples. Bake at 350° for 35-45 minutes or until a knife inserted into the cream cheese layer comes out clean.

5. Cool on a wire rack. Chill thoroughly. To serve, top with dollops of whipped topping; sprinkle with the remaining pumpkin pie spice. **Yield:** 8 servings.

Frozen Strawberry Pie

Prep: 25 min. + freezing

Awynne Thurstenson, Siloam Springs, Arkansas

This convenient recipe makes two yummy, attractive pies using store-bought chocolate crumb crusts. I serve each slice with a dollop of whipped cream, a strawberry and chocolate curls.

- 1 package (8 ounces) cream cheese, softened
- 1 cup sugar
- 1 teaspoon vanilla extract
- 4 cups chopped fresh strawberries
- 1 carton (12 ounces) frozen whipped topping, thawed
- 1/2 cup chopped pecans, toasted
- 2 chocolate crumb crusts (9 inches)

1. In a large bowl, beat the cream cheese, sugar and vanilla until smooth. Beat in the strawberries. Fold in the whipped topping and pecans. Pour into crusts.

2. Cover; freeze for 3-4 hours or until firm. Remove from the freezer 15-20 minutes before serving. **Yield:** 2 pies (6 servings each).

🎗🎗🎗
Chocolate Raspberry Pie

Prep: 30 min. + chilling **Bake:** 15 min. + cooling

Ruth Bartel, Morris, Manitoba

After tasting this heavenly pie at my sister-in-law's house, I just had to have the recipe. The smooth chocolate and tangy raspberry layers are separated by a rich cream-cheese filling.

- 1 unbaked pastry shell (9 inches)
- 3 tablespoons sugar
- 1 tablespoon cornstarch
- 2 cups fresh or frozen unsweetened raspberries, thawed

FILLING:
- 1 package (8 ounces) cream cheese, softened
- 1/3 cup sugar
- 1/2 teaspoon vanilla extract
- 1/2 cup heavy whipping cream, whipped

TOPPING:
- 2 ounces semisweet chocolate
- 3 tablespoons butter

1. Line unpricked pastry shell with a double thickness of heavy-duty foil. Bake at 450° for 8 minutes. Remove foil; bake 5 minutes longer. Cool on a wire rack.

2. In a large saucepan, combine sugar and cornstarch. Stir in the raspberries; bring to a boil over medium heat. Boil and stir for 2 minutes. Remove from heat; cool for 15 minutes. Spread into shell; refrigerate.

3. In a large bowl, beat the cream cheese, sugar and vanilla until fluffy. Fold in whipped cream. Carefully spread over raspberry layer. Cover and refrigerate for at least 1 hour.

4. In a microwave, melt chocolate and butter; stir until smooth. Cool for 4-5 minutes. Pour over filling. Cover; chill for at least 2 hours. Store in refrigerator. **Yield:** 6-8 servings.

🎗🎗🎗
Peachy Rhubarb Pie

Prep: 15 min. **Bake:** 1 hour

Phyllis Galloway, Roswell, Georgia

We have an abundance of rhubarb in our garden, so I save every recipe for it that I can find. My husband especially loves this pretty pie, which adds the mellow sweetness of peaches.

- 1 can (8-1/2 ounces) sliced peaches
- 2 cups chopped fresh or frozen rhubarb, thawed and drained
- 1 cup sugar
- 1/4 cup flaked coconut
- 3 tablespoons quick-cooking tapioca
- 1 teaspoon vanilla extract

Pastry for double-crust pie (9 inches)
- 1 tablespoon butter

1. Drain peaches, reserving syrup; chop the peaches. Place peaches and syrup in a large bowl. Add the rhubarb, sugar, coconut, tapioca and vanilla; toss to coat. Let stand for 15 minutes.

2. Line a 9-in. pie plate with the bottom crust; trim pastry even with edge. Fill with rhubarb mixture; dot with butter. Roll out remaining pastry; make a lattice crust. Trim, seal and flute edges.

3. Bake at 350° for 1 hour or until crust is golden brown and filling is bubbly. **Yield:** 6-8 servings.

Editor's Note: If using frozen rhubarb, measure rhubarb while still frozen, then thaw completely. Drain in a colander, but do not press liquid out.

Apple Crisp with a Twist, p. 227

Irish Creme Chocolate Trifle, p. 223

Cranberry Cheesecake, p. 219

Just Desserts

Creamy cheesecakes…golden fruit cobblers…rich and elegant tarts…you'll find all of those sweet treats and more in this chapter. So turn here when you need a fabulous finale for holiday feasts, dinner parties, potlucks or anytime at all.

Cran-Apple Crisp 208
Sweet Cherry Cheese Dessert............208
Chocolate Walnut Tart..................209
Strawberry Tartlets............................209
Strawberry Swirl Cheesecake.............210
Caramel Apple Crunch.....................211
Ginger-Lime Pear Cobbler.....................211
Blueberry Cornmeal Cobbler.............212
Apple Crumble 212
Almond Fruit Crisp............................214
Mousse Tarts 214
Cinnamon Roll Cherry Cobbler........215

Miracle Baklava 216
Granola Banana Sticks 217
Pumpkin Torte...............................217
Baked Cherry Pudding......................218
Grilled Apple Crisp..........................218
Cranberry Cheesecake......................219
Carrot Cheesecake............................220
Glazed Apricot Sorbet......................221
Blackberry Cobbler 221
Strawberry Rhubarb Cobbler...............222
Black Forest Cheesecake....................222
Irish Creme Chocolate Trifle..............223
Raspberry Pear Crisp........................223
Double-Berry Crisp 224
Apple Pie in a Goblet.......................224
Strawberry Puff Pastry Dessert............225
Peach Cobbler.................................226
Strawberry Popovers 227
Apple Crisp with a Twist..................227

Strawberry Puff Pastry Dessert, p. 225

2 snack-size cups (4 ounces *each*) vanilla
   pudding
1 cup eggnog
3/4 cup sugar
2 tablespoons all-purpose flour
5 cups thinly sliced peeled tart apples
2 cups fresh *or* frozen cranberries, thawed

TOPPING:

1 cup quick-cooking oats
3/4 cup packed brown sugar
2/3 cup all-purpose flour
1/2 teaspoon ground cinnamon
1/2 cup cold butter, cubed

1. In a small bowl, combine the pudding and eggnog until blended; cover and refrigerate until serving. In a large bowl, combine the sugar and flour. Add apples and cranberries; toss to coat. Transfer to an ungreased 13-in. x 9-in. baking dish.

2. In a large bowl, combine the oats, brown sugar, flour and cinnamon; cut in butter until crumbly. Sprinkle over fruit mixture.

3. Bake at 375° for 35-40 minutes or until the filling is bubbly and the topping is golden brown. Cool for 10 minutes. Serve crisp with the eggnog sauce. **Yield:** 12-14 servings.

Editor's Note: This recipe was tested with commercially prepared eggnog.

🎗️🎗️🎗️

Cran-Apple Crisp

Prep: 30 min. **Bake:** 35 min. + cooling

Mary Lou Timpson, Colorado City, Arizona

An easy eggnog sauce gives this crunchy crisp a distinctive flavor. With that topping plus apples and cranberries, it's a natural choice for Christmas and winter celebrations.

- -

🎗️🎗️🎗️

Sweet Cherry Cheese Dessert

Prep: 30 min. + chilling

Diane Lombardo, New Castle, Pennsylvania

I love the combination of the soft, creamy filling with the crunchy cookie crust in this crowd-pleasing treat. The layer of cherries on top makes for a beautiful presentation.

1/2 cup cold butter, cubed
2-1/2 cups crushed pecan shortbread cookies
2 cans (21 ounces *each*) cherry pie filling
1 teaspoon almond extract
1 teaspoon vanilla extract
1 package (8 ounces) cream cheese, softened
2 cups confectioners' sugar
1 carton (12 ounces) frozen whipped topping,
   thawed

1. In a large bowl, cut butter into crushed cookies until mixture resembles coarse crumbs. Press into an ungreased 13-in. x 9-in. baking pan. Bake at 350° for 15-18 minutes or until crust is lightly browned. Cool on a wire rack.

2. In a large bowl, combine the pie filling and extracts; set aside. In a large bowl, beat the cream cheese and confectioners' sugar until fluffy. Fold in the whipped topping. Spread over crust. Top with filling. Cover and refrigerate for 1-2 hours or until set. **Yield:** 15 servings.

🎗🎗🎗
Chocolate Walnut Tart

Prep: 20 min. **Bake:** 25 min.

Sue Shank, Harrisonburg, Virginia

This elegant dessert looks impressive but is actually simple to prepare in either a 9-inch or 11-inch pan. Slices are wonderful served warm with ice cream or whipped topping.

> 1 sheet refrigerated pie pastry
> 1 cup (6 ounces) semisweet chocolate chips
> 1 cup coarsely chopped walnuts
> 3 eggs, lightly beaten
> 3/4 cup dark corn syrup
> 1/2 cup packed brown sugar
> 1/4 cup butter, melted
> 1 teaspoon vanilla extract
> Whipped cream, optional

1. On a lightly floured surface, roll out pastry to fit an 11-in. fluted tart pan with removable bottom. Transfer pastry to pan; trim edges. Sprinkle with chocolate chips and walnuts. In a small bowl, whisk the eggs, corn syrup, brown sugar, butter and vanilla. Pour over chips and nuts.

2. Bake at 350° for 25-30 minutes or until a knife inserted near the center comes out clean. Cool on a wire rack. Serve with whipped cream if desired. **Yield:** 8-10 servings.

🎗🎗🎗
Strawberry Tartlets

Prep: 25 min. **Bake:** 10 min. + cooling

Joy Van Meter, Thornton, Colorado

Here's a great way to present fresh strawberries when entertaining. The elegant-looking tartlets are a breeze to assemble, and the cute wonton "cups" can be made in advance.

> 12 wonton wrappers
> 3 tablespoons butter, melted
> 1/3 cup packed brown sugar
> 3/4 cup Mascarpone cheese
> 2 tablespoons honey
> 2 teaspoons orange juice
> 3 cups fresh strawberries, sliced
> Whipped cream and fresh mint, optional

1. Brush one side of each wonton wrapper with the butter. Place brown sugar in a shallow bowl; press buttered side of wontons into the sugar to coat. Press wontons sugared side up into greased muffin cups.

2. Bake at 325° for 7-9 minutes or until the edges are lightly browned. Remove to a wire rack to cool.

3. In a small bowl, combine the cheese, honey and orange juice. Spoon about 1 tablespoon into each wonton cup. Top with strawberries. Garnish with whipped cream and mint if desired. **Yield:** 1 dozen.

Hulling How-To

Use a strawberry huller or the tip of a serrated grapefruit spoon to easily remove a berry's stem/hull. Just insert the spoon's tip into the berry next to the stem and cut around the stem.

Strawberry Swirl Cheesecake

Prep: 1 hour **Bake:** 1-1/4 hours + chilling

Mary Ellen Friend, Ravenswood, West Virginia

This doubly delightful cheesecake features two creamy layers— one strawberry, one vanilla. To avoid cracking, run the knife through just the very top when swirling the berry puree.

1-1/4 **cups all-purpose flour**
   1 **tablespoon sugar**
   1 **teaspoon grated lemon peel**
 1/2 **cup cold butter**

FILLING:
   4 **packages (8 ounces *each*) cream cheese, softened**
1-1/3 **cups sugar**
   2 **tablespoons all-purpose flour**
   2 **tablespoons heavy whipping cream**
   4 **eggs, lightly beaten**
   1 **tablespoon lemon juice**
   2 **teaspoons vanilla extract**
   1 **cup pureed fresh strawberries, *divided***
 8 to 10 **drops red food coloring, optional**

1. In a small bowl, combine flour, sugar and lemon peel; cut in butter until crumbly. Pat dough onto bottom and 1 in. up the sides of a greased 9-in. springform pan. Place on a baking sheet. Bake at 325° for 15-20 minutes or until lightly browned. Cool on a wire rack.

2. In a large bowl, beat the cream cheese, sugar, flour and cream until smooth. Add eggs; beat on low speed just until combined. Beat in lemon juice and vanilla just until blended. Pour 2-1/2 cups batter into a bowl; set aside.

3. Stir 3/4 cup pureed strawberries and food coloring if desired into remaining batter. Pour into crust. Place pan on a double thickness of heavy-duty foil (about 16 in. square). Securely wrap foil around pan. Place in a large baking pan. Add 1 in. of hot water to larger pan. Bake for 35 minutes.

4. Carefully pour reserved batter over bottom layer. Spoon the remaining berries over batter in three concentric circles. Carefully cut through only the top layer with a knife to swirl. Bake 40-50 minutes longer or until center is almost set. Remove pan from water bath. Cool on a wire rack for 10 minutes. Carefully run a knife around edge of pan to loosen; cool 1 hour longer. Refrigerate overnight. **Yield:** 12 servings.

🏅🏅🏅
Caramel Apple Crunch

Prep: 25 min. **Bake:** 45 min. + cooling

Melissa Williams, Peoria, Illinois

I combined the ingredients from various crisp recipes to create this nutty, fall-flavored version. The sweetness of the caramels perfectly balances out the tart apples.

      8 cups sliced peeled tart apples
     33 caramels, *divided*
      2 tablespoons plus 2 teaspoons milk, *divided*
    3/4 cup all-purpose flour
    3/4 cup quick-cooking oats
    3/4 cup packed brown sugar
    1/2 cup chopped walnuts
    1/8 teaspoon salt
Dash ground cinnamon
    1/2 cup cold butter, cubed
Vanilla ice cream, optional

1. Place the apples in a greased 13-in. x 9-in. baking dish. In a heavy saucepan, melt 25 caramels with 2 tablespoons milk, stirring often; drizzle over apples.

2. In a large bowl, combine the flour, oats, brown sugar, walnuts, salt and cinnamon; cut in the butter

until mixture resembles coarse crumbs. Sprinkle over the apples.

3. Bake at 375° for 45-50 minutes or until golden brown. Cool for 10 minutes. Meanwhile, in a heavy saucepan, melt remaining caramels with remaining milk, stirring often until smooth. Drizzle over dessert and ice cream if desired. **Yield:** 12-16 servings.

🏅🏅🏅
Ginger-Lime Pear Cobbler

Prep: 25 min. **Bake:** 50 min. + cooling

Heather Naas, Lompoc, California

We have a huge pear tree in our yard, and the abundance of fruit it yields led me to create this recipe. Tart lime and tangy ginger make the homey, comforting cobbler extra special.

    3/4 cup sugar
    1/8 teaspoon ground ginger
      5 cups sliced peeled fresh pears
      2 tablespoons finely chopped crystallized ginger
      2 tablespoons lime juice
    1/2 cup butter, melted
BATTER:
    3/4 cup all-purpose flour
    1/2 cup sugar
      2 teaspoons baking powder
      1 teaspoon grated lime peel
    1/8 teaspoon salt
Pinch ground ginger
    3/4 cup milk

1. In a large bowl, combine sugar and ground ginger. Stir in the pears, crystallized ginger and lime juice; set aside.

2. Pour the butter into an ungreased 11-in. x 7-in. baking dish. In a small bowl, combine the flour, sugar, baking powder, lime peel, salt and ginger. Stir in milk. Pour over butter (do not stir). Spoon the pear mixture over the top.

3. Bake at 350° for 50-55 minutes or until bubbly and golden brown. Cool for 10 minutes before serving. **Yield:** 8-10 servings.

2 teaspoons grated lemon peel
1 teaspoon ground cinnamon
1/4 to 1/2 teaspoon ground nutmeg
TOPPING:
1/2 cup butter, softened, *divided*
1 cup confectioners' sugar
1 egg
1 cup all-purpose flour
1/2 cup cornmeal
2 teaspoons baking powder
1/2 teaspoon baking soda
1/2 teaspoon salt
3/4 cup buttermilk
2 tablespoons maple syrup

🎀 🎀 🎀

Blueberry Cornmeal Cobbler

Prep: 20 min. + standing **Bake:** 35 min.

Judy Watson, Tipton, Indiana

Corn bread, blueberries and maple syrup butter give this special cobbler a taste that's delightfully different. I came across the recipe many years ago and have served it countless times.

4 cups fresh blueberries
1 cup plus 2 tablespoons sugar
1 tablespoon quick-cooking tapioca

1. In a large bowl, combine the blueberries, sugar, tapioca, lemon peel, cinnamon and nutmeg. Let stand for 15 minutes. Pour into a greased 11-in. x 7-in. baking dish.

2. In a small bowl, beat 1/4 cup butter and confectioners' sugar. Add egg; beat well. Combine the flour, cornmeal, baking powder, baking soda and salt; add to creamed mixture alternately with buttermilk, beating just until combined. Pour over berry mixture. Bake at 375° for 35-40 minutes or until a toothpick inserted near the center comes out clean.

3. In a small saucepan, melt remaining butter over low heat. Remove from the heat; stir in the syrup. Brush over corn bread. Broil 4-6 in. from the heat for 1-2 minutes or until bubbly. Serve warm. **Yield:** 12 servings.

Apple Crumble

Prep: 30 min. **Bake:** 40 min. + cooling

8 sheets phyllo dough (14 inches x 9 inches)
Butter-flavored cooking spray
1/2 cup packed brown sugar
2 tablespoons all-purpose flour
1/2 teaspoon ground ginger
1/2 teaspoon ground cinnamon
4 medium tart apples, peeled and sliced
TOPPING:
1/2 cup all-purpose flour
1/2 cup packed brown sugar
1/2 cup soft whole wheat bread crumbs
1/4 teaspoon ground ginger
1/4 teaspoon ground cinnamon
1/2 cup cold butter
1/4 cup slivered almonds

1. Place phyllo dough on a work surface; cut in half. Spritz one sheet with butter-flavored spray. Repeat with remaining sheets of phyllo, placing each layer, sprayed side up, in a greased 8-in. square baking dish. (Keep remaining phyllo covered with plastic wrap and a damp towel to prevent it from drying out.)

2. In a large bowl, combine the brown sugar, flour, ginger and cinnamon; add apples and toss to coat. Spoon over phyllo dough.

3. In another large bowl, combine the flour, brown sugar, bread crumbs, ginger and cinnamon; cut in butter until mixture resembles coarse crumbs. Add almonds; sprinkle over apple mixture.

4. Bake at 350° for 40-45 minutes or until the filling is bubbly and the topping is golden brown. Cool for 10 minutes before serving. **Yield:** 9 servings.

CAROL SIMPKINS SANTA CRUZ, CALIFORNIA

I watched this dessert being prepared while visiting friends in New Zealand. Back at home, I experimented in the kitchen to come up with my own version. Try topping off each serving with vanilla ice cream or fresh whipped cream.

Grand Prize Winner

★ ★ ★
Almond Fruit Crisp

Prep: 35 min. + standing **Bake:** 20 min. + cooling

Elizabeth Sicard, Summerfield, Florida

Sliced almonds add crunch to these individual crisps made with plums and either nectarines or peaches. I like to serve each warm-from-the-oven dish with a scoop of ice cream. The recipe yields 10 desserts—perfect for a get-together.

1-1/2 pounds nectarines or peaches, cubed
1-1/2 pounds red plums, cubed

1/4 cup lemon juice
  1 cup sugar
  2 tablespoons quick-cooking tapioca
Dash salt
ALMOND TOPPING:
  1 cup all-purpose flour
1/2 cup sugar
1/2 teaspoon baking powder
Dash salt
1/4 cup cold butter, cubed
  3 tablespoons almond paste
  1 egg, lightly beaten
1/4 teaspoon almond extract
1/3 cup sliced almonds

1. In a large bowl, combine nectarines and plums. Drizzle with lemon juice; toss to coat. Combine the sugar, tapioca and salt; sprinkle over the fruit and toss to coat evenly. Let stand for 15 minutes. Spoon into 10 greased 6-oz. custard cups.

2. In a large bowl, combine the flour, sugar, baking powder and salt. Cut in the butter and almond paste until crumbly. Combine egg and extract; stir into crumb mixture just until blended. Sprinkle over fruit. Top with almonds.

3. Place on a baking sheet coated with cooking spray. Bake, uncovered, at 400° for 20-25 minutes or until fruit is bubbly and topping is golden brown. Cool for 15-20 minutes before serving. **Yield:** 10 servings.

★ ★ ★
Mousse Tarts

Prep/Total Time: 10 min.

Angela Lively, Cookeville, Tennessee

Decadent white chocolate and whipped cream combine wonderfully in these fast-to-fix, berry-topped treats. They make great desserts for special events—I simply double the recipe.

  3 ounces white baking chocolate, chopped
  1 cup heavy whipping cream
1/2 cup sweetened condensed milk
1/4 teaspoon vanilla extract
  6 individual graham cracker tart shells
 18 fresh raspberries
  6 mint sprigs

1. In a microwave, melt the white chocolate at 70% power for 1 minute; stir. Microwave at additional 10- to 20-second intervals, stirring until smooth. Cool for 1 minute, stirring several times. Meanwhile, in a small bowl, beat cream until stiff peaks form; set aside.

2. In another small bowl, combine the milk, vanilla and melted chocolate. Add half of the whipped cream; beat on low speed just until combined. Fold in the remaining whipped cream. Spoon into the tart shells. Garnish with raspberries and mint. **Yield:** 6 servings.

🎗🎗🎗
Cinnamon Roll Cherry Cobbler

Prep: 30 min. **Bake:** 25 min. + cooling

Betty Zorn, Eagle, Idaho

Red-hot candies and tart cherries are the highlights of this memorable dessert from my childhood. I hadn't had the cobbler in years, so when I found my mother's recipe, I just had to make it to see if the taste was as good as I remembered. It was!

      1 can (14-1/2 ounces) pitted tart cherries
  1/2 cup sugar
      2 tablespoons cornstarch
  1/2 cup water
      3 tablespoons red-hot candies
CINNAMON ROLL TOPPING:
1-1/2 cups all-purpose flour
      6 tablespoons brown sugar, *divided*
      2 teaspoons baking powder
  1/2 teaspoon salt
  1/4 cup shortening
      1 egg, lightly beaten
  1/4 cup milk
      1 tablespoon butter, softened
  1/3 cup finely chopped pecans

  1/2 teaspoon ground cinnamon
LEMON GLAZE:
  1/2 cup confectioners' sugar
      1 tablespoon lemon juice

1. Drain cherries, reserving juice; set cherries aside. In a small saucepan, combine the sugar, cornstarch, water and reserved juice until smooth. Stir in red-hot candies. Bring to a boil, stirring constantly; cook 1-2 minutes longer or until thick and bubbly and the red-hot candies are melted. Stir in cherries; heat through. Transfer to a greased 8-in. square baking dish.

2. In a large bowl, combine flour, 3 tablespoons brown sugar, baking powder and salt. Cut in the shortening until crumbly. Combine egg and milk; stir into crumb mixture just until blended.

3. Turn onto a lightly floured surface; knead 3-4 times. Roll into a 14-in. x 10-in. rectangle. Spread with the butter; sprinkle with pecans. Combine cinnamon and remaining brown sugar; sprinkle over top.

4. Roll up, jelly-roll style, starting with a short side. Cut into eight slices; place the cut side down over the cherry filling.

5. Bake at 400° for 25-30 minutes or until golden brown. Cool for 10 minutes. Combine the glaze ingredients; drizzle over cobbler. **Yield:** 8 servings.

🎖🎖🎖
Miracle Baklava

Prep: 1 hour 25 min. **Bake:** 40 min.

Sue Klima, Northlake, Illinois

I'm always asked to bring baklava for special-occasion meals, and I created this lighter version to help everyone cut back on calories and fat. The layers of phyllo dough make it very flaky.

✓ This recipe includes Nutrition Facts and Diabetic Exchange.

  1 package (12 ounces) vanilla wafers, crushed
  2 tablespoons sugar
  1 teaspoon ground cinnamon
Refrigerated butter-flavored spray (about 4 ounces)
  1 package frozen phyllo dough (16 ounce, 14-inch x 9-inch sheet size), thawed
SYRUP:
  1 cup sugar
  1 cup water
  1/2 cup honey
  1 teaspoon grated lemon peel
  1 teaspoon vanilla extract

1. In a large bowl, combine wafer crumbs, sugar and cinnamon; set aside. Spritz a 13-in. x 9-in. baking pan with butter-flavored spray. Unroll phyllo sheets. Place one sheet of phyllo in the pan; spritz with butter-flavored spray and brush to coat evenly. Repeat seven times, spritzing and brushing each layer. (Keep remaining phyllo dough covered with plastic wrap to avoid drying out.)

2. Sprinkle 1/4 cup crumb mixture over phyllo in pan. Layer with two sheets of phyllo, spritzing and brushing with butter-flavored spray between each. Sprinkle with 1/4 cup crumb mixture; repeat 11 times. Top with one phyllo sheet; spritz and brush with butter-flavored spray. Repeat seven more times, spritzing and brushing each layer.

3. Cut into 15 squares; cut each square in half diagonally, creating triangles. Bake at 350° for 40-45 minutes or until golden brown.

4. Meanwhile, in a saucepan, bring the sugar, water, honey and lemon peel to a boil. Reduce the heat; simmer, uncovered, for 20 minutes. Remove from the heat; stir in vanilla. Cool to lukewarm. Pour syrup over warm baklava. **Yield:** 30 servings.

Nutrition Facts: 1 piece equals 154 calories, 4 g fat (1 g saturated fat), 1 mg cholesterol, 154 mg sodium, 30 g carbohydrate, 1 g fiber, 2 g protein. **Diabetic Exchange:** 2 starch.

🎀🎀🎀
Granola Banana Sticks

Prep/Total Time: 20 min.

Diane Toomey, Allentown, Pennsylvania

My daughter and I won an award at our local fair when we entered these crunchy peanut-butter bananas. I like to have the ingredients on hand so my kids can whip up the sticks for a snack when they get home from school. Sometimes we substitute rice cereal for the crushed granola bars.

- 1/4 cup peanut butter
- 2 tablespoons plus 1-1/2 teaspoons honey
- 4-1/2 teaspoons brown sugar
- 2 teaspoons milk
- 3 medium firm bananas
- 6 Popsicle sticks
- 2 crunchy oat and honey granola bars, crushed

1. In a small saucepan, combine the peanut butter, honey, brown sugar and milk; cook until heated through, stirring occasionally.

2. Peel bananas and cut in half widthwise; insert a Popsicle stick into one end of each banana half. Spoon the peanut butter mixture over the bananas to coat completely. Sprinkle with granola. Serve immediately or place on a waxed paper-lined baking sheet and freeze. **Yield:** 6 servings.

🎀🎀🎀
Pumpkin Torte

Prep: 30 min. **Bake:** 25 min. + cooling

Trixie Fisher, Piqua, Ohio

This beautiful layered dessert has a creamy filling with a mild pumpkin flavor and hint of spice—perfect for fall and winter. Toasted pecans and caramel topping add a nice finishing touch.

- 1 package (18-1/4 ounces) yellow cake mix
- 1 can (15 ounces) solid-pack pumpkin, *divided*
- 1/2 cup milk
- 4 eggs
- 1/3 cup canola oil
- 1-1/2 teaspoons pumpkin pie spice, *divided*
- 1 package (8 ounces) cream cheese, softened
- 1 cup confectioners' sugar
- 1 carton (16 ounces) frozen whipped topping, thawed
- 1/4 cup caramel ice cream topping
- 1/3 cup chopped pecans, toasted

1. In a large bowl, combine cake mix, 1 cup pumpkin, milk, eggs, oil and 1 teaspoon pumpkin pie spice; beat on low speed for 30 seconds. Beat on medium for 2 minutes. Pour into two greased and floured 9-in. round baking pans.

2. Bake at 350° for 25-30 minutes or until a toothpick inserted near the center comes out clean. Cool for 10 minutes before removing from pans to wire racks to cool completely.

3. In a large bowl, beat the cream cheese until light and fluffy. Add the confectioners' sugar and the remaining pumpkin and pumpkin pie spice; beat until smooth. Fold in whipped topping.

4. Cut each cake horizontally into two layers. Place bottom layer on a serving plate; spread with a fourth of the filling. Repeat layers three times. Drizzle with caramel topping; sprinkle with pecans. Store in the refrigerator. **Yield:** 10-12 servings.

1-2/3 cups sugar, *divided*
   1 cup all-purpose flour
   2 teaspoons baking powder
1/8 teaspoon salt
2/3 cup milk
   1 can (14-1/2 ounces) pitted tart cherries, undrained
   1 tablespoon butter

1. In a small bowl, combine 2/3 cup sugar, flour, baking powder and salt. Stir in the milk. Spread into a greased 11-in. x 7-in. baking dish; set aside.

2. In a small saucepan, combine the cherries, butter and remaining sugar. Bring to a boil; cook and stir for 1-2 minutes or until sugar is dissolved. Spoon over crust. Bake at 350° for 30-35 minutes or until golden brown. Serve warm. **Yield:** 6 servings.

🎗🎗🎗
Baked Cherry Pudding

Prep: 10 min. **Bake:** 30 min.

Loretta Broderick, Plattsburg, Missouri

One of my brothers was especially fond of Mom's cherry pudding. Every time he came home, she would bake this cake-like treat. Now, I surprise him with it when he visits me.

Baking Powder Pointer

Baking powder will keep in your cupboard for about 6 months. To test if it's still active, stir 1 teaspoon baking powder into 1/3 cup of hot water. If it bubbles, it is fine to use.

🎗🎗🎗
Grilled Apple Crisp

Prep: 20 min. **Grill:** 20 min.

Margaret Riley, Tallahassee, Florida

The first time I sampled this old-fashioned apple dessert, I couldn't believe it was made on the grill. Served warm with a scoop of vanilla ice cream on top, the cinnamon-spiced crisp will earn you rave reviews from everyone.

  10 cups thinly sliced peeled tart apples (about 8 medium)
   1 cup old-fashioned oats
   1 cup packed brown sugar
1/4 cup all-purpose flour
   3 teaspoons ground cinnamon
   1 teaspoon ground nutmeg
1/4 teaspoon ground cloves
1/4 cup cold butter, butter
Vanilla ice cream, optional

1. Place the apple slices on a double thickness of heavy-duty foil (about 24 in. x 12 in.). In a small bowl, combine the oats, brown sugar, flour, cinnamon, nutmeg and cloves; cut in butter until mixture is crumbly. Sprinkle over apples.

2. Fold foil around apple mixture and seal tightly. Grill, covered, over medium heat for 20-25 minutes or until apples are tender. Open foil carefully to allow steam to escape. Serve warm with vanilla ice cream if desired. **Yield:** 6 servings.

🎗️🎗️🎗️
Cranberry Cheesecake

Prep: 40 min. **Bake:** 65 min. + chilling

Mary Simonson, Kelso, Washington

The cranberry topping in this recipe is so good, I serve it all by itself as a Thanksgiving side dish! On the sweet cheesecake, it adds a wonderful, tongue-tingling tartness.

  9 **whole cinnamon graham crackers, crushed**
  1 **tablespoon plus 1 cup sugar, *divided***
1/4 **cup butter, melted**
  2 **packages (8 ounces *each*) reduced-fat cream cheese, cubed**
  1 **package (8 ounces) fat-free cream cheese, cubed**
3/4 **cup fat-free sour cream**
  3 **egg whites, lightly beaten**
  1 **tablespoon lemon juice**
  2 **teaspoons vanilla extract**
  1 **teaspoon rum extract**
TOPPING:
3/4 **cup sugar**
1/4 **cup orange juice**
  2 **tablespoons water**
1-1/2 **teaspoons grated orange peel**
1/4 **teaspoon minced fresh gingerroot**
  2 **cups fresh *or* frozen cranberries**
1/4 **cup chopped pecans**

1. Combine the cracker crumbs, 1 tablespoon sugar and butter. Press onto the bottom and 1 in. up the sides of a 9-in. springform pan coated with cooking spray. Place on a baking sheet. Bake at 350° for 10 minutes. Cool on a wire rack.

2. In a large bowl, beat the cream cheese, sour cream and remaining sugar until smooth. Add egg whites; beat on low just until combined. Stir in lemon juice and extracts. Pour into crust.

3. Place pan on a double thickness of heavy-duty foil (about 16 in. square). Securely wrap foil around pan. Place in a larger baking pan. Add 1 in. of hot water to larger pan.

4. Bake for 55-60 minutes or until center is just set. Remove pan from the water bath. Cool on a wire rack for 10 minutes. Carefully run a knife around edge of pan to loosen; cool 1 hour longer. Remove the foil. Chill overnight.

5. In a small saucepan, combine the first five topping ingredients; bring to a boil. Add cranberries. Cook over medium heat until berries pop, about 10 minutes. Stir in pecans; cool. Cover and chill for at least 1 hour.

6. Spoon topping over cheesecake to within 1 in. of edges. Refrigerate leftovers. **Yield:** 16 servings.

✦✦✦
Carrot Cheesecake

Prep: 25 min. **Bake:** 65 min. + chilling

Misty Wellman, Scottsdale, Arizona

My family loves this creamy, cinnamon-spiced dessert. It's a great recipe when you want something you can make ahead of time. Unlike traditional cheesecake, it features a streusel topping sprinkled over the filling.

- 2 cups graham cracker crumbs
- 1/4 cup sugar
- 1/3 cup butter, melted

FILLING:
- 3 packages (8 ounces *each*) cream cheese, softened
- 1-1/4 cups sugar
- 2 tablespoons brown sugar
- 3 eggs, lightly beaten
- 1/4 cup heavy whipping cream
- 2 tablespoons cornstarch
- 1 tablespoon sour cream
- 1-1/2 teaspoons vanilla extract
- 1 teaspoon lemon juice
- 1/2 teaspoon ground cinnamon
- 1-1/3 cups chopped carrots, cooked and pureed

TOPPING:
- 1 cup graham cracker crumbs
- 2 tablespoons brown sugar
- 1-1/2 teaspoons ground cinnamon
- 1/4 cup butter, melted

1. In a small bowl, combine crumbs and sugar; stir in butter. Press onto the bottom and 2 in. up the sides of a greased 9-in. springform pan. Place on a baking sheet. Bake at 350° for 6-8 minutes. Cool on a wire rack.

2. In a large bowl, beat cream cheese and sugars until smooth. Add the eggs; beat on low speed just until combined. Stir in the cream, cornstarch, sour cream, vanilla, lemon juice and cinnamon. Fold in carrots.

3. Pour into crust. Place pan on a double thickness of heavy-duty foil (about 16 in. square). Securely wrap foil around pan. Place in a larger baking pan. Add 1 in. of hot water to larger pan. Bake at 350° for 55-60 minutes until center is just set.

4. Combine topping ingredients; sprinkle over filling. Bake 7-10 minutes longer. Remove pan from water bath. Cool on a wire rack for 10 minutes. Carefully run a knife around edge of pan to loosen; cool 1 hour longer. Refrigerate overnight. **Yield:** 10-12 servings.

★★★
Glazed Apricot Sorbet

Prep: 10 min. + freezing

Nina Rohlfs, Unadilla, Nebraska

This fruity dessert is refreshingly cool and light with just a hint of richness. When serving it to company, I like to present it in sherbet glasses with mint sprigs for an elegant look.

> 1 can (20 ounces) apricot halves, drained
> 1 jar (10 ounces) apricot preserves
> 1-1/2 teaspoons grated orange peel
> 2 tablespoons lemon juice
> 5 tablespoons heavy whipping cream

1. In a food processor, combine the apricots, preserves, orange peel and lemon juice; cover and process until smooth. Pour into a freezer container; cover and freeze for at least 3 hours. May be frozen for up to 3 months.

2. Remove from freezer at least 15 minutes before serving. Scoop into dessert dishes; drizzle with cream. **Yield:** 5 servings.

★★★
Blackberry Cobbler

Prep: 15 min. **Bake:** 45 min. + cooling

Kimberly Reisinger, Spring, Texas

I tweaked this recipe a few times until I hit on this version. Lime zest complements the fruit, and the sour cream pastry is delightful. I use fresh blackberries when available.

> 6 cups fresh *or* frozen blackberries
> 1/2 cup sugar
> 3 tablespoons cornstarch
> 1 teaspoon grated lime peel
> **SOUR CREAM PASTRY:**
> 1-1/3 cups all-purpose flour
> 3 tablespoons sugar, *divided*
> 3/4 teaspoon baking powder
> 1/2 teaspoon salt
> 1/4 teaspoon baking soda
> 7 tablespoons cold butter, *divided*
> 1/2 cup sour cream
> 1/4 cup heavy whipping cream

1. Place the blackberries in a large bowl. Combine the sugar, cornstarch and lime peel; sprinkle over berries and gently toss to coat. Pour into a greased 9-in. square baking dish.

2. In a large bowl, combine the flour, 2 tablespoons sugar, baking powder, salt and the baking soda; cut in 5 tablespoons butter until crumbly. Combine the sour cream and heavy cream; gradually add to the crumb mixture, tossing with a fork until mixture forms a ball.

3. Roll out to fit top of baking dish; place pastry over filling. Trim and seal edges; cut slits in top. Melt the remaining butter; brush over pastry. Sprinkle with remaining sugar.

4. Bake, uncovered, at 375° for 30 minutes. Cover and bake 15-20 minutes longer or until filling is bubbly and the crust is golden brown. Cool for 15 minutes before serving. **Yield:** 6-8 servings.

Editor's Note: If using frozen blackberries, do not thaw before assembling cobbler.

🏵 🏵 🏵
Strawberry Rhubarb Cobbler

Prep: 25 min. **Bake:** 20 min. + cooling

Sabrina Musk, Caledonia, Michigan

When you want to use up homegrown rhubarb, consider this recipe. The comforting, ruby-red cobbler has an old-fashioned look and flavor that just can't be beat. Tender golden brown biscuits top the thick filling loaded with fruit.

  3/4 **cup sugar**
    2 **tablespoons cornstarch**
  1/8 **teaspoon salt**

    3 **cups chopped fresh** *or* **frozen rhubarb**
1-1/2 **cups sliced fresh strawberries**
TOPPING:
    1 **cup all-purpose flour**
    1 **tablespoon sugar**
1-1/2 **teaspoons baking powder**
  1/4 **teaspoon salt**
  1/4 **cup cold butter, cubed**
    1 **egg, lightly beaten**
  1/4 **cup milk**
Additional sugar

1. In a large saucepan, combine the sugar, cornstarch and salt. Add the rhubarb and strawberries; toss to coat. Let stand for 5 minutes. Bring to a boil; cook and stir for 1 minute. Pour mixture into a greased 8-in. square baking dish.

2. In a large bowl, combine the flour, sugar, baking powder and salt; cut in butter until mixture resembles coarse crumbs. Combine egg and milk; stir into crumb mixture just until moistened. Drop by tablespoonfuls onto fruit. Sprinkle with additional sugar.

3. Bake at 400° for 20-25 minutes or until the filling is bubbly and the topping is golden brown. Cool for 10 minutes before serving. **Yield:** 6-8 servings.

Editor's Note: If using frozen rhubarb, measure rhubarb while still frozen, then thaw completely. Drain in a colander, but do not press liquid out.

🏵 🏵 🏵
Black Forest Cheesecake

Prep: 20 min. + chilling

Christine Ooyen, Winnebago, Illinois

I came up with this chocolate-cherry cheesecake over 10 years ago, and I've been getting requests for it ever since.

    1 **package (8 ounces) cream cheese, softened**
  1/3 **cup sugar**
    1 **cup (8 ounces) sour cream**
    2 **teaspoons vanilla extract**
    1 **carton (8 ounces) frozen whipped topping, thawed**
    1 **chocolate crumb crust (8 inches)**
  1/4 **cup baking cocoa**
    1 **tablespoon confectioners' sugar**
    1 **can (21 ounces) cherry pie filling**

1. In a large bowl, beat cream cheese and sugar until smooth. Beat in sour cream and vanilla. Fold in whipped topping. Spread half of the mixture evenly into crust. Fold cocoa and confectioners' sugar into remaining whipped topping mixture; carefully spread over cream cheese layer. Refrigerate for at least 4 hours.

2. Cut into slices; top each slice with the cherry pie filling. Refrigerate leftovers. **Yield:** 6-8 servings.

❧❧❧
Irish Creme Chocolate Trifle

Prep: 20 min. **Bake:** 30 min. + chilling

Margaret Wilson, Sun City, California

I created this rich, decadent trifle when I was given a bottle of Irish cream liqueur as a gift and had some leftover peppermint candy. This version of the recipe uses coffee creamer.

    1 package (18-1/4 ounces) devil's food cake mix
    1 cup refrigerated Irish creme nondairy creamer
3-1/2 cups cold milk
    2 packages (3.9 ounces *each*) instant chocolate pudding mix
    3 cups whipped topping
   12 spearmint candies, crushed

1. Prepare and bake the cake according to package directions, using a greased 13-in. x 9-in. baking pan. Cool on a wire rack for 1 hour.

2. With a meat fork or wooden skewer, poke holes in cake about 2 in. apart. Slowly pour creamer over cake; refrigerate for 1 hour.

3. In a large bowl, whisk the milk and chocolate pudding mixes for 2 minutes. Let stand for 2 minutes or until soft-set.

4. Cut the cake into 1-1/2-in. cubes; place a third of the cubes in a 3-qt. glass bowl. Top with a third of the pudding, whipped topping and candies; repeat layers twice. Store in the refrigerator. **Yield:** 14-16 servings.

❧❧❧
Raspberry Pear Crisp

Prep: 15 min. **Bake:** 25 min. + cooling

Fancheon Resler, Bluffton, Indiana

We grow red raspberries, enjoy them fresh when they're ripe and freeze some for winter. This recipe combines those tangy berries with fresh pears and a crunchy cereal topping.

    2 cups sliced peeled fresh pears
    2 cups fresh *or* frozen raspberries
3/4 cup packed brown sugar, *divided*
    1 teaspoon ground cinnamon, *divided*
1/2 cup all-purpose flour
    3 tablespoons cold butter
    1 cup cranberry almond whole grain cereal, lightly crushed
Vanilla ice cream, optional

1. In a large bowl, combine pears, raspberries, 1/4 cup brown sugar and 1/2 teaspoon cinnamon. Spoon into a greased 9-in. pie plate.

2. In a small bowl, combine the flour and remaining brown sugar and cinnamon; cut in the butter until mixture resembles coarse crumbs. Stir in the cereal. Sprinkle over fruit.

3. Bake at 375° for 25-30 minutes or until the filling is bubbly and the topping is golden brown. Cool for 10 minutes. Serve with vanilla ice cream if desired. **Yield:** 6 servings.

Editor's Note: If using frozen raspberries, do not thaw before adding to batter.

1 cup sugar
1/4 cup cornstarch
2 tablespoons orange juice
1 teaspoon grated orange peel
2 cups fresh *or* frozen raspberries
2 cups fresh *or* frozen blueberries
1 cup old-fashioned oats
1/2 cup cornflakes
1/2 cup packed brown sugar
1/2 teaspoon ground cinnamon
1/4 teaspoon salt
1/4 cup butter, melted

1. In a large saucepan, combine sugar, cornstarch, orange juice, orange peel and berries until blended. Bring to a boil; cook and stir for 2 minutes or until thickened and bubbly. Pour into a greased 8-in. square baking dish.

2. In a large bowl, combine the oats, cornflakes, brown sugar, cinnamon and salt; stir in butter. Sprinkle over berry mixture. Bake at 350° for 25-30 minutes or until filling is bubbly. Cool for 10 minutes before serving. **Yield:** 6 servings.

Editor's Note: If using frozen raspberries, do not thaw before adding to batter.

🏵 🏵 🏵

Double-Berry Crisp

Prep: 20 min. **Bake:** 25 min. + cooling

Bernadette Beaton, Goose River, Prince Edward Island

This sweet-tart treat has an extra-crispy topping, thanks to the addition of cornflakes. Orange juice and orange peel bring a refreshing citrus accent to the blueberries and raspberries.

🏵 🏵 🏵

Apple Pie in a Goblet

Prep: 10 min. **Cook:** 25 min.

Renee Zimmer, Gig Harbor, Washington

I got this recipe from a church cooking class. The easy dessert has all the homey taste of traditional apple pie without the fuss. You can serve it in bowls, but I always get more oohs and aahs when I put it in lovely goblets.

3 large tart apples, peeled and coarsely chopped
1/4 cup sugar
1/4 cup water
3/4 teaspoon ground cinnamon
1/4 teaspoon ground nutmeg
12 shortbread cookies, crushed
2 cups vanilla ice cream
Whipped cream

1. In a large saucepan, combine the apples, sugar, water, cinnamon and nutmeg. Bring to a boil. Reduce heat; cover and simmer for 10 minutes or until apples are tender. Uncover; cook 9-11 minutes longer or until most of liquid has evaporated. Remove from heat.

2. In each of the four goblets or parfait glasses, layer 1 tablespoon cookie crumbs, 1/2 cup ice cream and a fourth of the apple mixture. Top with remaining cookie crumbs and whipped cream. Serve immediately. **Yield:** 4 servings.

Strawberry Puff Pastry Dessert

Prep: 30 min. **Bake:** 15 min. + cooling

Anna Ginsberg, Austin, Texas

My attempt to make a triple-layer strawberry malt mousse resulted in this scrumptious dessert. My husband declared it one of the best he's ever had! I don't bake with puff pastry often, but it was easy to work with.

- 1 package (17.3 ounces) frozen puff pastry
- 5 cups sliced fresh strawberries, *divided*
- 6 ounces white baking chocolate, chopped
- 1 package (8 ounces) cream cheese, softened
- 1 teaspoon vanilla extract
- 1 cup confectioners' sugar
- 1/3 cup malted milk powder
- 2 cups heavy whipping cream, whipped

Strawberry syrup, optional

1. Thaw one puff pastry sheet (save remaining sheet for another use). Unfold the pastry; cut lengthwise into three 3-in.-wide strips. Cut each strip into thirds, making nine squares.

2. Place 1 in. apart on ungreased baking sheets. Bake at 400° for 11-13 minutes or until golden brown. Remove to wire racks to cool.

3. Place 2-1/2 cups strawberries in a blender; cover and puree; set aside. In a large microwave-safe bowl, melt the white chocolate at 70% power for 1 minute; stir. Microwave at additional 10- to 20-second intervals, stirring until smooth; cool slightly. Add the cream cheese and vanilla; beat until smooth. Beat in the confectioners' sugar and malted milk powder until smooth. Stir in the puree. Fold in whipped cream.

4. Split pastry squares in half horizontally. Line an ungreased 13-in. x 9-in. dish with bottom pastry halves, cut side up; spread with 3-1/2 cups strawberry cream. Top with 1 cup of sliced berries. Cover with pastry tops, cut side down.

5. Spread with remaining strawberry cream. Sprinkle with remaining berries. Drizzle with strawberry syrup if desired. Refrigerate leftovers. **Yield:** 12 servings.

Best Berries

Aren't going to use your fresh berries right away? They should be stored covered in your refrigerator and washed just before using. Use them within 10 days of purchase.

🎀🎀🎀
Peach Cobbler

Prep: 20 min. + standing **Bake:** 50 min. + cooling

Ellen Merick, North Pole, Alaska

The tender cake-like topping of this cobbler pairs perfectly with the fruit filling and butterscotch sauce, which should be served warm. Canned peaches make this dessert quick to assemble.

    2 cans (29 ounces *each*) sliced peaches
1/2 cup packed brown sugar
    6 tablespoons quick-cooking tapioca
    1 teaspoon ground cinnamon, optional
    1 teaspoon lemon juice
    1 teaspoon vanilla extract
TOPPING:
    1 cup all-purpose flour
    1 cup sugar
    1 teaspoon baking powder
1/2 teaspoon salt
1/4 cup cold butter, cubed
    2 eggs, lightly beaten
BUTTERSCOTCH SAUCE:
1/2 cup packed brown sugar
    2 tablespoons all-purpose flour
1/8 teaspoon salt
1/4 cup butter, melted
    2 tablespoons lemon juice
Vanilla ice cream, optional

1. Drain peaches, reserving 1/2 cup syrup for the sauce. In a large bowl, combine peaches, brown sugar, tapioca, cinnamon if desired, lemon juice and vanilla. Transfer to an ungreased 11-in. x 7-in. baking dish. Let stand for 15 minutes.

2. In a large bowl, combine the flour, sugar, baking powder and salt; cut in butter until mixture resembles coarse crumbs. Stir in eggs. Drop by spoonfuls onto peach mixture; spread evenly. Bake at 350° for 50-55 minutes or until the filling is bubbly and a toothpick inserted in the topping comes out clean. Cool for 10 minutes.

3. In a small saucepan, combine the brown sugar, flour, salt, butter and the reserved peach syrup. Bring to a boil over medium heat; cook and stir for 1 minute or until thickened. Remove from the heat; add lemon juice. Serve with cobbler and ice cream if desired. **Yield:** 10-12 servings.

🎀🎀🎀 Strawberry Popovers

Prep: 20 min. **Bake:** 30 min.

Sandy Holton-Vanthoff, San Diego, California

These tender treats "pop up" nicely in the oven and hold a delicate cream filling dotted with chopped fresh strawberries. If you don't have a popover pan on hand, try muffin cups.

  1 cup heavy whipping cream
1/3 cup sugar
  1 teaspoon vanilla extract
  2 cups chopped fresh strawberries
4-1/2 teaspoons shortening
POPOVERS:
  4 eggs
  2 cups milk
  2 cups all-purpose flour
  1 tablespoon sugar
  1 teaspoon salt

1. In a large bowl, beat the cream until it begins to thicken. Gradually add sugar and vanilla; beat until stiff peaks form. Fold in the strawberries. Cover and refrigerate until serving.

2. Using 1/2 teaspoon shortening for each cup, grease the bottom and sides of nine popover cups. In a small bowl, beat eggs; beat in milk. Add the flour, sugar and salt; beat until smooth (do not overbeat). Fill prepared cups half full.

3. Bake at 450° for 15 minutes. Reduce heat to 350°; bake 15 minutes longer or until very firm.

4. Immediately cut a slit in the top of each popover to allow steam to escape. Spoon the strawberry filling into popovers. Serve immediately. **Yield:** 9 servings.

🎀🎀🎀 Apple Crisp with a Twist

Prep: 15 min. **Bake:** 35 min.

Marilynn Ostrander, Lehigh Acres, Florida

Nicely spiced apple crisp gets a delightful twist in this recipe, which features apricot jam over the traditional crumb topping. Served warm, it's wonderful with ice cream or frozen yogurt.

  1 large tart apple, peeled and sliced
1/4 cup sugar
  1 tablespoon all-purpose flour
1/2 teaspoon ground cinnamon
1/8 teaspoon ground nutmeg
TOPPING:
1/2 cup all-purpose flour
1/4 cup sugar
1/4 cup cold butter, cubed
  3 tablespoons chopped pecans
1/3 cup apricot jam
Vanilla ice cream, optional

1. In a small bowl, combine the apple, sugar, flour, cinnamon and nutmeg. Transfer to a 3-cup baking dish coated with cooking spray.

2. For topping, combine the flour and sugar in a small bowl; cut in butter until mixture is crumbly. Stir in pecans. Sprinkle over apple mixture. Drop jam by teaspoonfuls over the top.

3. Bake, uncovered, at 350° for 35-40 minutes or until the apple slices are tender. Serve the crisp warm with vanilla ice cream if desired. Refrigerate leftovers. **Yield:** 4 servings.

General Recipe Index

This handy index lists every recipe by food category, major ingredient and/or cooking method, so you can easily locate recipes to suit your needs.

✓ Recipe includes Nutrition Facts and Diabetic Exchanges

APPETIZERS & SNACKS
Appetizers
  Bacon Nachos, 17
  Bacon-Wrapped Stuffed Jalapenos, 14
  Chocolate Fruit Dip, 11
  Dilly Veggie Pizza, 13
  Fried Shoestring Carrots, 11
  Honey-Mustard Turkey Meatballs, 19
  Mini Bagelizzas, 10
  Pepper Avocado Salsa, 16
  Roasted Carrot Dip, 9
  Sauerkraut Ham Balls, 10
  Sweet Gingered Chicken Wings, 15
Snacks
  Granola Trail Mix, 19
  Italian Snack Mix, 8
  Sweet 'n' Crunchy Mix, 18
  Swiss Walnut Cracker Snack, 13

APPLES
Apple Crisp with a Twist, 227
Apple Crumble, 212
Apple Pie in a Goblet, 224
Apple Puff Pancake, 62
✓Apple-Stuffed Pork Tenderloin, 86
Blue Cheese 'n' Fruit Tossed Salad, 27
Caramel Apple Cake, 195
Caramel Apple Cream Pie, 204
Caramel Apple Crunch, 211
Chock-full of Fruit Snackin'
  Cake, 201
Cran-Apple Crisp, 208
Cran-Apple Tea Ring, 64
Cranberry Apple Saute, 134
Grilled Apple Crisp, 218
Popover Apple Pie, 189
Puffy Apple Omelet, 62
Upside-Down Apple Pie, 193

ASPARAGUS
Asparagus Berry Salad, 22
✓Spicy Asparagus Spears, 120
Wild Rice Brunch Casserole, 66

AVOCADOS
Pepper Avocado Salsa, 16
Zesty Garlic-Avocado Sandwiches, 49

BACON & CANADIAN BACON
Bacon 'n' Egg Salad Sandwiches, 53
Bacon-Cheese Topped Chicken, 85
Bacon Clam Chowder, 48
Bacon Mashed Potatoes, 123
Bacon Nachos, 17
Bacon-Wrapped Stuffed Jalapenos, 14
Onion-Bacon Baby Carrots, 127

BANANAS
Apricot Banana Bread, 153
Banana Shakes, 14
Buttermilk Banana Cake, 190
French Banana Pancakes, 70
Granola Banana Sticks, 217

BARS
Almond Truffle Brownies, 176
Blond Brownies a la Mode, 174
✓Blondies with Chips, 168
Chocolate Peanut Squares, 166
Coffee 'n' Cream Brownies, 174
Creamy Cashew Brownies, 180
Frosted Cookie Brownies, 163
Fudgy Oat Brownies, 159
Hazelnut Brownies, 169
Irish Mint Brownies, 162
Meringue Coconut Brownies, 171
Mocha Mousse Brownies, 164
Peanut Butter Blondies, 179
Peanut Lover's Brownies, 173
Pecan Caramel Bars, 163
Raisin Pumpkin Bars, 172
Raspberry Coconut Bars, 177
Ribbon Crispies, 176

BEANS
Bean and Pork Chop Bake, 113

Beef 'n' Chili Beans, 97
Black Bean Soup with Fruit Salsa, 44
Blue Cheese Green Beans, 131
Chipotle Turkey Chili, 49
✓Garbanzo Bean Medley, 134
Green Bean Tossed Salad, 22
Rocky Ford Chili, 40

BEEF & GROUND BEEF
Appetizers
Bacon Nachos, 17
Breakfast & Brunch
Reuben Brunch Bake, 73
Tacoed Eggs, 73
Main Dishes
Beef 'n' Chili Beans, 97
Beef and Potato Moussaka, 104
✓Beef Fillets with Portobello Sauce, 98
Louisiana Barbecue Brisket, 95
Marinated Chuck Roast, 102
Mongolian Beef, 93
Mustard-Herb Grilled Tenderloin, 102
Ole Polenta Casserole, 90
✓Spinach-Stuffed Beef Tenderloin, 117
Salad
✓Beef Fajita Salad, 28
Soup & Sandwiches
Beef Gyros, 56
Beefy Mushroom Soup, 44
Grilled Beef Tenderloin Sandwiches, 46
Hearty Country Burgers, 48
Pineapple-Stuffed Burgers, 58
Roast Beef Barbecue, 52

BEVERAGES
Banana Shakes, 14
Cherry Berry Smoothies, 18
Cranberry Spritzer, 17
Crimson Cranberry Punch, 8
Sensational Slush, 12

BLUEBERRIES
Blueberry Cornmeal Cobbler, 212
✓Lemon Blueberry Muffins, 144

BREADS & ROLLS (also see Coffee Cakes; Muffins; Pancakes, Waffles & French Toast)
Almond Chip Scones, 64
Almond Streusel Rolls, 80
Apricot Banana Bread, 153
Berry Bread with Spread, 140
Caramel Sweet Rolls, 76

Cheery Cherry Loaf, 155
Christmas Bread, 145
Dilly Bran Refrigerator Rolls, 154
Easy Potato Rolls, 152
Garlic Herb Twists, 152
Maple-Pecan Corn Bread, 145
Maraschino Cherry Almond Bread, 150
Marmalade Monkey Bread, 142
✓Mashed Potato Kolachkes, 77
Mini Italian Biscuits, 141
Oregano-Swiss Slices, 149
PB&J Spirals, 150
✓Quilt-Topped Corn Bread, 146
Spiced Walnut Loaf, 140
Sunshine Sweet Rolls, 63
Sweet Potato Bread, 142

BREAKFAST & BRUNCH
Almond Chip Scones, 64
Almond Streusel Rolls, 80
Apple Puff Pancake, 62
Brunch Lasagna, 78
Caramel Sweet Rolls, 76
Cherry Cream Cheese Coffee Cake, 72
Chocolate-Cherry Cream Crepes, 79
Chocolate Croissants, 67
Cinnamon-Nut Coffee Cake, 76
Coconut-Chip Coffee Cake, 78
Cran-Apple Tea Ring, 64
Florentine Egg Bake, 70
French Banana Pancakes, 70
French Toast Supreme, 66
Great-Grandma's Prune Roll, 66
✓Mashed Potato Kolachkes, 77
Peach Coffee Cake, 69
Pecan-Stuffed Waffles, 68
Puffy Apple Omelet, 62
Pumpkin Coffee Cake, 80
Pumpkin Pancakes, 79
Reuben Brunch Bake, 73
Salmon Quiche, 74
Special Stuffed French Toast, 72
Speedy Sausage Squares, 69
Strawberry Cream Crepes, 74
Sunshine Sweet Rolls, 63
Tacoed Eggs, 73
Turkey Potato Pancakes, 67
Wild Rice Brunch Casserole, 68

CABBAGE & SAUERKRAUT
Colorful Coleslaw, 31
Reuben Brunch Bake, 73
Sauerkraut Ham Balls, 10

CAKES *(also see Coffee Cakes)*

Berry Pinwheel Cake, 202
Buttermilk Banana Cake, 190
Caramel Apple Cake, 195
Chock-full of Fruit Snackin' Cake, 201
Chocolate Carrot Cake, 192
Chocolate Potato Cake, 198
Cranberry Bundt Cake, 189
Layered Carrot Cake, 199
Pecan Angel Food Cake, 187
Sunflower Potluck Cake, 194
Sweet Potato Mini Cakes, 184
Triple Layer Brownie Cake, 188
Triple-Layer Lemon Cake, 200

CANDY

Butter Pecan Fudge, 171
Butterscotch Hard Candy, 179
Caramel Truffles, 160
Coconut Snowmen, 170
Cookie Dough Truffles, 164
Elegant Dipped Cherries, 181
✓Frosty Peanut Butter Cups, 169
Hazelnut Toffee, 180
Hint-of-Berry Bonbons, 178
✓Nutty Chocolate Fudge, 160
Pecan Clusters, 166
Peppermint Taffy, 158
S'more Drops, 172
White Candy Bark, 159

CARROTS

Carrot Cheesecake, 220
Chocolate Carrot Cake, 192
Fried Shoestring Carrots, 11
✓Glazed Carrot Coins, 123
Horseradish Creamed Carrots, 124
Layered Carrot Cake, 199
Onion-Bacon Baby Carrots, 127
Party Carrots, 132
Pickled Baby Carrots, 136
Roasted Carrot Dip, 9
Sunny Carrot Salad, 26
Sunshine Sweet Rolls, 63

CASSEROLES

Main Dishes
Bean and Pork Chop Bake, 113
Beef and Potato Moussaka, 104
Brunch Lasagna, 78
Chicken Pie in a Pan, 94
Creamy Baked Macaroni, 87
Eggplant Sausage Casserole, 106

Florentine Egg Bake, 70
Old-Fashioned Chicken Pot Pie, 84
Ole Polenta Casserole, 90
Reuben Brunch Bake, 73
✓Roasted Pepper Ravioli Bake, 109
Wild Rice Brunch Casserole, 68
Side Dishes
Golden Mashed Potato Bake, 128
Herbed Baked Spinach, 132
Horseradish Creamed Carrots, 124
Onion-Bacon Baby Carrots, 127
Party Carrots, 132
Pretzel-Topped Sweet Potatoes, 127
Swirled Potato Bake, 121

CHEESE *(also see Cream Cheese)*

Bacon-Cheese Topped Chicken, 85
Blue Cheese 'n' Fruit Tossed Salad, 27
Blue Cheese Green Beans, 131
Blue Cheese Pear Salad, 35
Cheese Fries, 135
Creamy Baked Macaroni, 87
Fresh Mozzarella Sandwiches, 40
Oregano-Swiss Slices, 149
Ricotta Nut Pie, 194
Swiss Walnut Cracker Snack, 13

CHERRIES

Baked Cherry Pudding, 218
Black Forest Cheesecake, 222
Cheery Cherry Loaf, 155
Cherry Berry Smoothies, 18
Cherry Cream Cheese Coffee Cake, 72
Cherry-Glazed Roast Pork, 88
Chocolate-Cherry Cream Crepes, 79
Christmas Bread, 145
Cinnamon Roll Cherry Cobbler, 215
Elegant Dipped Cherries, 181
Maraschino Cherry Almond Bread, 150
Special Stuffed French Toast, 72
Sweet Cherry Cheese Dessert, 208
White Chocolate Mousse Cherry Pie, 196

CHICKEN

Appetizers
Sweet Gingered Chicken Wings, 15
Main Dishes
Asian Chicken Thighs, 101
Bacon-Cheese Topped Chicken, 85
Barbecued Chicken Legs, 101
Brined Roasting Chicken, 89
✓Chicken and Shrimp Satay, 92

Chicken Pepper Stir-Fry, 97
Chicken Pie in a Pan, 94
Chicken Rice Bowl, 109
✓Chicken-Stuffed Cubanelle Peppers, 112
✓Chicken with Mushroom Sauce, 96
Grilled Raspberry Chicken, 116
Herbed Cranberry Chicken, 93
✓Honey-Citrus Chicken Kabobs, 111
Old-Fashioned Chicken Pot Pie, 84
Pecan-Crusted Chicken, 94
Primavera Chicken, 114
Shrimp-Stuffed Chicken Breasts, 105
Southern Barbecued Chicken, 99
Spinach Crab Chicken, 106

Salads
✓Chicken Salad with Crispy Wontons, 26
Crispy Chicken Strip Salad, 34
Fiery Chicken Spinach Salad, 24
Grilled Chicken and Pear Salad, 28
Summer Chicken Salad, 24

Soups & Sandwiches
Buffalo Chicken Sandwiches, 57
Buffalo Chicken Wraps, 52
Chicken Tortilla Soup, 58
Curried Chicken Salad Sandwiches, 42
Florentine Chicken Soup, 50
Italian Chicken Wraps, 45
Southwestern Chicken Soup, 56

CHOCOLATE
Almond Chip Scones, 64
Almond Truffle Brownies, 176
Black Forest Cheesecake, 222
Caramel Truffles, 160
Chocolate Carrot Cake, 192
Chocolate-Cherry Cream Crepes, 79
Chocolate Chip Muffins, 141
Chocolate Croissants, 67
Chocolate Fruit Dip, 11
Chocolate Mint Wafers, 158
Chocolate Peanut Squares, 166
Chocolate Potato Cake, 198
Chocolate Raspberry Pie, 205
Chocolate Walnut Tart, 209
Coconut-Chip Coffee Cake, 78
Coffee 'n' Cream Brownies, 174
Cookie Dough Truffles, 164
Creamy Cashew Brownies, 180
Frosted Cookie Brownies, 163
Fudgy Oat Brownies, 159
German Chocolate Pie, 186
Hazelnut Brownies, 169
Hazelnut Toffee, 180

Hint-of-Berry Bonbons, 178
Irish Creme Chocolate Trifle, 223
Irish Mint Brownies, 162
Meringue Coconut Brownies, 171
Mocha Mousse Brownies, 164
Mud Pie, 198
✓Nutty Chocolate Fudge, 160
Peanut Lover's Brownies, 173
Pumpkin Chip Muffins, 146
S'more Drops, 172
Sunflower Potluck Cake, 194
Triple Layer Brownie Cake, 188
White Chocolate Mousse Cherry Pie, 196

COCONUT
Coconut Snowmen, 170
German Chocolate Pie, 186
Meringue Coconut Brownies, 171
Raspberry Coconut Bars, 177

COFFEE CAKES *(also see Cakes)*
Cherry Cream Cheese Coffee Cake, 72
Cinnamon-Nut Coffee Cake, 76
Coconut-Chip Coffee Cake, 78
Cran-Apple Tea Ring, 64
Great-Grandma's Prune Roll, 66
Peach Coffee Cake, 69
Pumpkin Coffee Cake, 80

CONDIMENTS
Cranberry Apple Saute, 134
Pickled Baby Carrots, 136
Spiced Cranberry Ketchup, 130
Three-Pepper Chutney, 129

COOKIES
Berry-Cream Cookie Snaps, 167
Chocolate Mint Wafers, 158
Noel Cookie Gems, 168
✓Pistachio Cranberry Biscotti, 161

CORN & CORNMEAL
Blueberry Cornmeal Cobbler, 212
Corn Muffins with Honey Butter, 149
Country Corn, 135
Maple-Pecan Corn Bread, 145
✓Quilt-Topped Corn Bread, 146
Tilapia with Corn Salsa, 117

CRANBERRIES
✓Calico Cranberry Couscous Salad, 36
Cran-Apple Crisp, 208

CRANBERRIES *(continued)*
Cran-Apple Tea Ring, 64
Cranberry Apple Saute, 134
Cranberry Bundt Cake, 189
Cranberry Cheesecake, 219
Cranberry Pear Pie, 202
Cranberry Spritzer, 17
Crimson Cranberry Punch, 8
Eggnog Cranberry Pie, 199
✓Flavorful Cranberry Gelatin Mold, 37
Herbed Cranberry Chicken, 93
Orange Cranberry Gems, 154
✓Pistachio Cranberry Biscotti, 161
Spiced Cranberry Ketchup, 130

CREAM CHEESE
Black Forest Cheesecake, 222
Caramel Apple Cream Pie, 204
Carrot Cheesecake, 220
Cherry Cream Cheese Coffee Cake, 72
Chocolate-Cherry Cream Crepes, 79
Cranberry Cheesecake, 219
Creamy Cashew Brownies, 180
Pecan-Stuffed Waffles, 68
Pumpkin Cheesecake Pie, 187
Special Stuffed French Toast, 72
Strawberry Cream Crepes, 74
Strawberry Swirl Cheesecake, 210
Sweet Cherry Cheese Dessert, 208

DESSERTS *(also see Bars; Cakes; Candy; Cookies; Pies)*
Almond Fruit Crisp, 214
Apple Crisp with a Twist, 227
Apple Crumble, 212
Apple Pie in a Goblet, 224
Baked Cherry Pudding, 218
Black Forest Cheesecake, 222
Blackberry Cobbler, 221
Blueberry Cornmeal Cobbler, 212
Caramel Apple Crunch, 211
Carrot Cheesecake, 220
Chocolate Walnut Tart, 209
Cinnamon Roll Cherry Cobbler, 215
Cran-Apple Crisp, 208
Cranberry Cheesecake, 219
Double-Berry Crisp, 224
Ginger-Lime Pear Cobbler, 211
Glazed Apricot Sorbet, 221
Granola Banana Sticks, 217
Grilled Apple Crisp, 218
Irish Creme Chocolate Trifle, 223
✓Miracle Baklava, 216

Mousse Tarts, 214
Peach Cobbler, 226
Pumpkin Torte, 217
Raspberry Pear Crisp, 223
Strawberry Popovers, 227
Strawberry Puff Pastry Dessert, 225
Strawberry Rhubarb Cobbler, 222
Strawberry Swirl Cheesecake, 210
Strawberry Tartlets, 209
Sweet Cherry Cheese Dessert, 208

EGGS
Bacon 'n' Egg Salad Sandwiches, 53
Brunch Lasagna, 78
Eggnog Cranberry Pie, 199
Florentine Egg Bake, 70
Lemon Pie in Meringue Shell, 196
Puffy Apple Omelet, 62
Reuben Brunch Bake, 73
Salmon Quiche, 74
Speedy Sausage Squares, 69
Tacoed Eggs, 73
Wild Rice Brunch Casserole, 68

FISH & SEAFOOD
Breakfast & Brunch
Salmon Quiche, 74
Main Dishes
✓Chicken and Shrimp Satay, 92
✓Easy Crab Cakes, 105
✓Peking Shrimp, 113
Shrimp-Stuffed Chicken Breasts, 105
Spinach Crab Chicken, 106
Swordfish Shrimp Kabobs, 87
Tilapia with Corn Salsa, 117
Salads
Cajun Potato Salad, 27
Polynesian Shrimp Salad, 23
Soups & Sandwiches
Bacon Clam Chowder, 48
Mexican Shrimp Bisque, 54
Open-Faced Crab Salad Sandwiches, 53
Tuna Puff Sandwiches, 41

FRUIT *(also see specific kinds)*
Almond Fruit Crisp, 214
Black Bean Soup with Fruit Salsa, 44
Blackberry Cobbler, 221
Blue Cheese 'n' Fruit Tossed Salad, 27
Chock-full of Fruit Snackin' Cake, 201
Glazed Apricot Sorbet, 221
Grapefruit Pie, 192
Tangerine Tossed Salad, 23

GRAND PRIZE WINNERS

Breads & Rolls
Marmalade Monkey Bread, 142
PB&J Spirals, 150
Pumpkin Chip Muffins, 146

Breakfast & Brunch
Almond Streusel Rolls, 80
Cran-Apple Tea Ring, 64
Florentine Egg Bake, 70
Strawberry Cream Crepes, 74

Cakes & Pies
Butter Pecan Pumpkin Pie, 184
Cranberry Pear Pie, 202
Martha Washington Pies, 190
White Chocolate Mousse Cherry Pie, 196

Cookies, Bars & Candy
Blond Brownies a la Mode, 174
Cookie Dough Truffles, 164

Desserts
Apple Crumble, 212

Main Dishes
Ole Polenta Casserole, 90
Southern Barbecued Chicken, 99
Spinach Crab Chicken, 106

Salads
Fiery Chicken Spinach Salad, 24
Grilled Chicken and Pear Salad, 28
Spicy Pork Tenderloin Salad, 32

Side Dishes & Condiments
Party Carrots, 132
Swirled Potato Bake, 121
✓Tomatoes with Horseradish Sauce, 124

Soups & Sandwiches
Curried Chicken Salad Sandwiches, 42
Mexican Shrimp Bisque, 54
Pineapple-Stuffed Burgers, 58
✓Sweet Pepper Sandwiches, 50
Turkey Pasta Soup, 46

GRILLED RECIPES

Appetizers
Bacon-Wrapped Stuffed Jalapenos, 14

Dessert
Grilled Apple Crisp, 218

Main Dishes
Brazilian-Style Turkey with Ham, 103
✓Chicken and Shrimp Satay, 92
Grilled Raspberry Chicken, 116
Grilled Veggie Pork Bundles, 88
Grilled Veggie Sausage Pizza, 108
✓Honey-Citrus Chicken Kabobs, 111
Louisiana Barbecue Brisket, 95
✓Mexican Pork Tenderloins, 100
Molasses-Glazed Baby Back Ribs, 90
Mustard-Herb Grilled Tenderloin, 102
Shrimp-Stuffed Chicken Breasts, 105
Southern Barbecued Chicken, 99
Swordfish Shrimp Kabobs, 87

Sandwiches
Grilled Beef Tenderloin Sandwiches, 46
Hearty Country Burgers, 48
Pineapple-Stuffed Burgers, 58

GROUND BEEF *(see Beef & Ground Beef)*

HAM

Brazilian-Style Turkey with Ham, 103
Brunch Lasagna, 78
Creamy Prosciutto Pasta, 116
Florentine Egg Bake, 70
Hearty Muffuletta, 54
Sauerkraut Ham Balls, 10
Wild Rice Brunch Casserole, 68

LEMONS

Frosty Lemon Pie, 188
✓Lemon Blueberry Muffins, 144
✓Lemon Ginger Muffins, 153
Lemon Pie in Meringue Shell, 196
Triple-Layer Lemon Cake, 200

MICROWAVE RECIPES

Bacon Nachos, 17
Caramel Truffles, 160
Chocolate Mint Wafers, 158
Fiery Chicken Spinach Salad, 24
Harvest Green Salad, 37
Kitchen-Sink Soft Tacos, 110
Rocky Ford Chili, 40
S'more Drops, 172
White Candy Bark, 159

MINT

Chocolate Mint Wafers, 158
Grasshopper Pie, 201
Irish Creme Chocolate Trifle, 223
Irish Mint Brownies, 162
Peppermint Taffy, 158

MUFFINS

Almond Berry Muffins, 148
Almond Peach Muffins, 155
Berry Cream Muffins, 144
Chocolate Chip Muffins, 141

MUFFINS (continued)

Corn Muffins with Honey Butter, 149
✓Lemon Blueberry Muffins, 144
✓Lemon Ginger Muffins, 153
Orange Cranberry Gems, 154
Pumpkin Chip Muffins, 146

MUSHROOMS

✓Beef Fillets with Portobello
  Sauce, 98
Beefy Mushroom Soup, 44
✓Chicken with Mushroom Sauce, 96
Mushroom Potato Soup, 45

NUTS & PEANUT BUTTER

Almond Berry Muffins, 148
Almond Chip Scones, 64
Almond Fruit Crisp, 214
Almond Peach Muffins, 155
Almond Streusel Rolls, 80
Almond Truffle Brownies, 176
Butter Pecan Fudge, 171
Butter Pecan Pumpkin Pie, 184
Chocolate Peanut Squares, 166
Chocolate Walnut Tart, 209
Cinnamon-Nut Coffee Cake, 76
Creamy Cashew Brownies, 180
✓Frosty Peanut Butter Cups, 169
Hazelnut Brownies, 169
Hazelnut Toffee, 180
Maple-Pecan Corn Bread, 145
Maraschino Cherry Almond Bread, 150
✓Nutty Chocolate Fudge, 160
PB&J Spirals, 150
Peanut Butter Blondies, 179
Peanut Butter Pie, 195
Peanut Lover's Brownies, 173
Pecan Angel Food Cake, 187
Pecan Caramel Bars, 163
Pecan Clusters, 166
Pecan-Crusted Chicken, 94
Pecan Spinach Salad, 30
Pecan-Stuffed Waffles, 68
✓Pistachio Cranberry Biscotti, 161
Ricotta Nut Pie, 194
Spiced Walnut Loaf, 140
Sweet 'n' Sour Cashew Pork, 115
Swiss Walnut Cracker Snack, 13

OATS

Caramel Apple Crunch, 211
Cran-Apple Crisp, 208

Double-Berry Crisp, 224
Fudgy Oat Brownies, 159
Grilled Apple Crisp, 218

ONIONS

Onion-Bacon Baby Carrots, 127
✓Pork Tenderloin with Glazed Red Onions, 110

ORANGES

Marmalade Monkey Bread, 142
Orange Cranberry Gems, 154

OVEN ENTREES (also see Casseroles)
Beef
  Marinated Chuck Roast, 102
Chicken
  Bacon-Cheese Topped Chicken, 85
  Barbecued Chicken Legs, 101
  Brined Roasting Chicken, 89
  ✓Chicken-Stuffed Cubanelle Peppers, 112
  Spinach Crab Chicken, 106
Fish & Seafood
  Spinach Crab Chicken, 106
  Tilapia with Corn Salsa, 117
Pork
  ✓Apple-Stuffed Pork Tenderloin, 86
  Caribbean Roast Pork Loin, 84
  Cherry-Glazed Roast Pork, 88
  ✓Pork Tenderloin with Glazed Red Onions, 110
  ✓Spinach-Stuffed Beef Tenderloin, 117

PANCAKES, WAFFLES & FRENCH TOAST

Apple Puff Pancake, 62
Chocolate-Cherry Cream Crepes, 79
Chocolate Croissants, 67
French Banana Pancakes, 70
French Toast Supreme, 66
Pecan-Stuffed Waffles, 68
Pumpkin Pancakes, 79
Special Stuffed French Toast, 72
Strawberry Cream Crepes, 74

PASTA

Brunch Lasagna, 78
✓Calico Cranberry Couscous Salad, 36
Creamy Baked Macaroni, 87
Creamy Prosciutto Pasta, 116
✓Cucumber Couscous Salad, 31
Ginger Garlic Linguine, 130
Polynesian Shrimp Salad, 23
Primavera Chicken, 114

✓Roasted Pepper Ravioli Bake, 109
Turkey Pasta Soup, 46

PEACHES
Almond Peach Muffins, 155
Peach Cobbler, 226
Peach Coffee Cake, 69
Peachy Rhubarb Pie, 205

PEARS
Blue Cheese Pear Salad, 35
Cranberry Pear Pie, 202
Ginger-Lime Pear Cobbler, 211
Grilled Chicken and Pear Salad, 28
Raspberry Pear Crisp, 223

PEPPERS
Bacon-Wrapped Stuffed Jalapenos, 14
✓Beef Fajita Salad, 28
Chicken Pepper Stir-Fry, 97
✓Chicken-Stuffed Cubanelle Peppers, 112
Chipotle Turkey Chili, 49
Pepper Avocado Salsa, 16
✓Roasted Pepper Ravioli Bake, 109
✓Sweet Pepper Sandwiches, 50
Three-Pepper Chutney, 129

PIES
Butter Pecan Pumpkin Pie, 184
Caramel Apple Cream Pie, 204
Chocolate Raspberry Pie, 205
Cranberry Pear Pie, 202
Eggnog Cranberry Pie, 199
Frosty Lemon Pie, 188
Frozen Strawberry Pie, 204
German Chocolate Pie, 186
Grapefruit Pie, 192
Grasshopper Pie, 201
Lemon Pie in Meringue Shell, 196
Martha Washington Pies, 190
Mud Pie, 198
Peachy Rhubarb Pie, 205
Peanut Butter Pie, 195
Popover Apple Pie, 189
Pumpkin Cheesecake Pie, 187
Ricotta Nut Pie, 194
Upside-Down Apple Pie, 193
White Chocolate Mousse Cherry Pie, 196

PORK *(also see Bacon & Canadian Bacon; Ham; Sausage)*
Main Dishes
  ✓Apple-Stuffed Pork Tenderloin, 86

Bean and Pork Chop Bake, 113
Caribbean Roast Pork Loin, 84
Cherry-Glazed Roast Pork, 88
Grilled Veggie Pork Bundles, 88
✓Mexican Pork Tenderloins, 100
Molasses-Glazed Baby Back Ribs, 90
✓Pork Tenderloin with Glazed Red Onions, 110
Sweet 'n' Sour Cashew Pork, 115
Salad
  Spicy Pork Tenderloin Salad, 32

POTATOES & SWEET POTATOES
Bacon Mashed Potatoes, 123
Beef and Potato Moussaka, 104
Cajun Potato Salad, 27
Cheese Fries, 135
Chili-Seasoned Potato Wedges, 131
Chocolate Potato Cake, 198
Dilly Stuffed Potatoes, 137
Easy Potato Rolls, 152
Golden Diced Potatoes, 122
Golden Mashed Potato Bake, 128
✓Mashed Potato Kolachkes, 77
Mushroom Potato Soup, 45
Pretzel-Topped Sweet Potatoes, 127
Sweet Potato Bread, 142
Sweet Potato Mini Cakes, 184
Swirled Potato Bake, 121
Tangy Potato Salad, 36
Turkey Potato Pancakes, 67
✓Two-Potato Soup, 42

PUMPKIN
Butter Pecan Pumpkin Pie, 184
Pumpkin Cheesecake Pie, 187
Pumpkin Chip Muffins, 146
Pumpkin Coffee Cake, 80
Pumpkin Pancakes, 79
Pumpkin Torte, 217
Raisin Pumpkin Bars, 172

RASPBERRIES
Berry Cream Muffins, 144
Cherry Berry Smoothies, 18
Chocolate Raspberry Pie, 205
Double-Berry Crisp, 224
Grilled Raspberry Chicken, 116
Raspberry Coconut Bars, 177
Raspberry Pear Crisp, 223

RHUBARB
Peachy Rhubarb Pie, 205
Strawberry Rhubarb Cobbler, 222

RICE

Chicken Rice Bowl, 109
Herbed Rice, 126
Wild Rice Brunch Casserole, 68

SALADS

Main-Dish Salads

✓Beef Fajita Salad, 28
✓Chicken Salad with Crispy Wontons, 26
Crispy Chicken Strip Salad, 34
Fiery Chicken Spinach Salad, 24
Grilled Chicken and Pear Salad, 28
Polynesian Shrimp Salad, 23
Spicy Pork Tenderloin Salad, 32
Summer Chicken Salad, 24
✓Vegetarian Taco Salad, 32

Side Salads

Asparagus Berry Salad, 22
Blue Cheese 'n' Fruit Tossed Salad, 27
Blue Cheese Pear Salad, 35
Cajun Potato Salad, 27
✓Calico Cranberry Couscous Salad, 36
Colorful Coleslaw, 31
✓Cucumber Couscous Salad, 31
✓Flavorful Cranberry Gelatin Mold, 37
Frozen Date Salad, 34
✓Greek Veggie Salad, 30
Green Bean Tossed Salad, 22
Harvest Green Salad, 37
Misty Melon Salad, 35
Pecan Spinach Salad, 30
Sunny Carrot Salad, 26
Tangerine Tossed Salad, 23
Tangy Potato Salad, 36

SANDWICHES

Cold Sandwiches

Bacon 'n' Egg Salad Sandwiches, 53
Curried Chicken Salad Sandwiches, 42
Hearty Muffuletta, 54
Zesty Garlic-Avocado Sandwiches, 49

Hot Sandwiches

Beef Gyros, 56
Buffalo Chicken Sandwiches, 57
Buffalo Chicken Wraps, 52
Fresh Mozzarella Sandwiches, 40
Genoa Sandwich Loaf, 41
Grilled Beef Tenderloin Sandwiches, 46
Hearty Country Burgers, 48
Italian Chicken Wraps, 45
Open-Faced Crab Salad Sandwiches, 53

Pineapple-Stuffed Burgers, 58
Roast Beef Barbecue, 52
✓Sweet Pepper Sandwiches, 50
Tuna Puff Sandwiches, 41

SAUSAGE

Bacon-Wrapped Stuffed Jalapenos, 14
Eggplant Sausage Casserole, 106
Genoa Sandwich Loaf, 41
Grilled Veggie Sausage Pizza, 108
Hearty Muffuletta, 54
Mini Bagelizzas, 10
Pizza Quesadillas, 114
Skillet Sausage Stuffing, 122
Speedy Sausage Squares, 69

SIDE DISHES

Bacon Mashed Potatoes, 123
Blue Cheese Green Beans, 131
Cheese Fries, 135
Chili-Seasoned Potato Wedges, 131
Country Corn, 135
Creamy Zucchini, 136
Dilly Stuffed Potatoes, 137
✓Garbanzo Bean Medley, 134
Garden Vegetable Medley, 128
Ginger Garlic Linguine, 130
✓Glazed Carrot Coins, 123
Golden Diced Potatoes, 122
Golden Mashed Potato Bake, 128
Herbed Baked Spinach, 132
Herbed Rice, 126
Horseradish Creamed Carrots, 124
Onion-Bacon Baby Carrots, 127
Party Carrots, 132
Pretzel-Topped Sweet Potatoes, 127
Skillet Sausage Stuffing, 122
✓Spanish Squash Medley, 126
✓Spicy Asparagus Spears, 120
Swirled Potato Bake, 121
✓Tomatoes with Horseradish Sauce, 124

SOUPS & CHILI

Bacon Clam Chowder, 48
Beefy Mushroom Soup, 44
Black Bean Soup with Fruit Salsa, 44
Chicken Tortilla Soup, 58
Chipotle Turkey Chili, 49
Florentine Chicken Soup, 50
Garlic Tomato Soup, 57
Mexican Shrimp Bisque, 54
Mushroom Potato Soup, 45

Rocky Ford Chili, 40
Southwestern Chicken Soup, 56
Turkey Pasta Soup, 46
✓Two-Potato Soup, 42

SPINACH

Fiery Chicken Spinach Salad, 24
Florentine Chicken Soup, 50
Florentine Egg Bake, 70
Herbed Baked Spinach, 132
Pecan Spinach Salad, 30
Spinach Crab Chicken, 106
✓Spinach-Stuffed Beef Tenderloin, 117

SQUASH & ZUCCHINI

Creamy Zucchini, 136
✓Spanish Squash Medley, 126

STOVETOP ENTREES

Beef
  ✓Beef Fillets with Portobello Sauce, 98
  Mongolian Beef, 93
Chicken
  Asian Chicken Thighs, 101
  Chicken Pepper Stir-Fry, 97
  Chicken Rice Bowl, 109
  ✓Chicken with Mushroom Sauce, 96
  Herbed Cranberry Chicken, 93
  Pecan-Crusted Chicken, 94
  Primavera Chicken, 114
Pork, Ham & Sausage
  Creamy Prosciutto Pasta, 116
  Pizza Quesadillas, 114
  Sweet 'n' Sour Cashew Pork, 115
Seafood
  ✓Easy Crab Cakes, 105
  ✓Peking Shrimp, 113

STRAWBERRIES

Almond Berry Muffins, 148
Asparagus Berry Salad, 22
Berry Bread with Spread, 140
Berry-Cream Cookie Snaps, 167
Berry Pinwheel Cake, 202
Frozen Strawberry Pie, 204
Hint-of-Berry Bonbons, 178
Martha Washington Pies, 190
Sensational Slush, 12
Strawberry Cream Crepes, 74
Strawberry Popovers, 227
Strawberry Puff Pastry Dessert, 225
Strawberry Rhubarb Cobbler, 222
Strawberry Swirl Cheesecake, 210
Strawberry Tartlets, 209

TOMATOES

Garlic Tomato Soup, 57
✓Tomatoes with Horseradish Sauce, 124

TURKEY

Brazilian-Style Turkey with Ham, 103
Chipotle Turkey Chili, 49
Honey-Mustard Turkey Meatballs, 19
Turkey Pasta Soup, 46
Turkey Potato Pancakes, 67

VEGETABLES *(also see specific kinds)*

Dilly Veggie Pizza, 13
Garden Vegetable Medley, 128
✓Greek Veggie Salad, 30
Grilled Veggie Pork Bundles, 88
Grilled Veggie Sausage Pizza, 108
Harvest Green Salad, 37
Primavera Chicken, 114
✓Vegetarian Taco Salad, 32

Alphabetical Index

*This handy index lists every recipe in alphabetical order,
so you can easily find your favorite recipes.*

✓ Recipe includes Nutrition Facts and Diabetic Exchanges

A

Almond Berry Muffins, 148
Almond Chip Scones, 64
Almond Fruit Crisp, 214
Almond Peach Muffins, 155
Almond Streusel Rolls, 80
Almond Truffle Brownies, 176
Apple Crisp with a Twist, 227
Apple Crumble, 212
Apple Pie in a Goblet, 224
Apple Puff Pancake, 62
✓Apple-Stuffed Pork Tenderloin, 86
Apricot Banana Bread, 153
Asian Chicken Thighs, 101
Asparagus Berry Salad, 22

B

Bacon 'n' Egg Salad Sandwiches, 53
Bacon-Cheese Topped Chicken, 85
Bacon Clam Chowder, 48
Bacon Mashed Potatoes, 123
Bacon Nachos, 17
Bacon-Wrapped Stuffed
    Jalapenos, 14
Baked Cherry Pudding, 218
Banana Shakes, 14
Barbecued Chicken Legs, 101
Bean and Pork Chop Bake, 113
Beef 'n' Chili Beans, 97
Beef and Potato Moussaka, 104
✓Beef Fajita Salad, 28
✓Beef Fillets with Portobello
    Sauce, 98
Beef Gyros, 56
Beefy Mushroom Soup, 44
Berry Bread with Spread, 140
Berry-Cream Cookie Snaps, 167
Berry Cream Muffins, 144
Berry Pinwheel Cake, 202
Black Bean Soup with Fruit
    Salsa, 44
Black Forest Cheesecake, 222
Blackberry Cobbler, 221
Blond Brownies a la Mode, 174
✓Blondies with Chips, 168

Blue Cheese 'n' Fruit Tossed
    Salad, 27
Blue Cheese Green Beans, 131
Blue Cheese Pear Salad, 35
Blueberry Cornmeal
    Cobbler, 212
Brazilian-Style Turkey with
    Ham, 103
Brined Roasting Chicken, 89
Brunch Lasagna, 78
Buffalo Chicken Sandwiches, 57
Buffalo Chicken Wraps, 52
Butter Pecan Fudge, 171
Butter Pecan Pumpkin Pie, 184
Buttermilk Banana Cake, 190
Butterscotch Hard Candy, 179

C

Cajun Potato Salad, 27
✓Calico Cranberry Couscous
    Salad, 36
Caramel Apple Cake, 195
Caramel Apple Cream Pie, 204
Caramel Apple Crunch, 211
Caramel Sweet Rolls, 76
Caramel Truffles, 160
Caribbean Roast Pork Loin, 84
Carrot Cheesecake, 220
Cheery Cherry Loaf, 155
Cheese Fries, 135
Cherry Berry Smoothies, 18
Cherry Cream Cheese Coffee
    Cake, 72
Cherry-Glazed Roast Pork, 88
✓Chicken and Shrimp Satay, 92
Chicken Pepper Stir-Fry, 97
Chicken Pie in a Pan, 94
Chicken Rice Bowl, 109
✓Chicken Salad with Crispy
    Wontons, 26
✓Chicken-Stuffed Cubanelle
    Peppers, 112
Chicken Tortilla Soup, 58
✓Chicken with Mushroom
    Sauce, 96
Chili-Seasoned Potato Wedges, 131

Chipotle Turkey Chili, 49
Chock-full of Fruit Snackin'
    Cake, 201
Chocolate Carrot Cake, 192
Chocolate-Cherry Cream
    Crepes, 79
Chocolate Chip Muffins, 141
Chocolate Croissants, 67
Chocolate Fruit Dip, 11
Chocolate Mint Wafers, 158
Chocolate Peanut Squares, 166
Chocolate Potato Cake, 198
Chocolate Raspberry Pie, 205
Chocolate Walnut Tart, 209
Christmas Bread, 145
Cinnamon-Nut Coffee Cake, 76
Cinnamon Roll Cherry
    Cobbler, 215
Coconut-Chip Coffee Cake, 78
Coconut Snowmen, 170
Coffee 'n' Cream Brownies, 174
Colorful Coleslaw, 31
Cookie Dough Truffles, 164
Corn Muffins with Honey
    Butter, 149
Country Corn, 135
Cran-Apple Crisp, 208
Cran-Apple Tea Ring, 64
Cranberry Apple Saute, 134
Cranberry Bundt Cake, 189
Cranberry Cheesecake, 219
Cranberry Pear Pie, 202
Cranberry Spritzer, 17
Creamy Baked Macaroni, 87
Creamy Cashew Brownies, 180
Creamy Prosciutto Pasta, 116
Creamy Zucchini, 136
Crimson Cranberry Punch, 8
Crispy Chicken Strip Salad, 34
✓Cucumber Couscous Salad, 31
Curried Chicken Salad
    Sandwiches, 42

D

Dilly Bran Refrigerator Rolls, 154
Dilly Stuffed Potatoes, 137

Dilly Veggie Pizza, 13
Double-Berry Crisp, 224

E

✓Easy Crab Cakes, 105
Easy Potato Rolls, 152
Eggnog Cranberry Pie, 199
Eggplant Sausage Casserole, 106
Elegant Dipped Cherries, 181

F

Fiery Chicken Spinach Salad, 24
✓Flavorful Cranberry Gelatin
    Mold, 37
Florentine Chicken Soup, 50
Florentine Egg Bake, 70
French Banana Pancakes, 70
French Toast Supreme, 66
Fresh Mozzarella Sandwiches, 40
Fried Shoestring Carrots, 11
Frosted Cookie Brownies, 163
Frosty Lemon Pie, 188
✓Frosty Peanut Butter Cups, 169
Frozen Date Salad, 34
Frozen Strawberry Pie, 204
Fudgy Oat Brownies, 159

G

✓Garbanzo Bean Medley, 134
Garden Vegetable Medley, 128
Garlic Herb Twists, 152
Garlic Tomato Soup, 57
Genoa Sandwich Loaf, 41
German Chocolate Pie, 186
Ginger Garlic Linguine, 130
Ginger-Lime Pear Cobbler, 211
Glazed Apricot Sorbet, 221
✓Glazed Carrot Coins, 123
Golden Diced Potatoes, 122
Golden Mashed Potato Bake, 128
Granola Banana Sticks, 217
Granola Trail Mix, 19
Grapefruit Pie, 192
Grasshopper Pie, 201
Great-Grandma's Prune Roll, 66
✓Greek Veggie Salad, 30
Green Bean Tossed Salad, 22
Grilled Apple Crisp, 218
Grilled Beef Tenderloin
    Sandwiches, 46
Grilled Chicken and Pear Salad, 28
Grilled Raspberry Chicken, 116
Grilled Veggie Pork Bundles, 88
Grilled Veggie Sausage Pizza, 108

H

Harvest Green Salad, 37
Hazelnut Brownies, 169
Hazelnut Toffee, 180
Hearty Country Burgers, 48
Hearty Muffuletta, 54
Herbed Baked Spinach, 132
Herbed Cranberry Chicken, 93
Herbed Rice, 126
Hint-of-Berry Bonbons, 178
✓Honey-Citrus Chicken
    Kabobs, 111
Honey-Mustard Turkey
    Meatballs, 19
Horseradish Creamed Carrots, 124

I

Irish Creme Chocolate Trifle, 223
Irish Mint Brownies, 162
Italian Chicken Wraps, 45
Italian Snack Mix, 8

K

Kitchen-Sink Soft Tacos, 110

L

Layered Carrot Cake, 199
✓Lemon Blueberry Muffins, 144
✓Lemon Ginger Muffins, 153
Lemon Pie in Meringue Shell, 196
Louisiana Barbecue Brisket, 95

M

Maple-Pecan Corn Bread, 145
Maraschino Cherry Almond
    Bread, 150
Marinated Chuck Roast, 102
Marmalade Monkey Bread, 142
Martha Washington Pies, 190
✓Mashed Potato Kolachkes, 77
Meringue Coconut Brownies, 171
✓Mexican Pork Tenderloins, 100
Mexican Shrimp Bisque, 54
Mini Bagelizzas, 10
Mini Italian Biscuits, 141
✓Miracle Baklava, 216
Misty Melon Salad, 35
Mocha Mousse Brownies, 164
Molasses-Glazed Baby Back
    Ribs, 90
Mongolian Beef, 93
Mousse Tarts, 214
Mud Pie, 198
Mushroom Potato Soup, 45

Mustard-Herb Grilled
    Tenderloin, 102

N

Noel Cookie Gems, 168
✓Nutty Chocolate Fudge, 160

O

Old-Fashioned Chicken Pot
    Pie, 84
Ole Polenta Casserole, 90
Onion-Bacon Baby Carrots, 127
Open-Faced Crab Salad
    Sandwiches, 53
Orange Cranberry Gems, 154
Oregano-Swiss Slices, 149

P

Party Carrots, 132
PB&J Spirals, 150
Peach Cobbler, 226
Peach Coffee Cake, 69
Peachy Rhubarb Pie, 205
Peanut Butter Blondies, 179
Peanut Butter Pie, 195
Peanut Lover's Brownies, 173
Pecan Angel Food Cake, 187
Pecan Caramel Bars, 163
Pecan Clusters, 166
Pecan-Crusted Chicken, 94
Pecan Spinach Salad, 30
Pecan-Stuffed Waffles, 68
✓Peking Shrimp, 113
Pepper Avocado Salsa, 16
Peppermint Taffy, 158
Pickled Baby Carrots, 136
Pineapple-Stuffed Burgers, 58
✓Pistachio Cranberry Biscotti, 161
Pizza Quesadillas, 114
Polynesian Shrimp Salad, 23
Popover Apple Pie, 189
✓Pork Tenderloin with Glazed
    Red Onions, 110
Pretzel-Topped Sweet Potatoes, 127
Primavera Chicken, 114
Puffy Apple Omelet, 62
Pumpkin Cheesecake Pie, 187
Pumpkin Chip Muffins, 146
Pumpkin Coffee Cake, 80
Pumpkin Pancakes, 79
Pumpkin Torte, 217

Q

✓Quilt-Topped Corn Bread, 146

R

Raisin Pumpkin Bars, 172
Raspberry Coconut Bars, 177
Raspberry Pear Crisp, 223
Reuben Brunch Bake, 73
Ribbon Crispies, 176
Ricotta Nut Pie, 194
Roast Beef Barbecue, 52
Roasted Carrot Dip, 9
✓Roasted Pepper Ravioli
    Bake, 109
Rocky Ford Chili, 40

S

Salmon Quiche, 74
Sauerkraut Ham Balls, 10
Sensational Slush, 12
Shrimp-Stuffed Chicken
    Breasts, 105
Skillet Sausage Stuffing, 122
S'more Drops, 172
Southern Barbecued Chicken, 99
Southwestern Chicken Soup, 56
✓Spanish Squash Medley, 126
Special Stuffed French Toast, 72
Speedy Sausage Squares, 69
Spiced Cranberry Ketchup, 130
Spiced Walnut Loaf, 140

✓Spicy Asparagus Spears, 120
Spicy Pork Tenderloin Salad, 32
Spinach Crab Chicken, 106
✓Spinach-Stuffed Beef
    Tenderloin, 117
Strawberry Cream Crepes, 74
Strawberry Popovers, 227
Strawberry Puff Pastry Dessert, 225
Strawberry Rhubarb Cobbler, 222
Strawberry Swirl Cheesecake, 210
Strawberry Tartlets, 209
Summer Chicken Salad, 24
Sunflower Potluck Cake, 194
Sunny Carrot Salad, 26
Sunshine Sweet Rolls, 63
Sweet 'n' Crunchy Mix, 18
Sweet 'n' Sour Cashew Pork, 115
Sweet Cherry Cheese Dessert, 208
Sweet Gingered Chicken Wings, 15
✓Sweet Pepper Sandwiches, 50
Sweet Potato Bread, 142
Sweet Potato Mini Cakes, 184
Swirled Potato Bake, 121
Swiss Walnut Cracker Snack, 13
Swordfish Shrimp Kabobs, 87

T

Tacoed Eggs, 73

Tangerine Tossed Salad, 23
Tangy Potato Salad, 36
Three-Pepper Chutney, 129
Tilapia with Corn Salsa, 117
✓Tomatoes with Horseradish
    Sauce, 124
Triple Layer Brownie Cake, 188
Triple-Layer Lemon Cake, 200
Tuna Puff Sandwiches, 41
Turkey Pasta Soup, 46
Turkey Potato Pancakes, 67
✓Two-Potato Soup, 42

U

Upside-Down Apple Pie, 193

V

✓Vegetarian Taco Salad, 32

W

White Candy Bark, 159
White Chocolate Mousse Cherry
    Pie, 196
Wild Rice Brunch Casserole, 68

Z

Zesty Garlic-Avocado
    Sandwiches, 49